"*The 12-Step Buddhist* is as relevant—and necessary—today as when I first read it while I was in treatment in 2008."

— Annie McCullough, cofounder and executive director of
Faces and Voices of Recovery Canada

"Darren Littlejohn's *The 12-Step Buddhist* is a down-to-earth presentation of the tools that helped him become familiar with his mind and how to change it. The 12 Steps, in their emphasis on looking inside, taking responsibility, and having the courage to change, fit the Buddhist approach like a glove.

We're all addicts, it's just a question of degree. When we understand that the nature of attachment is dissatisfaction—the aching sense of never being enough, never having enough, always wanting more   this can begin to make sense. What Buddha's saying is deceptively simple: fulfillment, happiness, satisfaction, contentment are within our grasp."

—Venerable Robina Courtin, executive director of the
Liberation Prison Project, USA and Australia

"*The 12-Step Buddhist* is one of those rare books that transcends genres by seamlessly integrating the 12-Step approach, Buddhist principles, and a compelling personal struggle with addiction and a quest for spiritual awakening. With its refreshingly direct, tell-it-like-it-is style, this book takes a systematic approach to blending the 12 Steps with timeless Buddhist meditations and wisdom.

The 12-Step Buddhist is an important guidebook to living life 'just as it is'—beyond the insanity of addiction and recovery. This book is ideal for both spiritual seekers and those who feel that their life is out of control. As a former Buddhist monk and a practicing psychotherapist who works with recovering addicts, I highly recommend this book!"

—Donald Altman, MA, LPC, author of *Living Kindness* and *Meal by Meal*

"This book is written not based on theory or assumption, but by a person who actually went through the experience of recovery and from that experience has seen the benefits of this system as a way to help other people who are facing the same circumstances. This will be an important contribution to the literature of Buddhism and of recovery in the West."

—Yangsi Rinpoche, Tibetan Buddhist teacher and president of Maitripa Institute

"*The 12-Step Buddhist* is a unique synthesis of the traditional 12-Step model and the liberating wisdom of Dharma, bridging the divide between traditional programs, which suffer from problematic terminology and pedagogy, and Buddhist teachings, which aren't equipped to address some of the specific needs and concerns of the modern addict."

—*Mandala* Magazine

"Darren's book is an insightful, personal meditation on the many fruitful intersections between 12-Step recovery programs, science, and Buddhism. For those seeking recovery, but put off by what seems like a heavy Judeo-Christian orientation in many 12-Step programs, Darren's story will be a refreshing eye-opener to alternative possibilities."

—James Blumenthal, professor of Buddhist Studies, Oregon State University and Maitripa College, author of *The Ornament of the Middle Way*

"Addiction makes your life completely meaningless. . . . It blocks your path to enlightenment, your spiritual path. But overcoming addiction is not easy because there are so many habits from the past. Studying Dharma is unbelievably important and is something that should be done right now, because death can come at any time. It is also the main thing for achieving everlasting happiness, total liberation from samsara, and from all suffering. It is the foundation for achieving enlightenment, for the benefit of others. Thus the benefit of practicing meditation is not just overcoming addiction."

—Venerable Lama Thubten Zopa Rinpoche, spiritual director of the Foundation for the Preservation of the Mahayana Tradition

"If the 12 Steps lead to recovery, Buddhist practice and philosophy can provide the spiritual underpinnings needed to stabilize that recovery. [Darren Littlejohn's] interpretation of the 12 Steps as seen through the lens of this wisdom tradition is fascinating and useful. A very practical and inspired guide."

—Susan Piver, author of *How Not to Be Afraid of Your Own Life*

"Written out of the fire of his own journey through the darkness, Littlejohn cuts right to the heart of the addictive personality in all of us and shows how the spiritual dimension can unlock healing in a uniquely powerful way.

—Dr. Reginald Ray, Buddhist Studies at Naropa University, Spiritual Director of the Dharma Ocean Foundation, and author of *Touching Enlightenment*

The
12-Step
Buddhist

The
12-Step
Buddhist

Enhance Recovery from
Any Addiction

Darren Littlejohn
Foreword by Robert Thurman

ATRIA PAPERBACK
New York London Toronto Sydney New Delhi

BEYOND WORDS
Hillsboro, Oregon

ATRIA PAPERBACK
A Division of Simon & Schuster, Inc.
1230 Avenue of the Americas
New York, NY 10020

BEYOND WORDS
8427 N.E. Cornell Road, Suite 500
Hillsboro, Oregon 97124-9808
503-531-8700 / 503-531-8773 fax
www.beyondword.com

Managing editor: Lindsay S. Easterbrooks-Brown
Editor: Ali McCart
Copyeditor: Gretchen Stelter
Proofreaders: Robert Vaughn, Ashley Van Winkle
Design: Sara E. Blum and Devon Smith
Composition: William H. Brunson Typography Services

This publication contains the opinions and ideas of its author. It is intended to provide helpful and informative material on the subjects addressed in the publication. It is sold with the understanding that the author and publisher are not engaged in rendering medical, health, or any other kind of personal professional services in the book. The reader should consult his or her medical, health, or other competent professional before adopting any of the suggestions in this book or drawing inferences from it. The author and publisher specifically disclaim all responsibility for any liability, loss, or risk, personal or otherwise, which is incurred as a consequence, directly or indirectly, of the use and application of any of the contents of this book.

First Beyond Words/Atria Paperback edition November 2019

For more information about special discounts for bulk purchases, please contact Simon & Schuster Special Sales at 1-800-456-6798 or business@simonandschuster.com.

Manufactured in the United States of America

10 9 8 7 6 5 4 3 2 1

Library of Congress Cataloging-in-Publication Data

The 12-Step Buddhist : enhance recovery from any addiction / Darren Littlejohn.
     p.   cm.
Includes bibliographical references and index.
     1. Twelve-step programs—Religious aspects—Buddhism.   2. Religious life—Buddhism.   3. Self-help techniques.   I. Title.

BQ4570.T85L58 2009
294.3'4442—dc22

2008044310

ISBN 978-1-58270-714-3 (pbk)
ISBN 978-1-98211-572-2 (ebook)

The corporate mission of Beyond Words Publishing, Inc.: *Inspire to Integrity*

For my brother, Darryl,
who wanted to be free of suffering—just like me

Contents

x   **Contents**

Foreword

I am deeply moved by Darren Littlejohn's remarkable story, and his broad grasp of everything that can possibly help us all to find more freedom from our various forms of addiction. He is talking real talk and walking a real walk. It comes through in every line of this no-nonsense and intensely compassionate book.

His Holiness the Dalai Lama never pushes some sort of "Buddhism" as a panacea for our problems, but always teaches us to look toward the teachings of compassion, tolerance, and peace in all spiritual traditions, while also taking advantage of whatever insight and technique science has to offer. Darren's book works in this same spirit, not pushing the 12 Steps or Buddhism as a panacea, but drawing on a wide range of experiences and traditions to provide a powerful, illuminating path that will benefit all who read or encounter it.

On the surface, it might seem strange to combine a Judeo-Christian recovery program with a Buddhist psychology and spiritual practice. But the way Darren puts them together in a non-dogmatic, essentially pragmatic way, makes sense. He speaks out to all of us, whether we are officially addicts or not. Understanding the pervasiveness of addictive habits is the only way to help our dear ones who are in trouble, while also facing the areas where we ourselves are also bound. Traveling this road with Darren helps us realize we are all attached—addicted—to something. And we all suffer as a result of such attachments. We all crave the kind of peace that will never come from a bottle or from a drug, but from understanding ourselves and the power of our minds.

Darren shows great honesty in sharing the nitty-gritty of his own life, the struggle he faced and still faces. His brave stance of absolute openness makes a bridge for all readers, whether they are in the full struggle after facing their addiction or are feeling helpless while witnessing a loved one's self-destruction. By reading this book, confronting the powerful emotions and absorbing the startling statistics, it becomes easier to feel compassion for those around us who are not yet free from the grip of addictive diseases and behaviors. It helps us get over the usual barriers, judge less punitively, and love more effectively.

The 12-Step Buddhist provides meditations and exercises that will be life changing for those who apply themselves with discipline and patience. Illuminating the unique states of mind that the addict must confront, this book reflects our inner truth—that we achieve the freedom and peace we desire by releasing attachment, not by clinging to things that drag us down. His "Aspects of Self" exercises also aid in that shift from outer to inner awareness.

As nations strive to dominate each other due to their inability to see themselves clearly and confront their addictions to racism, fanaticism, greed, and hatred—so tragically exemplified in the half-a-century-long oppression of Tibet by China—it is essential to keep hope alive by envisioning the possibility of solving the situation through realistic understanding and compassionate action. For individuals who struggle with sickness, desperation, depression, and addiction, and all their loving friends, it is essential to envision realistic steps toward liberation. My reading of *The 12-Step Buddhist* and my encounter with the keen intellect and the great heart of Darren Littlejohn have shown me how to be more free myself, and have given me real hope that those I love will find their way to greater freedom. I welcome the book, congratulate the author, and recommend the work to all of you.

—Robert Thurman
Jey Tsong Khapa Professor of Buddhist Studies, Columbia University
President, Tibet House US
Author of *Why the Dalai Lama Matters*

Introduction

Buddhism isn't a substitute for the 12 Steps. I don't care how devout you are in any religion, whether you've meditated with the Dalai Lama or had an audience with the pope. Also, this book is not a substitute for the 12 Steps. Use it as a *supplement to*, not a *substitute for*, active participation in a 12-Step program: regular meeting attendance, step work, sponsorship, and service. Spiritual work is difficult. When engaging in deeper spiritual practices, you'll need support in and out of the 12-Step community. Share this book with your sponsor (who guides you through the 12 Steps), doctor, therapist, spiritual adviser, and family.

Since I published this book in 2009, much has happened in the recovery and Buddhist worlds. Ten years is a long time for things like research, trial and error, attempts and failures. The book was an integration of what we knew about the power of the 12 Steps as the application of spiritual principles, and the power of Buddhist teachings to eradicate suffering. I incorporated those with some useful dynamics of Western psychology, especially in the Aspects of Self dialogues.

At the time we had no form of Buddhist recovery. There was a significant gap in understanding between Buddhists and those involved in their own recovery, not to mention the treatment of recovering addicts. All of this has changed. Some for the good, and some of it, like the scandal that destroyed Against the Stream and has left Refuge Recovery in shambles, has left many with even deeper wounds. It remains a valid path, though.

Those rebels among us who have been interested in Buddhism as a spiritual path for a while now have also been swooped up in the proliferation of mainstream "McMindfulness" in the past decade. With hundreds of books on the subject of mindfulness making Buddhism drastically more accessible, you can't throw a rock without hitting someone who just got back from a retreat or workshop. Back in the day, if you had a tattoo you were considered a biker outlaw. Now you'll be getting your ink at the strip mall, likely next to a twenty-two-year-old computer science major who's never even bloodied his knuckles. To be Buddhist used to be a kind of esoteric, mysterious thing. To be a tattooed Buddhist in recovery these days is certainly not as unusual as it once was. In fact, it's pretty trendy.

What's still missing from many of these developments—if you can call them that—is really the absolute, most important, central principle to all Dharma, all spirituality, and recovery: compassion fused with mindful wisdom.

If you mention mindfulness to your mother, your barber, or your Uber driver, they're likely to be informed enough to discuss it with you. But as easy as it is to be informed on everything in the information age, it's still just as difficult to learn it, internalize it, and integrate it into daily life—if not more so.

We've also learned enough about the brain science of addiction, trauma, and compassion to make it mainstream. Neuroscience courses and conferences on the latest research abound in the treatment world. We now know a lot more about trauma and the body's and brain's responses to it, including substance abuse disorder, PTSD, complex PTSD, and addiction. Treatment centers are more holistic, offering mindfulness and yoga as standard fare. Part of the premise of this book is that the 12 Steps are a necessary component to healing from addictions. For those who want to find an alternative to the 12-Step model, there are groups like Refuge Recovery, SMART Recovery, and Y12SR, a version of yoga for recovery. I can't speak to the efficacy of these groups because I haven't participated in them. But I have heard from many people over the years that they find help using these alternatives. They're out there, and you should always explore a variety of tools in recovery, as I've always said.

We have definitely come a long way. But as the saying goes, we have as far to go as we have come. This new, updated edition talks about all of this.

When I wrote my first book in 2008, I'd been blogging for a few years, but I really just sat down and hammered out my thoughts and experiences. At the time I had "recovered my recovery" with ten years clean and sober after relapsing with ten years in 1994. I had been a practicing Zen Buddhist since the mid-1980s and had been involved with the Tibetans for several years too.

Now, in late 2018, I just celebrated twenty-one years clean and sober. Over the course of the past decade, I've led dozens of retreats and led weekly 12-Step Buddhist groups. I became a yoga teacher in 2011 and have been practicing daily since then too. I've put out several more books on Buddhism, yoga, and recovery.

I've received hundreds of emails and messages on social media from people who got sober using *The 12-Step Buddhist* and continue to enjoy years of sobriety today. Thank you so much for sending those. Keep 'em coming!

One thing that was interesting is that many people told me they were given *The 12-Step Buddhist* by their counselors in treatment when they balked at the 12-Step model. Apparently counselors felt the book was ahead of its time. Looking back, we can see where that's true. Buddhism is a thriving part of the recovery world as well as the psychotherapy world now.

This new edition is not only about doing the work that many of us in 12-Step programs overlook but also about exploring new developments in recovery that have happened in the past decade, especially around compassion. Whether you're a newcomer, an old-timer, or anything in between, the purpose of this book is to help you enjoy recovery and avoid a relapse. It doesn't matter what your addiction is. To begin with, you may not be sure you're addicted to anything. But in my experience, most people aren't willing to do *any* work, let alone the difficult work, unless, as an old-timer used to say, their "ass is up against the wall, suckin' plaster." If you're an addict like me, you have a choice: a way of life based on compassion or the aloneness of addiction.

The work here is meaty but can be approached at any level of recovery or experience. You don't have to be a genius to benefit. But you do have to have some guts. I promise, if you give this approach a sustained effort, it will deepen and enhance your spiritual experience. Really. As we say in the program, "If it will work for me, it will work for anybody." So, who am I?

The book is my personal story, my critical analysis of treatment methods, and my practical advice on how to integrate Buddhism *with* a 12-Step recovery program. I also use therapy as part of my personal program and will share some thoughts on how that works for me. You don't have to have a therapist to begin, but at some point, it will help you to be open-minded about getting professional help. In my experience, good therapy *vastly* improves your chances for happiness and long-term sobriety.

We all know people with long-term sobriety who are a little, shall we say, tightly wound? Many of us in recovery get stuck, and many of us die. If the idea of therapy bothers you, relax. Just remember this: therapy can be a powerful spiritual tool when integrated with a recovery program. We all get stuck. It's OK to ask for help.

To make sense of a complex history, I'll delve into my recovery experience on a few different timelines. In doing this work, I've found that it makes sense to look at some of these dimensions separately.

To clear up some misconceptions, I'm going to lay out some new, updated research on the subject of addiction as a *brain disease* as well as the other side of the argument that says it's a mistake, and even detrimental, to consider addiction a disease at all. We have to get clear on the problem so we can forge an unambiguous vision of the solution. Going over data is boring, but one benefit of scientific study is that it helps us see the big picture and our place in it. For addicts, who usually feel alienated on some level, the macro perspective can be helpful and can "air out" our attitudes. I'll help you clarify.

The book is based on over thirty years of experience in 12-Step programs. I've tried many approaches combining addiction, sobriety, 12 Steps, Buddhism, and therapy; 12 Steps only; therapy only; psychiatric medication in and out of therapy with and without sobriety. You get the idea. Since the first edition, and with the more recent discoveries on trauma's link to addiction and various therapies to address trauma, I've even tried CBD and some psychedelic therapies, as I'll discuss. It's about what works for me and what doesn't. Hopefully, I can save you some time—and suffering—in figuring out what works for you.

This book will also talk about some of the scientific, psychological, and spiritual underpinnings of addiction. I'll offer suggestions that can prevent a relapse and actually enhance and deepen your spiritual life.

At the end of the book I'm going to give you a new final section that bridges 12-Step Buddhism with a new, developing paradigm: Compassionate Recovery, based on my book of the same name. Compassionate Recovery is a universal, inclusive, evidence-based, and trauma-informed approach to healing attachment and addiction. This program will offer a way to build on what we already do in 12 Steps, Buddhism, and other healing modalities. It will also open up the healing to more people. I'm excited about it, and I know that you will be too, because we're all in the same boat: We want to be free of suffering and its causes. We want happiness for ourselves and others. And there's just too damn much suffering in this world, so we can use as much help as we can get.

After more than thirty-four years in the recovery world, I feel that we need to use as many approaches as we can to offer as much healing as we can to as many people as we can. Let *The 12-Step Buddhist* and *Compassionate Recovery* serve as a foundation and adjunct to other solutions out there.

Why Buddhism?

Based on my experience and observations since 1984, I believe that Buddhism contains immeasurably powerful methods for everyone, especially addicts. If these methods are understood and practiced in the context of a recovery program, they will help you understand and realize your spiritual nature, which is the true mission of the 12 Steps. As the Alcoholics Anonymous literature states, "our job is to grow in understanding and effectiveness."[1] The purpose of this book is to help you achieve that within the context of your particular 12-Step program.

The point I've been rooted to since before I wrote the first edition is that if we understand Buddhism, we really don't have to go anywhere special to practice. We can learn to be comfortable in our own skin, wherever we are, which is what we really need in recovery. That said, the root of Buddhism—what I believe is the root of all religious and spiritual traditions as well as 12-Step recovery—is compassion. I think we'd do well for ourselves and those whom we would like to help if we can develop compassion using the principles and practices outlined here, as well as expanding and fine-tuning that to a life based on true compassion.

I've been practicing Zen since 1988 and Tibetan Buddhism since 2005. I have an associate's degree in behavioral science, a bachelor's degree in psychology, and all but the thesis completed of a master's in research psychology. I'm not sure I would have been a good psychologist. As a veteran of 12-Step life, I've always had the attitude, "Hey, you can't tell me shit. I've been to 'Nam!" I've never been in the service, but addiction causes a similar post-traumatic syndrome, which made me feel like I was a war veteran and others couldn't understand me because they hadn't been there.

It was interesting to study addicts from a researcher's outside perspective. But when I tried to view addiction from the eyes of a psychologist, I always felt like the field of psychology was missing something. Psychologists didn't understand people like me. I also felt this way while working as a mental health specialist in treatment centers and psych units. These professional treatment programs always left me with that hollow, hospital-waiting-room feeling. Contrast this with the warm fuzziness of 12-Step meetings—as a friend says, "like sitting on your couch in your jammies."

Who This Book Is For

This book is for all addicts and alcoholics, but I will use the term *addict* for the remainder of the book to cover the entire spectrum of addiction in all its forms. I won't get into the debate over whether alcoholics are different from addicts. The Alcoholics Anonymous liturature and the Narcotics Anonymous literature make clear their respective positions. While reading, you are free to substitute the word *addict* for whatever applies to you.

This book is especially for those in recovery looking for a broader spiritual perspective—in this case, by applying Buddhist principles. It is also for the six in ten of us who are dual-diagnosed with psychiatric disorders in addition to addiction.[2]

However, the notion of dual diagnosis as defined by the treatment community—"when an individual is affected by both chemical dependency and an emotional or psychiatric illness"—may be a misnomer since the *Diagnostic and Statistical Manual of Mental Disorders, Fifth Edition* (DSM-5) added Substance-Related and Addictive Disorders as an official clinical psychiatric disorder in 2013.[3] Therefore, addiction and mental illness can be seen as one diagnosis, not two. In fact, trauma can and should be included in a more comprehensive diagnosis.

That said, the details of diagnosis of the various types of substance and behavior disorders are up to you and your treatment staff or management team to determine. For our purposes it's important to know that as addicts, abusers, or those with serious attachments, we are dealing with complex and difficult-to-treat symptoms that require a lot of help from different sources to promote healing. I honestly don't think the specific diagnosis is as important for us personally as it is for insurance to pay for treatment. If we have a problem and we want to heal, that's really the important fact to keep in mind, not the label.

This book was also written for individuals, spiritual teachers, therapists, and anyone else interested in, related to, working with, or working for anyone who is addicted to one or more of the following: substances, events, processes, or people. And in a very real sense, this book is for all sentient beings. In Buddhism, sentient beings are all beings with consciousness, all beings who feel pain. We're related to them all.

What Addiction Looks Like

There are hundreds of specialty 12-Step programs, but I believe that at the core of all addictions lies the same beast. Below are some ways in which we practice our disease. If you identify with any of these "fixes," this book is for you:

- ✶ **Substances:** alcohol, illegal drugs, nicotine in all forms, prescription drugs. Also those things that aren't meant to be used as drugs: inhalants, sugar, and caffeine. The list goes on.
- ✶ **Events:** trauma, crisis, trouble, drama. Some of us live for the next stimulating event. When life is uneventful, we can get very depressed. Luckily, we have many news channels and websites to keep us hooked. And going. And going. At one point, I was a news junkie. Since 9/11, when I hit bottom, I've been almost 100 percent news-free. (Does C-SPAN count?)
- ✶ **Processes:** drama, violence, work, gambling, sex, shopping, social media. Some things that don't happen all at once, but are part of the cycle: building up, crisis stage, remorse stage, and eventually active addiction. All addictions involve processes and events. Process addictions are often hard to classify as addictions because they're part of normal life for "normal" people.
- ✶ **People:** codependency, the addiction to someone else's process of addiction and their need for you to cosign, care for, and otherwise enable it and them. Also, note the cycle of love addiction, which can become a predatory, life-threatening sociopathology. This takes more forms than you'd think, and our culture supports it. I suppose the paparazzi *do* serve an economic function. But then again, so do alcohol, nicotine, meth, etc. If *People* magazine is your crack, there might be a program for you.

Because of numerous forms of addiction in our culture, very few of us are left unaffected by the disease. It's said in 12-Step meetings that addicts affect at least ten other people with their shenanigans. I think that's an understatement. This book is about deepening the understanding of addiction and its solutions for everyone affected. It's about our collective spirituality in general and Buddhism in particular, and about the relationship these have with addiction and the 12 Steps.

Aren't the 12 Steps Enough?

This brings up the question: Aren't the 12 Steps enough? No, they're not. That is, unless you're right in the middle of the bell curve of white, middle-aged, middle-class, Christian-oriented, straight males who dominate the 12-Step meetings. Even they, however, have deeper problems. (Please don't bring this up at meetings. You might experience a non-spiritual reaction from staunch members.) Compassion for ourselves and others is a vital part of the underlying principles, as we'll see, in Buddhism and in the 12 Steps.

At first, the 12-Step program is pretty much all that recovering addicts can manage. But the road of recovery is long and bumpy. We have to dig deeper at some point if we're going to find happiness. It's my experience that only a few in the 12-Step community have really tapped into the depth of what the program has to offer. Far from becoming spiritual giants, many people stay pretty sick well into double-digit sobriety.

The AA literature talks about compelling spiritual experiences like being "rocketed into a fourth dimension of existence of which we had not even dreamed"[4] and "limitless expansion."[5] Chuck C. was one whom many regarded as a true spiritual giant.[6] My sponsor, John C., was also in this class. They lived happy, joyous, and free lives—the goal of the program. But in my experience, these superheroes of the 12-Step world, people who actually walk what they talk, are very rare. On the contrary, some 12-Step groups and their leaders can be a little "off."

Anyone who's been in 12-Step programs for years knows that recovery can get stale. As an unconscious alternative to digging deep, we easily switch to a less obvious addiction: work, food, or sex. We do fine with our compatriots in 12-Step meetings, yet remain crippled with unresolved family, financial, relationship, psychiatric, and spiritual issues.

The foreword to the first edition of the AA *Twelve Steps and Twelve Traditions* says that the steps are "a group of principles, spiritual in their nature, which, if practiced as a way of life, can expel the obsession to drink and enable the sufferer to become happily and usefully whole."[7] Many of us work very hard at recovery yet still don't experience this level. Frustrated, we often relapse, or worse. Even those seasoned in 12-Step programs hit a brick wall in their spiritual development—no matter how good they look or sound.

A typical example is what I call the Circuit Speaker Fairy Tale. Those of us who've been around a while have heard hundreds, if not thousands, of circuit speakers at conventions and 12-Step meetings. Circuit speakers are people who travel around the country, at the expense of local groups, telling their stories in an hour-long canned pitch—one that is well-rehearsed and routinely repeated from town to town. In much the same way a comedian times his deliveries, so the circuit speaker delivers his/her power talk. Some circuit speakers are as skilled as professional entertainers and, thus, are able to paint a rags-to-riches picture of recovery that looks very different from the life of the average addict. It can be inspiring or depressing, depending on your state of mind. And, as addicts know, our state of mind is subject to sudden, frequent, and drastic changes.

As polished as circuit speakers can be, their deeper truths are often left untold. For example, I remember a speaker who delivered his amazing, canned power pitch. It was the same story as the year before and the year before that. The talk was great, but I found out that he had, just days before, beat up his wife. He didn't mention that in his talk. If he had, someone may have been helped by the honesty. And someone may have been spared another beating. The speaker and his wife of many years later divorced. Soon after, he married a young, beautiful woman (his sponsee) with whom he'd been having an affair.

Another speaker whom I heard more recently shared that, while he had been a famous 12-Step circuit speaker for thirty years, he was secretly a liar, a con man! He eventually relapsed, tried to commit suicide, and went to prison. These two examples illustrate the point that, while we can seem to be living the program on the outside, on the inside something is amiss. We can have ourselves and everybody else completely snowed with our addict charms and dope-fiend scams. Sometimes we don't even know this is happening because we're so busy being successful 12-Steppers. But if we choose to sit still long enough to notice, it bares the fact that something is wrong in Soberland. If we're at a sober stuck point that my sponsor called the Funnel, a drink, fix, pill, or bullet may be the only option that makes sense.

The Funnel can kill you, and you might not even know you're in it. It can bring you to your knees in long-term sobriety, or even take you out. If you've been to a 12-Step convention, you've witnessed a sobriety countdown, in which people of ascending lengths of sobriety are asked to stand up and be counted. Most are between thirty days and six months of sobriety, and then there are large gaps as the increments ascend: four at one year, three at two years, a couple at four and five years, no one at six, seven, or eight, one at ten, one at thirteen, one at nineteen, one at twenty, one at thirty-five. What happens to all those enthusiastic newcomers? Why aren't the rooms filled with long-term members?

While it is an amazing miracle that any of us actually gets clean and sober at all, abstinence is often about as far as we get, despite honest, sincere efforts at working the program. We get stuck in a recovery rut. The timeframe is most often between six and twelve years but can occur in later sobriety. Visualize a funnel, wide at the top where the numbers in early sobriety are high, narrowing out as fewer and fewer addicts trickle through to long-term sobriety. This is the phenomenon I've witnessed since 1984.

When sober members lose their minds, they're in the Funnel. Some do everything *but* relapse on their drug of choice. Many of us with long-term sobriety also relapse. Some of us kill ourselves. I remember a guy in Long Beach with twelve years of sobriety who, after speaking at the Alano club one night, went home and put a shotgun in his mouth. Many others suffer but don't know how to get better, despite efforts to work harder at their program, sponsor more people, and take on more service commitments. For many of us, the 12 Steps provide surface-level remedies to treat the symptoms of addiction but don't address our deeper attachment to the addiction.

Dealing with attachment is fundamental to Buddhist practice. Even if you aren't an addict, if you can relate to what's being said in this book, you'll be better equipped to apply Buddhism to a less severe problem.

Addiction and attachment are on the same continuum. For this reason, an addict easily understands Buddhism on a conceptual level, but putting it into practice in daily life is an entirely different matter. I've found that Buddhist groups are a great place to apply the 12 Steps, and the 12 Steps provide an excellent vehicle for the application of Buddhism. The practices and meditations included here will help clarify important points in ways that you will not learn from typical Buddhist teachers, unless they have direct experience with addictions and 12-Step programs. While such teachers are rare, if they're Buddhist, they deal with attachment on some level.

Everyone suffers from attachment to some degree. While there are similarities between normal attachments and true addictions, real addicts suffer major life consequences due to their addictions. For example, I wouldn't call everyone who breathes air an addict, but if you hold your breath for a while, you'll get a sense of how attached you are to breathing. Noticing attachment in all areas of our lives is what Buddhism teaches.

Buddhists who understand attachment will find addiction fascinating (I hope as observers and not as participants). The similarities between attachment and addiction will become clearer as you explore yourself through listening, studying, and practicing. And at times, the line between them will blur. Here's an example of the similarity between addiction and attachment.

Attachment means we want what we want, and as we say in the 12 Steps, we're "willing to go to any lengths" to get it. One thing that everyone is seriously attached to is identity—who we *think* we are. In Buddhism, the fact that we think we exist at all as a separate self is said to be an illusion. My identity is a dream for which the "I" is willing to go to war, lie, cheat, steal, argue, and suffer. It's a hallucination. And we're attached, even addicted, to this illusion.

If you think this doesn't apply to you, I invite you to try an experiment. Go to work tomorrow and try to be someone else for a while. Seriously, try it. To avoid meeting men in white coats and five-point restraints, tell at least one person in advance that you're going to do this. When people try to interact with you, don't answer to your name. Tell your boss you're beyond names and conceptual thoughts. At lunch, go to your bank and try to draw out some money without showing your ID.

If you're not game for that, here's one you can try right now. Most people identify themselves with their past. Spend the next ten minutes being totally free of influence by your own personal history. Try to have one original thought that isn't based on a previous thought, your education, upbringing, place of birth, or anything else in your life experience. Go ahead. I'll wait.

We're all addicted to being alive. I don't think you'll argue that point, no matter how self-destructive you may have been at one time. Some of us, who I'll call nihilistic existentialists in phenomenological crisis, obsessively desire to not exist. Such people, who take these thoughts very seriously, wind up killing themselves and/or others. Buddhism would say that they're still addicted—to the desire to not exist. If you know one of these people—perhaps a philosophy major or poet in the family—don't share this perspective with them. They'll get more depressed. Give them this book instead.

We're all attached to something else: concepts. Our concepts form our identities, our selective, distorted memories, personalities, goals, dreams, complaints, and fears. And we love to have them. When we look at attachment from this angle, it's obvious that we're addicted to our thoughts. We're willing to go to the mat for our right to believe them, especially the ones that we think define who we are. "But, who are we?" the Buddhist would ask. Once, while meditating, I asked myself that Zen question, "Who *are you*?" My addict said, "Who's asking?" Go figure.

Recovery as a Multifaceted Program

Use this book as part of a comprehensive, multifaceted recovery program. Such a program includes multiple aspects. Do as many of the following as needed to help with your recovery and to live to your full potential:

- Commit to therapy.
- Facilitate therapy with medications as prescribed.
- Exercise your body and mind.
- Participate in spiritual groups.
- Volunteer in your local community.
- Accommodate a practice of self-care.

Commit to Therapy

Commit to trying different kinds of psychotherapies. There are many new forms currently being used with addicts that yield good results.

Cognitive behavioral therapy (CBT) is backed by new brain science that shows that people who learn to reframe—or think differently—about their addictions have a better chance of success in recovery. Dialectical behavior therapy (DBT) incorporates mindfulness techniques as well as communication skills and owning one's own behaviors. While the latter was designed for use with borderline personality disorder, it can also be very useful for addicts who don't have that disorder.

There are also techniques such as neurofeedback and EMDR—eye movement desensitization and reprocessing—that get a lot of press for their effectiveness in treating addiction as well as the underlying traumas that help create addicts in the first place.

Trauma itself has entered center stage in the understanding and treatment of addictions, and there are specific treatment modalities for trauma as well. We'll talk about it more in chapter 3. Any treatment provider who deals with addiction should be trauma informed. Your well-informed clinician will be up to date on the latest research and training on trauma and its relationship to addiction.

Part of your commitment to self-compassion and healing is to shop for a good therapist and therapeutic modality with as much consideration as you would give anything else, like a car or a good coffee maker.

Facilitate Therapy with Medications as Prescribed

To facilitate therapy, be open to taking medications as prescribed by a medical doctor who understands addiction *and* is willing to talk with your therapist. Since the first edition was published, I've made use of medications in my own recovery. I have a PhD psychotherapist who works with a psychiatrist to prescribe medication that helped me through a very difficult time. When it was time to get off of those meds, I consulted with the members of my recovery management team to wean off carefully and under supervision. I believe that this approach saved my sobriety and quite possibly my life, and I recommend that you seriously consider it if your team thinks it could help you in your recovery. But again, please do your research. Make sure that you know the effects of the medication on your long-term health. Work with your team, but remember that you are your number-one advocate.

Exercise Your Body and Mind

Exercise your body and mind. I can't emphasize this enough. When I wrote the first edition, I had yet to begin a serious yoga practice, but I was going to the gym regularly and still do. In my experience, there is nothing more beneficial to mood and energy than a good, strong cardio session. In 2010 I became a daily practitioner of heated power vinyasa, a very physically demanding yoga style. The goal in any exercise is to get your heart rate up in a manner that is safe for your age and physical characteristics. There are tools to calculate target heart rate at most gyms and online. Any form of healthy exercise will help your recovery, but yoga has the benefit of being mindfulness based, so it really fits in with a 12-Step Buddhist approach.

Introduction

Yoga and Recovery

If you feel you might not be flexible enough to do yoga or may be embarrassed if you take a class, don't worry. I felt the same way. There are all kinds of different classes and studios. If you look around a little bit, I'm sure you can find a class that meets your ability where you are.

At first I was embarrassed and frustrated. I didn't have the body for yoga and felt shame around all the other fit people in the class. But I did what we say in AA. I *kept coming back* until I eventually developed a daily practice.

I approach yoga from the perspective of recovery and spirituality. Yes, it's a physically demanding practice and does get the heart rate up while providing a ton of benefits for the body. But it also feeds my soul. I consider the practice of yoga to be a moving meditation—and an integration of body, breath, and mind. In fact, I even became a certified yoga instructor through CorePower Yoga in 2011. I've been teaching ever since. I created a group in Portland called Yogis in Recovery where we did yoga, meditation, and sharing. All of my yoga trainings and practices have informed my recovery and the way I live my life today.

The social part of yoga can support recovery too—and it can also present some challenges. When I go to 12-Step meetings, the "meeting after the meeting" typically takes place in the smoker's area outside. This is not the case after any yoga classes that I've ever been to. We can see there's a difference in wellness mentality between yoga practitioners and 12-Steppers.

On one hand, 12-Steppers often have poor boundaries, difficulty dealing with their extreme emotional highs and lows, and a tendency to engage in unhealthy habits like smoking, making poor nutrition choices, and engaging in toxic relationships. But they're in recovery and have an ability to be raw, authentic, and gut-level honest that you don't see much outside of 12-Step groups. Yogis, on the other hand, can be a pretty difficult crowd to feel comfortable in, especially for those in recovery. Yoga, as we see it in the West, is a practice of the privileged. It costs plenty of money and requires a certain amount of courage and self-esteem to begin for many people not comfortable in fitness settings. Yogis can be superficial, oversensitive, and forgetful of the principles and practices of yoga. In fact, there's a whole philosophy that goes contrary to Buddhism but I've heard some teachers promote: detox to retox. In other words, party as much as you want, then come to yoga to sweat it out so you can get back on the carousel and do it all again. This may or may not be addictive behavior, but I think it's against the main anti-harm and anti-intoxication principles of yoga.

As we discuss further on, the new brain science has mapped out exactly what happens in the addict's brain. One of the main points is that addiction hijacks the brain's reward system, making the body feel a need for that reward again and again. Trauma also changes the way the body reacts during stress, causing the person to lose the ability to rationalize under stress. Practices like yoga, tai chi, and martial arts work on the somatic—or body—level but also on the energy and chemical levels to literally build new brain patterns that help us cope with stress, difficult emotions, and traumas. These ancient Eastern practices can really work wonders. In fact, some researchers have shown that yoga and other somatic practices are more effective than any medication in relieving the suffering caused by trauma.[8]

Stay Integrated in Body, Energy, and Mind

In the 12-Step Buddhist retreats and weekly groups that I did for five years in the Portland area, we worked with many aspects of healing in an effort to bring integration to the recovery community. We worked with shamans, crystal bowl healers, several Tibetan lamas—I took people to initiations and connected them with many live teachings—acupuncture, therapeutic massage, Reiki masters, art therapists, Hindu teachers, and a great deal of yoga. All of this was based on the idea that there are many modalities available for people in recovery to utilize. But for the treatment providers who are not familiar with addicts, we tried to bridge the gap. For addicts unfamiliar with the different tools, we tried to connect them. As always, my approach is about integration of tools designed for healing.

Yoga is a great way to integrate body and energy, and it's very interesting to integrate Buddhism and yoga. Yoga as a spiritual practice is based upon the Vedas, the most ancient Hindu teachings in India. The Vedas were also the Buddha's foundation for Buddhism. There are many differences between Buddhism and yoga, but in my experience, there are enough similarities that the two can be practiced interchangeably. We won't go into all the super-deep philosophical insights that separate the Buddha's teachings from earlier yogas—that would take a whole book! But one of the main points is that while the Vedas attempted to define the end goal as connected to a god source, the Buddha more or less refused to elaborate on the topic.

I think the Buddha taught that we're our own gods of a sort. We're ultimately responsible for everything that we experience, good and bad, seen and unseen, traceable and so far back in our past lives that we'd literally have to be a Buddha to see the connection. In fact that is exactly what happened. The Buddha saw and could elaborate on all of his past lives to the beginningless beginning. The gurus and yogis before him could only go back so far.

But if we think about the Buddha as an enlightened being, that's probably too much for most of us to feel that we can aspire to. Stillness is the key point. We can do a simple, easy practice that can help us all right away without meditating for twelve hours a day or becoming a monk or nun.

The best thing about a yoga session is the two-minute *savasana*, or resting pose, at the end. After we move and breathe and push through our hour-long session, we get a moment to chill. In that space we can get a break from our minds, our to-do lists, and our worries. And because the savasana follows lots of effort, it's that much sweeter. We can get a few minutes of clarity, peace, and insight—and some glimpse of what the Buddha taught—in our savasana. And of course we can also do seated, still meditation practice in addition, or as an alternative.

For the mind, I read a ton and take courses in everything from web development to technical writing. I study intellectuals like Jordan Peterson and watch informative YouTube videos to learn everything I can. This kind of brain growth is key to my sobriety and spiritual development. Just as we have other practices to nurture our body and energy in recovery, feeding the mind is key, and it's easy to do in this information age.

Participate in Spiritual Groups

In AA we always say that it's vital to our sobriety to get involved. Get a service commitment of some kind in whatever group that you find yourself in. It really helps you feel connected. Believe it or not, one of the strongest ways to feel OK in your own skin is to feel connected to a group by being of service. Don't just sit there downloading information. Participate!

My teacher explained it like this. The Buddha said that there were some characteristics required to be on the path to end suffering. The first was our participation, which can also be thought of as faith or confidence in 12-Step terminology. But the idea is that without our interest, we don't participate, and if we don't participate, we have no vested interest in succeeding on the path. So participation is key, even if we're not feeling it at first or we don't really know what we're doing. Bring your body—your head will follow. Plus, we now have so many teachers doing live Instagram and Facebook feeds of their teachings, it's really created an exciting new level of accessibility for participating.

Volunteer in Your Local Community

Volunteer in your local community beyond 12-Step and meditation groups too. Participate in different types of groups—spiritual, secular, personal development. Community is key in recovery. Volunteering fosters a sense of responsibility, involvement, and connection. There are many ways to be involved. Most Dharma groups have opportunities like food distribution programs. It's better to get connected than to feel like an alien. Get up, suit up, show up, and get involved.

Accommodate a Practice of Self-Care

Don't forget regular self-care: get a massage, eat good foods slowly, take vitamins, and explore natural health remedies. Be nice to dogs and the elderly. It's called lovingkindness in Buddhism. Mix things up. By learning to balance the serious work of recovery with pleasure, you'll enjoy even the mundane aspects of life. Take it seriously but have fun.

Sexuality and Buddhism?

Sexuality can be a big source of shame for many people. Addicts are no exception. In fact, we probably carry more shame around sex than non-addicts. In our 12-Step Buddhist groups and retreats over the years, many LGBTQ (lesbian, gay, bisexual, transgender, and queer) members found comfort and acceptance in our community. I was told that it was because they had felt so much judgment and condemnation in other, more traditional religious settings. I've had the privilege of getting to know many LGBTQ addicts over the years and am honored to have had the opportunity to help people find self-compassion in the context of what could have been a lifetime of shame.

Through the process of serving the *whole* recovering community in this way, I found that I was able to deal with much of my own shame and hang-ups regarding my sexuality too. Back around 2011, I lost interest sexually in my long-term partner. When I moved out into my own place, I found myself perusing Craigslist anonymous ads one day and, out of curiosity, began experimenting sexually with men. Until I learned to practice compassion for myself and others through the practices of a 12-Step Buddhist, these experiences had always been a weird source of internal conflict for me. I consider myself heterosexual yet open, so how did these attractions fit? I was able to navigate this question with compassion.

It's more than internal conflict for many people too. LGBTQ individuals, unfortunately, are still being targeted by people who don't have compassion. It's not a good situation, even in very liberal areas of the country. I want the LGBTQ community to know that they are supported, wanted, needed, and welcome. This is how Buddhism and recovery work. It's not about hate, judgment, or criticism. It's about compassion for ourselves and each other. We've got a long way to go, but I believe in the common humanity that we all share and that it will one day be the main principle that guides our behavior toward one another. May we all be happy and free.

Some of the people who came to the 12-Step Buddhist groups identified as sex addicts. I'm a pretty sexual person and have always had high energy in that regard, so I explored some of the 12-Step groups and other literature on sex addiction to see if this applied to me as well. I didn't relate to the specific behaviors listed in the literature, but an addict is an addict. Our brains will do what addict brains do: seek reward, have consequences, withdraw, repeat.

I wanted to share this with my readers because maybe you have some shame around sexuality that you might want to address. I've had a lot of it myself. This is my experience, and I just hope that if you have something similar going on that you feel a little bit less alone. The practices of compassion that we talk about in the section on the 12 Steps can help you find relief. Compassion is the foundation of all the tools we use in recovery and in Buddhism. It is the first step in self-care, and it supports every aspect of a multifaceted recovery program.

The bottom line in dealing with any of our feelings—whether they're about shame, guilt, fear, or not accepting who we are—is that alienation kills more addicts than anything else.

So be free. Do you. And whomever else you want to as long as it's non-harming.

By an Addict, for Addicts

This book will help anyone who has dealt with addiction, Buddhism, and/or the 12 Steps. First, it offers practical techniques that are applicable to everyday situations in the life of the recovering addict. This isn't another memoir of half-truths, nor is it a story about how an addict became a Buddhist and lived happily ever after. It's about the reality of the spiritual path for all of us suffering sentient beings, and it is in language that the addict can understand. If this makes the addict in you nervous, it's OK. Tell the addict not to worry. No one is trying to kill him/her. The addict will survive, regardless of how sober, spiritual, or successful you become. I just want the rest of you to flourish and find lasting happiness. That is the promise of Buddhism for *all* beings. My aim is to make the workable tools of Buddhism available for those with the super-cunning personality of the addict.

Second, I wrote it from my experience as an addict. No matter what their credentials, experience, brilliance, or level of spirituality, I don't believe that anyone but an addict truly understands the disease of addiction. I remember doing my third step—turning my will and my life over to the care of a power greater than myself—with a Catholic priest. He got frustrated and said, "Hey, you're the expert on this; it's way out of my league."

It's common to meet this lack of understanding in those whom we ask for help. We've all looked into the eyes of our doctor, mother, employer, friend, children, and dog after one more in a seemingly endless series of addiction-related catastrophes to be met with blank disbelief. They just don't understand why we do this to ourselves and to them. They can empathize and socialize with us; they can criticize or even wish to euthanize us, but they cannot know addiction. The 12-Step literature says that we are "bodily and mentally different." I doubt that in the 1930s they had any idea that science would one day back this up, irrefutably. But we know how different we are. Don't we?

Third, I wrote this book from my experience as a Buddhist who understands addiction. I've had to learn to make the connections between Buddhism and my 12-Step program through my own work because, in my experience, Buddhist teachers don't understand addicts very well.

In 1995, I was in a very bad way and went to my Zen center for help. I was in a desperate, homicidal-suicidal state of mind. I couldn't function. At one point, I smoked six packs of Marlboros in one day. I cried out at large 12-Step meetings, begging for help. I reached out many times to individuals in the *sangha* (Buddhist community). The teacher, Ruben Habito, tried to help. He said some useful things such as, "Seven times I fall, eight I rise," and, "In Buddhism, we say it's a terrible tragedy to end one's own extremely precious life because it's so rare to be born human." But I knew from the look in his eyes that he hadn't been where

I was. In the long run, the center was not even remotely equipped to address the severity and peculiarity of my mental, emotional, and physical addiction and my spiritual situation.

I feel that Buddhism *does* have the tools that could have helped me then, because they're helping me now. What was and is missing are communities and teachers who are equipped to deal with the complexities that addicts face. The Dalai Lama—exiled political leader and reincarnated bodhisattva—himself admits that Buddhists have much to learn from other religions in terms of working in their local communities. Buddhist monks traditionally spend most of their time in monasteries working toward enlightenment, and not much time engaging with laypeople. You don't see many monks on staff in detoxification or acute psychiatric centers.

Many years after that incident, I still can't imagine going to one of the many local Buddhist centers around the country if I were in the midst of a bad run—drunk, blacked out, tripping, and tweaking. They don't know what to do with me now, with many years of sobriety, so I'm pretty sure that if I showed up in prime addict condition, they'd call 9-1-1. I understand Buddhism from the perspective of one who must apply it to live sober and sane. That's hard-won experience. While it sucked for me as I got this experience, I hope you can benefit from it.

Fourth, this book addresses mental illness, trauma, and addiction, because I have suffered from various mild forms of mental illness for much of my life. With the combined tools of therapy, medication, 12-Step work, and Buddhism, I've crawled up out of the worst of it. The 12-Step community calls this "problems other than alcohol" and tries not to address it. There are some special meetings, but if you've ever been to a Dual Diagnosis 12-Step group, you'll know that peace of mind isn't the strong point.

In my experience, neither the Buddhists nor the 12-Step community is properly equipped to deal with dual-diagnosed addicts. I've seen many therapists since childhood. They really couldn't help much until I learned how to apply and integrate recovery with therapy and Buddhism. This book is about how to do that. Don't worry, you don't have to be mentally ill to benefit, but everyone who deals with addiction should be aware of the mental health issues. With this knowledge, you'll be better equipped to help someone who needs it.

One of the most important reasons why this book will help you is this: it is my *intention* for it to help you. In Buddhism, intention combined with wisdom is everything. I seriously believe that, if my work is done with the intention of maximum benefit, then it *will be* of maximum benefit. My intention is thus, and I don't believe that I'm working alone. Tibetan Buddhism says that there are numberless bodhisattvas—beings committed to the enlightenment of all—who are ready, willing, and able to send out help to those who need it. All ya gots to do is ask.

Buddhism says that if we ask for the Buddha's help, the Buddha will help us. Helping us is his job, his promise, his *samaya*. That's why he's called the Buddha or Awakened One. He's awake to the reality that we're all interconnected, we all suffer, and we all need love. The Buddha really knows it, lives it, and *is* that awakened state. And there are numberless Buddhas available in the infinite dimensions where Buddhas dwell. It's pretty cool when you think about it.

Intention works both ways. The processes outlined in this book will help you if your intention is to be helped. In 12-Step rooms, we call this "willingness." I should warn you, though; even if you say you don't need any help, I'm certain that if you read and apply even a little of this book, you *will* notice change, a shift of consciousness.

In 12-Step language, a spiritual awakening is *the* result of the steps. You'll have to try it to prove me wrong. When you do, let me know what it's looking like down the road. Contact me at the12stepbuddhist.com.

If you honestly work through this book and determine it's just not for you, then by all means, give it to someone else. As you walk away, say a little prayer like, "May this action be of benefit." That will help you and the recipient. With that single action, you'll be practicing Buddhism and recovery, so maybe the book will have helped you after all.

Buddhism is the perfect tool for relief from suffering, but it's not enough to deal with serious addiction. I know, if you're a hard-core Buddhist, you might be saying that if we only practiced the true Buddhadharma—Buddhist enlightenment practice—we'd be free of all addictions. That may be true for some, but not if you're a real addict.

A 12-Step program is a necessary, but insufficient, route to complete recovery from addiction. Whole recovery is more than a twenty-year coin, a BMW, and a fat 401(k). If you're a hard-core 12-Stepper, you might be saying if we just *did* what the program and our sponsors told us, we wouldn't *need* anything else. Maybe you're one of those for whom that is true. But it's not true for everyone in recovery. In my experience, it's not true for most of us. If you think it's true for you, then you're the exception rather than the rule. Or, you may be in the Funnel.

If you're an addict who's lost jobs, families, relationships, aspirations, dignity, and freedom, I recommend a way of life in the 12 Steps. If you're one for whom the program is not enough, then the ancient teachings of Buddhism can help, particularly when they are applied in an integrated manner to developing, enhancing, and sustaining the spirituality that is the basis for your recovery.

I Am Not Your Guru

As you enter into the 12-Step Buddhist practice, I recommend keeping your focus on yourself and using the methods from your integrated therapy to guide you in recovery. For many years, followers of Buddhism emphasized the importance of a guru, but one of the things that's changed in the 12-Step Buddhist landscape in the last ten years is that we've had a lot of trouble with teachers abusing power and positions of authority. While I still feel that a legitimate teacher is indispensable, there is a move away from declaring the need for a guru and toward clinical instruction of mindfulness, compassion, and self-compassion.

In 2018, Noah Levine, author of *Refuge Recovery*, was one among many Western Dharma teachers accused of sexual misconduct. The huge meditation center Spirit Rock and its founder Jack Kornfield have revoked Levine's teacher status. The #metoo movement brought about many articles, including secret reports and police investigations.

Levine's Against the Stream nonprofit has dissolved over these allegations. His community of teachers and students has split. He claims innocence amid multiple investigations by separate organizations, and has not been charged with any crimes. Levine and I crossed paths, and I wrote about some of that in the first edition, so I'm even more saddened by the controversy.

There is no denying that the Refuge Recovery programs have become a worldwide recovery movement. There are meetings, retreats, podcasts, and forums dedicated to being a Buddhist in recovery. But now due to the controversies, there are legal battles over the rights to use the name, and at the time of this writing, the Refuge Recovery treatment center is closed.

When I wrote *The 12-Step Buddhist*, I just wanted to share my experiences as a Buddhist in recovery. I am not your guru. But you, my readers, are my sangha. I think it's time that we move into more science-based, evidence-backed practices that are supported by clinicians in the treatment field as well as peer-led communities and spiritual teachers. My book *Compassionate Recovery* takes this even further and lays out a simple program for recovery based in the principles that we use in this book and what we've learned over the years.

One benefit of being older is that it's easier to see that what we feel is important at one point in our lives fades into the distance in the long run. Think about your early high school years, how you thought you'd die when that first love broke your heart. What does it matter to you now? If you're anything like me, you can look back and see how the things that seemed so significant really weren't as important as you thought at the time.

The people we've idolized have often turned out to be less-than-stellar examples of enlightenment over time. For example, look at your favorite rock stars, Hollywood movie stars, sports heroes. Mine have been Prince, Robin Williams, and Elvis, to name a few. These idols showed their humanness. There are so many stories like this. One that hits close to home for me is the story of Trevor Tice, founder of Core-Power Yoga. When I met him in yoga teacher training, I was in awe of the man who'd created such an amazing company that brought yoga to so many people. I remember speaking with him about *The 12-Step Buddhist*, and he told me he needed it because of his own struggles. I gave him my number and offered to help. But that call never came.

What came, instead, was an article reporting on his death in 2017:

> CorePower Yoga founder Trevor Tice, found dead in his posh San Diego home in December, spent his last hours careering around the house, leaving pools of blood from a severe, self-inflicted head injury the medical examiner says killed him. . . . A toxicology report showed he was intoxicated and that he had non-toxic concentrations of antidepressant and antianxiety medications in his blood. He also suffered from liver disease, the coroner's report said.[9]

This story, like all the tragic stories of addiction without recovery, underscores the need to continue this work and to build on it in ways that will reach as many addicts as possible.

In AA we kind of idolize our sponsors. It makes sense because they do save our lives in a way. But I don't even believe in AA sponsorship for myself. I had a sponsor for many years, and I have sponsored people. My sponsor was a hard-core, solid AA member. When he died, he had married a newcomer with two years sober who was stealing his pain medication for cancer. She told me that he asked her for a shot of whiskey before he died. Be careful not to idolize. This is my point. In 12-Step programs, it can get weird, because as addicts we have expectations and demands that aren't always realistic. I don't currently have an AA sponsor, and I'm fairly certain that I never will again.

Don't make the wrong person your master. I still believe that to be serious on the Buddhist path, it is helpful to find a legitimate master. My teacher, Chogyal Namkhai Norbu, was real. He was a long-term Tibetan scholar and master practitioner, and he passed away on September 29, 2018. My practice grew immeasurably because of him. But since there are so many problems with teachers who abuse power, it might be better to go the way of current trends that use mindfulness and compassion practices in a scientific way to bring healing to addicts. If you really need to meet your guru, you will. But most of us just want to live a sober life and be comfortable in our own skin.

It Works If You Work It

The 12-Step Buddhist has been a bestseller for many years. It's brought me in touch with so many amazing people who felt the same as I have on the path of recovery. I know of many who read my book in treatment, were able to establish their own sobriety, and went on to become treatment counselors themselves.

I met one recently at a conference on addiction. She told me that she had read my book many years earlier and had used it to get sober. When I met her, she had become a leader in the treatment field and was responsible for helping thousands of people raise awareness on addiction and recovery. Another man told me a similar story. He was a presenter at the conference and had used *The 12-Step Buddhist* in his work over the years.

I'm so grateful to all the people who've come up to me across the country and told me how they've been helped by this work. I really wanted to update it because after ten years of integrating the practices into my life, especially in really difficult times, I feel even more strongly now about its value to recovery. As we say in 12-Step programs, "It works if you work it."

The ideas that I set forth in the first edition were new at the time. We didn't have much to go on. But the similarities and connections between the principles of the 12 Steps and those of Buddhism were undeniably strong and remain so to this day. I hope that you'll find the updates useful and will continue to contact me regarding your success with the material.

Darren's Story

Understanding that beneath the many broken memories, his
experience was like shattered glass. Seeing clearly the punctured
delicate ego reflecting the fragments each in full clarity.
Then to uncover the root of suffering as the basis for realization,
and necessary to appreciate happiness.

—*Tysa F.*

I'm sixteen, lying in a fetal position on the bathroom floor, my face
bruised from a beating, hair chopped, and my identity obliterated—
out of my mind with debilitating agony. I promise myself that "If I ever
get free of this hell, I'll come back and help people like me." It's thirty
years later, and I'm sober and reasonably sane. My life is blessed with an
amazing collection of spiritual tools that were powerful enough to end
much of my suffering and set me on the path of true happiness—which
includes sobriety but also much more. With this intention, I make an
offering—this book and my service work that I do—to those who can
benefit from my experience.

But, to understand the cure, you need to understand the disease.
I won't go into a long drunk-a-logue, a war story that you can hear at
any 12-Step meeting. I'm not interested in impressing anyone with the
severity of my illness or the extremes of my past behavior. The purpose
of disclosure, at a 12-Step meeting or in these pages, is twofold.

First, my story is motivation to do the work. Acknowledging and
understanding the depths of our true condition is the impetus of
spiritual progress. Real change requires real commitment. Superficial
changes, like abstinence from addiction, are necessary to begin the
process. But deep, fundamental change requires deep, fundamental

motivation—at the core. The condition I describe is overwhelming. *Totally incapacitating.* But honest disclosure is a necessary prerequisite to recovery for all of us. Without this basic motivation, most won't do the work necessary to grow spiritually and to stay sober. At spiritual programs, workshops, seminars, and retreats, you see weekend warriors who are like some Sunday churchgoers with no carryover into the workweek. For me, spiritual progress is not a hobby. It's a way of life.

Second, addicts require honest disclosure to identify their condition. We tend not to listen if we don't identify. If you can relate to the basic humanity that I share with you, you will feel connected to another human being who has suffered like you. I'm not saying, however, that I've suffered more or less than anyone else or that you should feel bad about my experiences. We all suffer and can relate if we're honest with ourselves. We just have to sit still long enough to let it touch us.

In recovery, when we're straight with ourselves and our 12-Step fellowship, we can address our addiction. Buddhism teaches that only when we feel our own pain can we feel compassion for ourselves and others. It's useful to recognize this parallel. In my experience, however, not many Buddhists engage in self-disclosure to the same degree as those in the 12-Step community.

As the token recovery guy in many spiritual groups, people are often shocked when I share the raw stuff commonly heard in 12-Step meetings. But without this level of self-awareness and disclosure, I can't progress on the spiritual path or help you to identify your own suffering. This is where the paths of Buddhists and recovering addicts cross, and where we can help each other.

The Roots of My Suffering

I was born in a south suburb of Chicago in 1962. My mother suffered from a litany of ailments: regulatory arthritis, uterine and breast cancer, chronic ulcers, you name it. She was also, according to post-mortem psychiatric analysis by my shrink, someone with bipolar disorder and a borderline personality. My dad, previously abandoned by his parents during the Depression, voluntarily enlisted for WWII service at seventeen. It was an escape from his upbringing in what he called "work farms," basically forced child labor. My parents had painful lives and tried, by all accounts, to live the American Dream. But for us, it never quite worked out that way.

When I was in fourth grade, we moved to Tucson, Arizona, where I developed a strange coping mechanism, later recognized as an obsessive-compulsive disorder. This was the compulsion to touch an object a certain number of times in just the right way. I'd walk by a doorknob, touch it, take a few steps, go back, and touch it again. Wash, rinse, repeat. This went on in my mind as well, in that I had to repeat words or parts of words over and over—useful these days for mantra recitation.

Another habit was saving things. I had a drawer filled with drinking straws, bottle caps, rocks, matchsticks, gum wrappers, etc. When I saw these solitary items on the ground, I was compelled to save them from being alone. Stuffing my pockets, I accumulated quite a trash collection. I was devastated when my parents, yelling at me for not throwing out my garbage, emptied my overflowing desk. They were always doing that. Throwing away bits and pieces of who I tried to be.

It wasn't until I took a college course called the Sociology of Prisons that I learned about these types of behaviors. They were defined as the primary and secondary identification mechanisms that we use to retain a sense of self. For example, upon entering an asylum, the patient is stripped of all the objects that defined his or her identity: hair, clothing, and personal possessions. With the primary identifications removed, individuality is lost—replaced by the uniform of the asylum or prison. To maintain a sense of self, the patient forms odd habits: collecting bottle caps, strands of hair, or developing an odd manner of speech. These are secondary identifications for which the prisoner becomes known.

The point of that course was to teach us that we are all institutionalized by society and forced to find a sense of self in clothes, cars, or by any means other than becoming familiar with who we are inside. According to the professor, marriage, career, and education are all secondary identifications. My method was to pick up lost little objects. You don't have to be an analyst to see that it was a neurotic attempt to save my self. It's a relief, frankly, that in Buddhism, there is no self to save.

First Meditation

Since I was in culture shock, had no friends, and had never lived anywhere but my suburban neighborhood, I played in the desert. I set traps outside of lizard holes, trying to catch an iguana or a desert chameleon. Never did snag me one, although I did catch a leg full of prickly pear desert cactus.

I was playing one afternoon when I turned to find myself surrounded by about a dozen sixth graders. They were pretty tough kids, known for bloody lunchtime belt fights in the schoolyard. I stayed in my room more after that, watching a nineteen-inch black-and-white television. All I got on the rabbit ears were a couple of local channels. When cartoons weren't on, I watched whatever else the channels had to offer. A public access karate instruction program became my favorite. My parents didn't want to pay for karate classes, so I was on my own trying to learn self-defense from this guy on television. He wore the traditional gi, a white karate uniform with a black belt tied around the waist.

I was busy learning how to kick those kids' asses when, at the end of the program, the teacher sat down on a cushion, knees bent and ankles crossed, and said, "And now we meditate." He said to close your eyes and follow your breathing. After a little while, he said something that stopped me in my mental tracks. I was already sitting down, but my mind even then ran a hundred miles a minute. He said, "Think of a pond in the middle of a forest, with no ripples."

I think that may have been the first sense of calm I'd experienced in my short life. I started watching that show all the time, even the reruns, practicing the karate kicks and meditating on my own. At some point, they stopped playing it, and I lost my first meditation teacher forever, but I never forgot about the pond with no ripples.

We moved again the next year, this time to San Jose, California. It was there, looking for books on martial arts, that I had my first real introduction to Eastern thought. I found the kung fu books mixed in with Zen, Hinduism, and Krishnamurti, and I used to thumb through all of them. One such book by Gichin Funakoshi, *Karate Do*, mystified and confused me, but I couldn't put it down. The book had mysterious philosophical thinking interspersed in between tricks and tips on how to seriously kick ass. The author talked about inner strength and amazing feats of endurance that he claimed anyone could do, and I believed him.

The show *Kung Fu* was on television at that time. I loved the show and the character Kwai Chang Caine. I watched every episode with total focus and tried to imitate both the kung fu moves and Caine's spiritual attitude. Somehow, even though this was just a Western with kicks replacing swinging fists, I began to get a sense of Eastern mysticism's real potential. The show affected me deeply in that the character always struggled between his American, aggressive side and his Chinese, Confucius side. Though for different reasons, inner conflict was to become a similar theme in my own life.

In fifth grade, I was given a battery of tests by the school district. My IQ at the time was around 138. That's when teachers started saying that I was smart and needed more challenges to keep me occupied. The real problem was, with no intellectual or emotional support at home, doing homework was impossible, whatever my IQ. I couldn't control my behavior and acted out constantly by hitting, kicking, and talking back. We now call this a behavior disorder, which qualifies kids for special education.

When I was in sixth grade, we moved to Northern California, the land of the hip, slick, and cool. My mom did me a great disservice by dressing me up for school every day. I showed up late to the first day of class looking like a used car salesman: greased-back hair; taped glasses; red, white, and blue sailor shirt; white pants; white belt; brown shoes poorly covered with white shoe polish. I continued learning to fight that year by reading books on karate and jujitsu.

My school desk was the kind with a lid that lifted up but was rounded inside so crayons and papers would never stay flat. I can still smell that wood top, where I had to lie with my head down for punishment so many times. My teacher said I was the kind of kid that he was going to read about in the paper someday. I didn't get the insult until many years later. I sat during reading time devouring the paperback of *The Exorcist*, wrapped in a homemade, brown paper grocery bag cover so it wouldn't get taken away. My mom knew I was reading it, but my teacher would be pissed because it was "dirty." I read an article in *Newsweek* not long after I finished the book about a family in Daly City that had knives and plates flying around their house. According to *Newsweek*, demonic possession was real. The night I read that article, I couldn't sleep. The feeling haunted me for many years. It was many years before I learned about Chod, a Tibetan Buddhist practice that deals with demons. Doing this practice teaches us to resolve even the most deeply rooted fears.

In seventh grade, my burgeoning hormones led me to find a new freedom. I refused to let my mom put grease in my hair, I took off my glasses, and I wore jeans and sneakers instead of slacks and dress shoes. Feeling light on my feet, I started practicing basketball so I could get into lunchtime games. After school, I worked incessantly at free throws, layups, and dribbling, but I couldn't catch up to even the dorkiest seventh graders. They had obviously been shooting hoops since birth.

I went to dances and made friends with some jocks. It was with them that I learned to guzzle champagne out of the bottle. I learned that while I couldn't play basketball at their level, they couldn't drink at mine. The worse I felt about not being athletic, the more I drank. The difference between me and the jocks was that while they could drink and act like assholes, they still made it to practices and won games. I just drank harder.

First Drug Use

In the summer before eighth grade, I noticed that my next-door neighbor had some interesting plants growing in her backyard. I jumped over the fence and snipped a few leaves. After drying them out on my windowsill, I pulled the tobacco from one of my dad's Winstons and stuffed the weed in. On the side of the house, alone, I smoked it.

I had discovered a magic method to end all my suffering and was in like Flynn. I needed more, and I knew right where to go. When I volunteered to babysit for that neighbor, I discovered her stash and commenced to smoke. This was during the first couple of seasons of *Saturday Night Live* with the original cast. I smoked ragweed and munched out while the kids . . . well, I'm not sure what they were doing. It was a great setup, until the neighbor found out and fired me. That was the first job I ever lost due to addiction.

By the time I was sixteen, I would lie stoned in bed for hours, head spinning. I'd watch fantastic Disney-esque cartoons race across the forefront of my consciousness. Everything was sharp and vivid. The sequences corresponded to my thoughts and emotions in a synchronized interplay of imagery and sensation. But this experience quickly degraded, and I chased down others in every way imaginable over the next several years. I knew in my bones that if I could concoct just the right mixture of drugs, people, and music, it would be cosmic and magical. But that never really happened, even when I dropped acid and sat in the doublewide trailer reading books about *Total Mind Power*. I was determined to get enlightenment, although I didn't have the language for it at the time. I had to transcend what we call in recovery the "consciousness of our intolerable situation."[1] I didn't even come close and had to run out and get as drunk as possible that night.

I won't deny that when I took four hits of Mr. Natural from an underground Rosicrucian Haight-Ashbury hippie dude and stood with sixty thousand people behind me at Led Zeppelin's Day on the Green in the late seventies, it was more than a pilgrimage to rock 'n' roll Mecca. It was a spiritual experience. But despite great hallucinations and the usual buzz, I never found any real peace.

Because of hallucinogens, I had the knowledge early on that things aren't what they appear to be; exploring this became something of a spiritual mission for me. A crazed friend told me, in some kind of pseudo-hypnotic late-night psychedelic whispering, that there was a secret that you could only figure out on acid. After that, I tried dozens of times in vain to get him to explain, sometimes to the point of rage. But he would never speak again of that mystery. Tortured, I vowed to discover it with or without his help.

So I took more acid, got more confused, smoked more weed, and drank more booze. I didn't get any smarter, nor did the habit increase my perceptiveness, emotional stability, or functionality. I drove myself deeper into the drug culture and further from school, home life, and the real world. When a hot blonde in denim cutoffs gave me some pot laced with PCP, I found out just how bad drugs could be. I blacked out and woke up in the park with a wino's hand down my pants. Grabbing someone else's bike, I bounced my head off the pavement all the way home, tore all the pictures off the wall, and finally slammed into my bedroom floor. It was so heavy, as we used to say, that I decided to smoke PCP at least twenty more times, even though once is enough to cause permanent brain damage. That's how my addict works. More, more, more, no matter what.

I effectively quit in the eighth grade to pursue pain relief full-time. I tried to go back—registered at five high schools—but never made it through more than a few weeks. Yet school officials kept passing me and my problem on to the next grade: freshman, sophomore, junior. I never even took one final.

My parents inconveniently kept finding and flushing my stash, but I kept using. In desperation, they told my drunk, raging, car mechanic older brother to come straighten me out. On a sunny Northern California afternoon, he found me at a neighbor's, where I was rolling around on the crisp lawn, blissed out on pot. I laughed like a drooling fool while listening to George Carlin reciting the seven words you can't say on television. No longer shocking; still funny.

My brother, Darryl, found me in the midst of that wanton freedom, and hated me for it. I saw his blue polyester overalls, sleeves rolled up past his forearms—buff from slinging Snap-on tools all day and adorned with a heart tattoo with his first wife's name crossed out. My guts sank into that warm earth. Like a flailing sledgehammer, he punched me straight in the face. My dog, Kida, a sweet, gray-brown husky with one blue eye and one brown, jumped at Darryl to protect me. He punched the dog too and threw Kida across the lawn. Then he dragged me into the house by the hair, bounced me off every wall, floor, and cabinet while beating me with his fists.

Adding to the torture and shock, my big brother tore down my meticulously gathered rock star posters, which had been acquired with illicit drug money. Next, he smashed all my drug paraphernalia and acid-head room decor and shoved it in the fireplace. He held me down on the floor and ruthlessly butchered my beautiful, long brown hair. Then he lit a match and held my face to the fireplace as I watched my primary identity burn.

In retaliation, I got more loaded, more often. The trauma of that beating scarred me for many years. I was determined to replace everything in an effort to reconstruct my world. It took about eighteen months. And just when all of my hair had grown back and my room was decorated with new Kiss, Zappa, Alice Cooper, Stones, and Hendrix posters, my brother repeated the scenario—more brutally. This time, after the beating, he took it a step further. He forced me to chop off my own hair, stuff my life into the fireplace, and light the match myself. My reaction again was to drink and drug even worse. When the pain is more intense, so is the pain relief.

One day, I came home to find that my parents had been arrested for food stamp fraud. They got fined and put on five years' probation. My middle-American, drug-free parents were now felons. My dad lost his job and the house. My dog got taken away, and we moved to a trailer park filled with blue-haired stiffs. Slightly disappointed at this turn of events, I naturally retaliated by cussing out the park manager, and within days, he served us eviction papers. My parents salvaged the situation by sending me to live with my brother. Recently divorced, he was less cheerful than ever.

My brother was a violent drunk but had never touched drugs. One of my new friends, the brother of a drug dealer, had access to cocaine. He suggested that I pay my brother back for what he'd done to me. So one night, we got him drunk and broke out the blow. We left him a freebie bindle of the white stuff as a hook. His ensuing fondness for the stuff ended his ability to call *us* dopers—and, eventually, his life. My brother went into rehab in 1984, right before I did. He stayed sober about 120 days, the most sobriety he would ever put together before dying—a crystal meth smoker—in 2000. For us addicts, the ride goes on until we stop it or it stops us.

Sobriety v.1.0

I entered rehab for the first time at twenty-two, having drunk, used, and been a mini-dealer for most of my teenage years. My brother was forced by his employer to get treatment for drug and alcohol abuse. On a visit to the facility with my parents, I attended mandatory group therapy. Family members described the drug use of the person in treatment and how it affected them. When it was time for me to share, the clock was all done ticking. I cried because my problem was *far* worse than my brother's. That's how I got "tricked" into treatment.

It was 1984. I went through the doors of the treatment facility. A message, crookedly burned into a pine plank above the door, said: *Through These Doors Pass the Most Beautiful People in the World.* Uncomfortably numb, a wad of yesterday's bile in my throat, spun out on yellow chicken crank and bong residue, I stared with disbelief. Who the hell were *they* talking about?

I did thirty-six days of rehab, consisting of reality (confrontation) therapy, sit-ups at 0'dark-thirty, lectures on nutrition and pharmacology, and—my favorite—a meditation class. On the wall of a visiting room in that converted surgical wing, over a cigarette-burned blue couch, I first encountered the 12 Steps. My eyes, which my dad often said looked like "two piss holes in the snow," shot down to the eleventh step: "Sought Through Prayer and Meditation to Improve Our Conscious Contact with God . . . and the 12th Step, Having Had a Spiritual Awakening as the Result of These Steps."[2]

In the treatment center, a lady named Margaret came to teach us meditation. She told us stories of sitting in retreats where you didn't move for hours at a time. Tears streaming down her face, she would continue in meditation until the teacher rang the bell, signaling to stop. I was awed by anyone who could have such discipline. Margaret was tough; she didn't take any crap from us smart-aleck druggies and insisted that we take the program seriously. She taught us some tai chi movements and how to meditate by staring at a candle. The sound of her voice guiding me through the process was strong and soothing. I was already attracted to the spiritual awakening they were talking about in the 12 Steps but hadn't met anyone who could guide me. This first real meditation instruction was enough to rekindle the interest that had been born back when I was a kid in Tucson, sitting like a pond with no ripples in the middle of a forest.

Having tried for years to figure out the secret that my trippin' buddy had proclaimed, the bits in the recovery program about conscious contact and spiritual awakening were big selling points. In the exit interview, my counselors asked about my clean and sober life plans. I had no idea, but they suggested that I consider the priesthood, given my spiritual leanings.

When I got out of the treatment center, I practiced the meditation with the candle alone in my room. I dove head-on into the 12-Step world of spirituality. All the newly sober young people went to meetings at noon, six, eight, and midnight. From there we stayed up until the wee hours in coffee shops talking spiritual matters. We shared our open wounds and our discoveries from meetings and step work. What fascinated me even then were the common threads that the 12 Steps shared with religion—minus the dogma, guilt, and shame.

When they said they had a wrench to fit every nut, I believed them. The first Friday night speaker I heard, over catcalls, was a priest named Doctor Fred. Through a wall of cigarette smoke, I saw that he was seventy going on about a hundred. He had white hair against black, priestly garb with a huge gothic cross on a chain that would make Flavor Flav jealous. When he introduced himself as a foxy, gay wino, I knew that if this crazy dude could stay sober, I was definitely going to make it. He was one of many colorful birds in that cuckoo's nest, and I loved it. Whatever keeps you coming back, as we say.

Going after the program like a puppy on a rawhide chew toy, I had a primary focus: the spiritual awakening they were all talking about. From where I sat, it sounded like what I'd been looking for all my life. I wanted what they had and wanted to get rid of what I showed up with—a life packed with nothing but agonizing misery.

From 1984 to 1994, I went to meetings and spent all of my extra time studying spirituality, reading spiritual books, going to retreats and meditation centers, and—my favorite—staying up late talking spiritual turkey with recovering folk. I picked the brains of anybody who I thought knew anything useful. I still talked nonstop, but now it was about spirituality. I learned to meditate and became conversant on metaphysical Christianity and its influence on the 12 Steps. For the first time, I was on a spiritual path that led somewhere.

I had trouble making a living, so it was time to figure out what to do with my life. Others told me they were impressed with my ability to read, remember, and apply spiritual teachings, so I decided to get a degree in psychology and become a spiritually oriented counselor. After years of scrambling from one sales job to another, selling everything from women's shoes to Hondas, I was ready for a meaningful goal.

Married with a baby, I moved to Southern California. I tried again—this time sober—to pick up my college career. This was a tremendous challenge with a fried mind and a seventh-grade education. Neither my wife nor I were emotionally stable enough to survive each other. She had a breakdown, changed sexual preferences, and went out on her own. I kept our son. I went to class and meetings and rode a moped to work double shifts on the lockdown unit at a psych hospital. The climb from the uneducated working class was harder than it looked, and it looked pretty hard.

For stability, I expanded my recovery program beyond meetings. I had weekly sessions at the university's counseling center, quit smoking, started running, and took martial arts classes in the evenings. As a psych major, I also took classes on Buddhism, Christianity, criminology, and sociology. While I grew in sobriety and progressed in my education, I felt like I had a pretty good overview of the human mind and its inner workings. This was the beginning of my interdisciplinary approach to recovery. Despite the difficulties, I got my bachelor's in psychology and went on to graduate school for my master's.

One evening, I came home to find that my girlfriend of three years had moved out. No warning, no notice. My reaction, with eight years of sobriety, was to get a tattoo, buy a Fender Strat, and start playing the blues.

At that point, I fell into a pretty serious depression. I'd been married and divorced, and the next long-term relationship failed. I should have jumped over to the counseling master's program and taken that degree, but my pride in being a scientist was too great. Then I got the brilliant idea to move to Dallas, Texas, home of Stevie Ray Vaughan, to study music while finishing my master's. The goal was to get another degree in the fledgling field of music therapy, thereby combining my early interests in music with a career in psychology. Another fine revision.

Unfortunately, the field of psychology left a lot to be desired. It was great to learn how to study, think critically, design surveys, and analyze data, but deep down, I never found what I was looking for. So, I turned back to an interest in music to find the real truth. I had also just finished three years of therapy with a cognitive behaviorist, and his conclusion was that therapy had taken me as far as it could. My dilemma was one of an existential nature now, and I would be wise to pursue my spirituality further. Instead I got a new, psychiatrically challenged girlfriend and stopped going to meetings. Eventually, I took some acid and sat meditating zazen style, as I'd learned from my Zen teachers.

Zen and the Art of Relapse

Back in my third year sober, a friend in the program recommended a Zen memoir by Janwillem van de Wetering, *The Empty Mirror*. It's about a merchant marine who traveled around the world looking for enlightenment and ended up spending a year in a Japanese Zen monastery. I knew that enlightenment was not only possible but my destiny, if only I could find the right book, the right teacher. But one program veteran who had been to the mountain, so to speak, said that I'd never find what I was looking for in a book. I wouldn't understand what he meant for a really long time.

Even though I had experienced meditation, I felt that many questions lined the recovery path. I continued to seek a teacher for this reason. I wanted to find a real Zen master, but settled for a lady practitioner. I found a lady in the Los Gatos Hills who was willing to teach me.

Standing on her porch in my T-shirt and jeans, I flicked an exhausted Marlboro Red into her bushes and rang the doorbell. She greeted and guided me through the hallways of what looked to me to be a mansion, filled with masks and statues from all over the world. We went into a room with nothing but pillows on the floor. We sat cross-legged, facing each other, and she told me to watch my breath for a few minutes. After-ward I said, "That's it?" and she said, "That's it." Somewhat less than thrilled, I left and went back to my books and meetings.

In 1990, around six years sober, I began to take Zen more seriously as a path. I read *Everyday Zen*; *Zen Mind, Beginner's Mind*; *The Three Pillars of Zen*; and others. My life had become more intense as a single parent and a full-time college student in recovery. One day, I just looked up Buddhist Groups in the Yellow Pages. I found a Zen group that con-sisted of a man and his wife. Zen practice is mostly about sitting still and silent, which is great for a mind like mine that never stops. I sat like this with them weekly for a few years at their Long Beach apartment.

The guy had seven years of sobriety at the time. I thought it was great that I had found someone in recovery who took meditation seri-ously. I noticed, though, that he didn't go to meetings very often. He relapsed on cocaine awhile later, but not before he took me to the Zen Center of San Diego to meet one of my favorite Zen authors, Charlotte Joko Beck. I had an interview with her and loved it. She told me to pay attention. I said, "To what?" and she responded, "Oh, I don't know, your eyebrow." I knew then that she was the real Zen teacher I'd been waiting to meet.

I continued to receive teachings by phone from Joko on a regular basis. This consisted of instructions to sit on a cushion, perfectly still,

watch my thoughts, question everything, notice all—the essence of
Zen. Joko's style was to offer this practice minus any trappings from her
training with the old-school Japanese master Taizan Maezumi Roshi,
by whom she was originally ordained. Meeting her and establishing a
teacher-student relationship was the beginning of a phase of the spiritual process from which, as Joko advised me, there is no return. (I'd
tried to give up the cushion—sitting practice—many times over the
years, but always found myself returning to the breath even when not
sitting formally.)

When meditating, I'd always found a lot of emotional content bub-
bled up for me. I feared that the practice could bring up more than I
could handle, so I always kept a therapist around. This was the early
phase of integrating Buddhism, the 12 Steps, and therapy, although I
didn't really know at the time that's what I was doing. I was just frantic
to stay on top of the emotional chaos that was my life. It was particularly difficult as a single parent and college student in recovery to stay
balanced. I knew meditation was a vital part of the process, but I also
knew that there was mud in the water that was bound to get stirred up.

In Texas, I got pretty sidetracked by trying to survive on a $5-an-hour
job and student loans with my son in special education as I was learning
music and getting over the culture shock of being a California trans-
plant in the middle of the great state of Texas. My Zen practice and my
recovery took a strange turn right about then.

Denton, Texas, has an annual event called the Fry Street Fair. Every
year around Cinco de Mayo, about ten thousand hippie-type, alternative, musically inclined kids come from everywhere for some good,
old-fashioned psychedelic fun. Dozens of bands perform. Everybody,
and I do mean everybody, trips. I thought I'd died and gone back to the
sixties. It was like a hot night in the Haight during the summer of love
that I'd missed out on growing up in the lame seventies.

It was there, standing in front of the Kharma Cafe with a fellow guitar student, the sole Black Sabbath fan in the jazz department, that I
had an epiphany. Bill Wilson, founder of Alcoholics Anonymous, said
in his biography *Pass It On* that he experimented with acid, séances, and

other fringe methods, without considering them relapses. After years of psychology education, Zen, spiritual development, therapy, and recovery, I suddenly realized that LSD was just what I needed to achieve my enlightenment. After all that work, I was sure to have a better, clearer, more insightful experience. Of course, I didn't.

My rationale was that I hadn't been ready for the cosmic experience as a troubled teenager, but over nine-plus years of sobriety, I'd learned so much. I guess I was trying to go back to the place I was in as a freaked out kid, to those days of hallucinogenic mystery, so I could finally figure out the meaning of it all. What I found out instead was that I was really depressed. The drugs just magnified it.

I'd thought I'd be able to unravel the mysteries of the universe with a quiet and still mind, highly trained in spirituality, well examined in therapy, and skillfully refined from graduate studies in psychology. Instead, I found myself staring at the carpet with the nauseous and dizzy realization that I wasn't going to learn anything new. The drug didn't move me beyond where meditation could take me. At that point, my existential dilemma was thicker than I could have ever imagined. I found myself on the phone with Joko, hungover and paranoid on cocaine and ecstasy. She again tried to pass on her teaching to me, to route me back to the present moment and the untruth of my thoughts. But it wasn't coming through to me; my receiver was tuned to another frequency. I was in my addiction. Neither the master, nor Zen Buddhism itself, could help me.

I left school and moved to Dallas for a job in television. There, I sought the help of Ruben Habito, a former Catholic priest who had become a Zen master. He tried to help me as my disease progressed, but I was insane, suicidal. I sat there, snot flowing from my nose, begging him to help me with my suffering. He said that in Buddhism, we value the preciousness of being born human and that if I killed myself it would be a waste of the opportunity. He told me to touch my infinite roots. These sayings make sense to "normal" Zen students, but I wasn't able to apply them to my addiction so easily.

He sent me to a guy with experience in the 12 Steps who told me that he'd sat zazen long enough that he could drink safely again—that it was all in my mind. I knew he was completely full of crap. That was the end of the conversation. I wasn't looking for an excuse to keep getting loaded. I was looking for a way to end my suffering without having to die trying.

More agitated than ever, I wound up taking designer drugs because I figured they were more advanced than acid, which was "so sixties." The newer drugs were designed for group therapy to help people feel comfortable. I found out too quickly that MDMA or ecstasy is mostly speed, and speed makes me paranoid. I needed some weed to calm me down. Once you're stoned, you get thirsty. So off I went, into the gates of insanity and hell.

I talked to Joko by phone, but she couldn't help me. I called my sponsor in California, and he couldn't help me either. I went to meetings and got sick of the drivel halfway through, stopping for vodka on the way home. I lost the television job, got a high-tech gig. As I got sicker and sicker, I was less and less able to manage my life.

Although I was no longer consciously practicing meditation, the mindful awareness was ingrained in me from previous years. It only served to make me acutely aware of the torment I was going through. I tried to drink and use my way to oblivion.

On Christmas 1995, I sat in my empty apartment. The landlord drove all night from Indiana to bust the door down and kick me out. My rent checks had bounced. I'd sent my son to my parents in Chicago because I wasn't able to take care of him and do cocaine at the same time. I checked in by phone with my brother in San Jose. He had just spent days looking out the window of a ghetto apartment, paranoid. Out of work, he traded hits of speed for the company of hookers. He said he always knew I wouldn't stay sober. What could I say? My life had completely fallen apart.

At a meeting, I found a guy who had relapsed after ten years of sobriety. He'd gone to a treatment center that specialized in relapse cases, so I borrowed the plane fare to Arizona from someone in the Zen group. I stopped in Chicago first because my mother was on her deathbed. While there, I went to a meeting in the basement of the hospital where I was born. I felt desperate and unable to connect with the program. I saw my mother, all sick and twisted up in that hospital bed, for what would be the last time.

It was a pretty weird experience being in the treatment center in Arizona after working in one and being sober all that time. I decided to leave AMA—against medical advice. I got back to Texas just in time to hit a dangerous emotional low. A lady I'd met in treatment offered to let me stay with her and her husband at their cabin in the Rockies. I arrived in Colorado with two backpacks. I would never see most of my belongings again. I left my apartment in Dallas with two cats, all of the pictures from my life, my books from college, all of my son's toys. Everything.

I got to the mountains and tried to start my life again. I got a tech job, went to meetings, and found a therapist. There were a lot of opportunities to do things I'd never tried in my life: mountain biking, kayaking, river fishing, skiing. After nine months of sobriety, I smoked some pot. That winter I skied, worked, drank, and smoked. I played my guitar, burned black tar, and wrote poetry on opium. I saved up for a car and drove, high, for twenty-four hours straight to get my son in Chicago. I got him back to Colorado and signed him up for school.

I made a big plan to buy a bunch of super weed and move to California. It was so strong that I fell asleep when I smoked it. I woke up one afternoon and the bag, and all of my moving money, was gone. My employer had had enough of me and offered a few paychecks to send me wherever I was going to go, as long as it was away from there. I decided that if I was going to be a drunk, stoned, depressed loser, I might as well do it on the beach. The craziest place I'd ever been was Santa Cruz, home of hippies, bikers, and kooks. I'd fit right in.

I loaded up the U-Haul and got to Santa Cruz with $300 in my pocket, a nine-year-old, and a truck full of hand-me-down furniture that I had accumulated in Colorado. I got a job as a graphic designer at a newspaper and proceeded to work, drink, and smoke. When I'd been sober in the eighties, I'd sponsored a seventeen-year-old guy. He was sober for seven years when he gave up on the 12 Steps. He was living in Santa Cruz, so I looked him up and we got high together.

At his apartment, I took mushrooms and puked all over his carpet. We argued, had an otherwise uncomfortable time, and he asked me to leave. I was higher than hell—mushrooming out of my head, drunk on cheap beer, and stoned on the strongest weed I'd ever had. I headed up to my rented room in the Santa Cruz Mountains where the California Highway Patrol was waiting for me. I was not only humiliated by being evicted by a guy for whom I'd been a spiritual adviser and authority figure for much of his adult life, I now found myself handcuffed in the back of a police car for drunk driving.

After nine months, I lost the newspaper job for being wasted at work. I was attending the Catholic church on Sundays, stoned out of my mind. I liked listening to the young priest talk about interesting spiritual topics. I decided to become a Catholic and planned to take the necessary classes, but they weren't really interested in having me on board. Go figure. Instead, I joined a manic-depressive self-help group that met on Wednesdays in the basement of a church.

Sobriety v.2.0

On December 4, 1997, I was at the bipolar group meeting when I heard a lot of noise upstairs. I went up there to yell at whoever it was. It turned out to be a Young People's 12-Step meeting going on. The cute secretary said, "Hi! Come on in, have a seat!" So I sat down. I've been clean and sober ever since.

I began sitting zazen again at home, in between meetings. After a while, I met Noah Levine in the Santa Cruz meetings. He represented what I had wanted for myself, namely to stay sober for ten years and to develop a good Buddhist practice, so I asked him to be my sponsor. This was several years before he wrote *Dharma Punx*. It was good to meet Noah and find someone as into meditation as I had once been. Although my sponsor relationship with him didn't work out, I am grateful to have had the experience of connecting with someone who saw beyond the 12 Steps to a deeper Buddhist perspective.

Over those first ten years of sobriety, the street drugs had grown stronger and I had grown older. There was less of a future to look forward to, and I frankly did not look too good out on the party scene. During my relapse, I had many experiences of devastating new levels of "pitiful and incomprehensible demoralization."[3] I guess I was just tired, so I started going to meetings again, got a new tech job, and met a new girlfriend.

The emotional problems I'd suffered since childhood were made worse by addiction and relapse. Because of this, the second period of sobriety has been difficult. To deal with it, I have to work on my recovery and spirituality nonstop.

In the desert hospital, the addiction shrink had diagnosed me with a plethora of conditions: bipolar disorder, post-traumatic stress disorder, poly-substance abuse, impulse control disorder, post-hallucinogenic perceptual disorder—which means that when I close my eyes, I see thousands of tiny, swimming particles of light. It's like being surrounded and engulfed by white noise. It never stops, and there's no cure or treatment for it. This is one reason why I need more than the 12 Steps to help me and a big reason why certain Buddhist practices are my only hope.

This time, I approached recovery with the knowledge that I have a mental illness—as do most addicts. Addiction is a brain disease—a serious, complex problem. While my 12-Step program is a vital part of my recovery and integral to my spiritual path, it alone is not enough. Over the ten years between getting sober again and writing the first edition, I developed my recovery into a flexible, dynamic approach that includes rigorous work in 12-Step programs, the use of medication combined with consistent, long-term medical psychotherapy, and intense Buddhist study and practice as well as community involvement, from creating dog parks to infusing spirit into the jazz scene.

A note on medications: I took antidepressant and mood-stabilizing medication for over ten years. I was able to wean off to the point that I use it only on rare occasions. I owe that to working a multifaceted, comprehensive recovery program that includes daily meditation practices with the help of my teachers and rigorous application of the principles of the 12 Steps, including regular attendance at meetings. With the doctor's guidance, I was able to slowly let go of the meds, one at a time.

I wanted to live without the side effects of agitation, sedation, and the like, so I needed to work really hard to get my moods under control with the other tools available. If you have psychiatric issues, I recommend that you find a psychiatrist who is willing to do therapy, instead of one who just throws drugs at you. I recommend that you follow the doctor's advice, be consistent, and stick with it.

This book is one big recommendation for combining approaches to recovery. I just want to be clear from the start that no matter what people in 12-Step programs may say:

a) **Meds are OK, especially when combined with therapy and used as a tool rather than a panacea.**

b) **Getting off meds eventually is OK if the doctor/therapist agrees and is willing to guide you through the process, no matter how long it takes.**

Additionally, this takes time, hard work, and a lot of meditation practice. For several years, my program was to go to meetings, see my psychiatrist, and practice Zen. It's a management team approach, and it works when you work it.

Despite the best of intentions, sometimes we can still face challenging times, as happened to me after the first edition of *The 12-Step Buddhist*.

The Funnel v.2.0: Addicted to Addiction

One of the most frequent comments that I get from readers is how they identified with the Funnel. As I said the first time around, this work is about helping people avoid falling into the Funnel. When I fell into it back in 1994, I lost ten years of sobriety and a fair amount of gray matter. Little did I know that after regaining my lost decade, pioneering the field of Buddhism and recovery, and being a bestselling author and retreat leader, I'd visit a deeper, darker Funnel than I had ever imagined possible.

When I got sober again in 1997, I met Tysa. We stayed together a long time. We didn't fight. She never lied to me or hurt me. We were a good team. But I lost interest sexually after about thirteen years. A couple of years of therapy and trial separation didn't change anything. We separated when I met someone half my age, and I had no idea that I'd find new levels of addiction—in sobriety. I became what is known as a self-defeating Caretaker. To cover up feelings of worthlessness that were based on childhood trauma—which I didn't even know was there—I took on that role. Author and marriage therapist Margalis Fjelstad describes it as

> . . . the most intense level of caretaking. You may find it hard to imagine success and happiness for yourself, yet you feel intense pain for others when they are not happy. This level of Caretaking can create depression, a sense of being overwhelmed, and sometimes emotional exhaustion, financial ruin, and a complete loss of your self-esteem. It will take work and a lot of help and support from others to move yourself out of this self-defeating mode of living, but don't you really, in your heart, want to give up your life of being a doormat, a personal slave, or a drudge for the benefit of others who don't really care about you?[4]

I fell into a pattern called trauma bonding (see chapter 3, the new section on trauma). I didn't lose my sobriety, but I almost gave up on my own life. I told myself it was for love. Because I was committed. I never gave up, and I never let go. All of this happened as a long-term sober member of the 12-Step community, bestselling author, and retreat leader. This was a slip, not out of sobriety, but into a deeper Funnel than I ever knew was possible. I had to dig deep into the principles and practices of this book and draw on many new resources in order to survive.

One thing that kept me going was the ongoing mail from readers who had used *The 12-Step Buddhist* in their own lives, to much success. Here are a few examples. I would read these and somehow make it through one more day.

"Thank you for the book. It has really helped me in my recovery."

"I came across the book when I made it to a prerelease center. Felony charges for possession of a dangerous drug [class] 2 is what had me in there. I was seeking help, and found *The 12-Step Buddhist* in our local library. It's also when I started attending our local mindfulness center. I've been a drug addict for so many years, so the meditations in the first step helped so much in doing a thorough first step with traditional 12-Step literature and sponsorship."

"Dear Darren, I just finished reading *The 12-Step Buddhist*. It is so very helpful to be able to see the steps through a Buddhist lens. It makes a huge difference for me. Your book will become a permanent, well-used, and often recommended part of my library. You did good. :)"

"During my alcoholic recovery 'early years' I found your book, *The 12 Step Buddhist*. I don't know how much it changed me, but I do tell anyone who wants to listen that you helped save my life. There was of course everyone at AA and the local sangha that I belong to as well. So it's a great privilege to say hi."

"I have had your *12-Step Buddhist* for years and often refer it to my recovery sisters and brothers."

"Hi, a friend of mine got me your book for my twenty-third birthday. Being clean for twenty-three years is good, but I was really unhappy about my life. I hadn't said anything, but your book has helped. She also has helped me on the spiritual path of Buddhism, so this was right on time. Not sure what will happen, as I'm still reading the book, but just wanted to say thanks. You are so freaking awesome! I'm your fan!"

When I learned about attachment theory, that helped me put the addiction to toxic relationships into context. In attachment theory, there are three main attachment styles, and knowing about these goes a long way to understanding ourselves and having compassion for how we are in relationships. In the book *Attached: The New Science of Adult Attachment and How It Can Help You Find—and Keep—Love*, Amir Levine describes the attachment styles as:

> Anxious: You love to be very close to your romantic partners and have the capacity for great intimacy. You often fear, however, that your partner does not wish to be as close as you would like him/her to be. Relationships tend to consume a large part of your emotional energy. You tend to be very sensitive to small fluctuations in your partner's moods and actions, and although your senses are often accurate, you take your partner's behaviors too personally. You experience a lot of negative emotions within the relationship and get easily upset. As a result, you tend to act out and say things you later regret. If the other person provides a lot of security and reassurance, however, you are able to shed much of your preoccupation and feel contented.
>
> Secure: Being warm and loving in a relationship comes naturally to you. You enjoy being intimate without becoming overly worried about your relationships. You take things in stride when it comes to romance and don't get easily upset over relationship matters. You effectively communicate your needs and feelings to your partner and are strong at reading your partner's emotional cues and responding to them. You share your successes and problems with your mate, and are able to be there for him or her in times of need.
>
> Avoidant: It is very important for you to maintain your independence and self-sufficiency and you often prefer autonomy to intimate relationships. Even though you do want to be close to others, you feel uncomfortable with too much closeness and tend to keep your partner at arm's

length. You don't spend much time worrying about your romantic relationships or about being rejected. You tend not to open up to your partners and they often complain that you are emotionally distant. In relationships, you are often on high alert for any signs of control or impingement on your territory by your partner.[5]

I recommend this book. It has a test you can take to find out your attachment style. I think I'm prone to anxious attachment—you can see what my patterns were of what I thought love was. What a way to live. I'm grateful it's behind me now.

The one good thing this brutal experience did for me was deepen my practice, in the way that only suffering can. In my healing regimen, I did my regular Buddhist practices, two hot power vinyasa yoga classes a day, regular therapy, psychiatrist appointments, meds, retreats at different Zen centers, shamanic healings, and AA meetings night after night after night reading the Big Book with old-timers.

But something my former partner Tysa told me rang true more than anything else. "Darren," she said, "*The 12-Step Buddhist* was a letter to your future self." And receiving all those letters from people telling me how much being a 12-Step Buddhist had helped them really reinforced the importance of this work and reminded me of the many thousands of people who were helped by it. To find a deeper recovery, I had to practice everything that I'd written about in 2008, and take it further.

CBD, Ayahuasca, and the Psychedelic Sobriety Movement

In around October 2016, I experienced some severe bouts of PTSD. A friend, who has a master's in drug treatment and worked at a major treatment center, offered me cannabidiol (CBD). CBD is derived from marijuana and is used as medicine for epilepsy and many other illnesses. It is approved by the FDA for epilepsy but is still being studied as a treatment for other ailments. Since pot had been my drug of choice when I was not sober, I was very reluctant to use anything derived from it. But I was in pain, and I was in crisis.

My friend explained that THC—which is the compound that gets you high when you ingest pot—was not part of the CBD formula, except for varieties used for severe chronic pain (like for those who suffer from brain cancer). I did some research and tried taking CBD in oil form.

Some die-hards in AA would tell you that CBD is a chemical and taking a chemical means you're not sober. But then again, they used to say the same thing about antidepressants, and it's well accepted now that antidepressants can be a healthy part of an integrated treatment plan. The CBD I take is a microdose of less than 5 milligrams and has either zero or trace amounts of THC, and I don't feel any kind of high or euphoria on it. I also don't crave chocolate chip cookies. What the oil does is it relaxes my brain from hyperarousal, PTSD, and major anxiety. I take it in combination with psychotherapy, spiritual healing work, and yoga. I believe that this combination has allowed me to carve new neural pathways in my brain; it helps my brain relax in ways that were never before possible. I have been using CBD ever since.

I don't give advice to others on whether or not they should try CBD. As with everything in this book, I only have my own experience to share, and my experience is that taking this derivation that does not cause a high has medicinal effects. I don't consider this a breach of my sobriety at all. That said, if other people do, that's their choice. My recommendation to you is that if you have anxiety, PTSD, sleep problems, or other issues that you think CBD can help with, consult with your support team and decide if you want to try it.

Another controversial part of treatment that has been helpful for many is ayahuasca. Last year I came in contact with some people who participate in sacred ceremony, namely, ayahuasca. I interviewed some on *The 12-Step Buddhist Podcast*, which you can find on Spotify, YouTube, and iTunes, and I was intrigued. Ayahuasca involves taking plant medicine and working with a shaman to experience a spiritual transformation. I did extensive research and one-on-one counseling with one of the group facilitators to make sure it was a good fit and that I would be safe. There are many fake shamans out there, and some people have become ill, suffered worse PTSD, and even died. It makes a lot of sense to do your research and be very careful.

The "grandmother," or "abuelita," as it is called, seemed to be psychically contacting me to participate. After months of preparation, which included reducing and ultimately stopping the mood regulators that my psychiatrist had prescribed, I took the first step and joined a San Pedro ceremony. This is the precursor to an ayahuasca ceremony and from what I have heard is much different. The San Pedro ceremony is a way of preparing your heart, mind, and soul for the deeper work that an ayahuasca ceremony brings.

I took the plant medicine journey with a shaman and his wife on a mountaintop in the desert outside San Diego. We sat for twelve hours in the pounding sun while the shaman called in the Four Directions and the helping spirits. We started the ceremony by acknowledging the wounds of the family. It was a long, ten-hour day in the sun, digging deep into those wounds and praying for healing with songs, chanting, and support from the community. The pain was so intense that, for most of the day, I could hardly breathe. I had no distractions and no defenses. I prayed and chanted and sang and begged and cried to all the Buddhas, the Divine Mother, the Four Directions, all of my teachers and ancestors. It was all I could do to survive. I sat still, lay down, walked in nature, and looked within, and I felt everything that I had been trying to avoid and hold back for over eighteen months. Breathing. Meditating. Praying.

At one point I told the group how I was feeling and explained that I just wanted to be in the present moment and feel the joy of being alive. The shaman came up to me and squatted down with his sun hat over his brow, taking long pulls of a hand-rolled tobacco offering. He said, "The medicine is cleaning the wound right now. Squeezing it. You're going to be uncomfortable for a while, but maybe tomorrow or in a couple of days, you will have healed."

He was right. By the next morning, the anxiety had started to calm. My spiritual epiphany was that I had been holding tension in my body, at the soul and core center of my being. That tension is the opposite of acceptance. It's the opposite of love. With PTSD, the brain doesn't know how to undo the trauma response. But the angels and I undid it. With the help of my spiritual guides, I managed to unyoke the chains of inner suffering that had been keeping me stuck.

I knew the work would be ongoing. There's no one-size-fits-all miracle mantra. There is no pill, no person who will do the work for you. I realized over the next few days what really needed to happen. I had to practice the inner yoga, the real yoga—not just the breath, postures, and movements that I had been doing daily for ten years. That inner yoga is self-compassion—I needed to love myself. Not just with words. Not just with actions. But with a feeling of contentment with myself, just as I am.

After seven months of compassion meditations and personal introspection, I decided to postpone the second stage of sacred ceremony. I felt that so much came up in the San Pedro ceremony that I should just keep doing what I'd been doing with my Tibetan practices, yoga, etc.

In the future I may opt to do the ayahuasca ceremony or another spiritual journey. I'm leaving that open for myself. Stay tuned on the12stepbuddhist.com and the podcast for ongoing reports from the field. For now I'm good with what I've learned and am integrating everything I knew from being a 12-Step Buddhist into the next phases of my recovery.

I have come across some people who are in some form of recovery, some who also have mental illness, who microdose on LSD, psilocybin, and other substances that traditionally make the blacklist of things we definitely do not typically do in sobriety. I'm going to go out on a long limb here and share with you that I have used psilocybin for spiritual purposes a few times in recent years. As with the plant medicine journey, the experience was nothing like a high or an escape. In fact, it was extremely challenging and required a lot of work to process difficult traumas. I worked extensively with my spiritual teachers and a licensed psychologist throughout these experiences. I don't personally feel that I want to do more of this, but it did open up some truths for me that I had not otherwise been able to obtain with my normal practices.

The main realization is that I am a Joyous Light Being. I'm totally free. Compassion is my way of life. The universe is available to explore and participate in. All the good and all the bad are rolled up into one experience. This impacts my views on Buddhism, sobriety, and my meditation and yoga practices. Why? Apparently, "psilocybin decreases activity in the parts of the brain that are overactive in depression, addiction and ingrained behaviors."[6] We'll look at some more of what researchers have found about the use of these kinds of substances to treat trauma and addiction in chapter 3.

I can't say that I recommend that you or anyone else take any drug at all to enhance your spiritual practice or your recovery. But I've found that where nothing else worked for me, CBD, plant medicine, and psilocybin have provided me support that later led to deeper understanding of myself and my sobriety.

This book is about how I learned to integrate what I needed to stay sober and get sane. It's about what went wrong in my first attempt to live sober and what's going right this time. Following are examples from my own experience learning to address addiction, mental illness, and a spiritual malady in a comprehensive manner. It's also about taking responsibility to "create the fellowship I crave."[7]

From Zen to Tibetan and Back

There once lived an addict named Darren
Who swapped drugs for the study of Zen
He turned round his Karma
By living in the Dharma
And for this he gets to twice turn ten.

*—Limerick written by Kate R. as a gift for my
ten-year sobriety anniversary in 2007*

When I moved to Portland, Oregon, in 2000, I decided that I wanted to find a good sitting group. I'd moved here to mellow out, and meditation was going to play a key role in my quest for serenity. I found the Zen Center of Portland referenced online. Then I met Larry, a clinical psychologist and student of Joko Beck who became one of her Dharma successors: someone in Zen who is given permission to teach. I thought the coincidence was fortuitous, and after a phone conversation with Joko to verify Larry's credibility, I started sitting with Larry and the group.

I spent several years at this center, served on the board of directors, developed its website, and tried to fit into the community. With Larry, I enjoyed something I never had in the past: private interview time every week. I was a bit edgy in those days. I still needed medication to remain calm, and I was very attached to the peacefulness of the Zen space, so I really prized this time with the teacher. Larry and I would have good talks about what my doctor and I had discussed in therapy and the differences and similarities between the 12 Steps and Zen practice. I even had Larry and my doctor check in with each other from time to time to compare notes.

This comprehensive recovery system worked well, as there was an Alano Club—facilities across the country where many types of 12-Step meetings are held—right up the street. In this way, therapy, step work, jazz, and Buddhism all worked together in one integrated process. I could go to a meeting and have counseling, jazz lessons, and the Zen Center all within a ten-block radius. This became a stabilizing routine for me.

Eventually, I left the Zen group and went to talk about my future in Tibetan Buddhism with the education director of the Foundation for the Preservation of the Mahayana Tradition (FPMT). I'd been to a teaching by a Tibetan Buddhist nun, Venerable Robina, a while before, and I was intrigued by the Tibetan teachings and had tried to incorporate some of what I'd learned into my Zen practice and recovery world. But there was so much depth to Tibetan Buddhism. I didn't know if I could ever understand it all.

Meeting the Lamas

About five years into sobriety v.2.0, at the direction of my sponsor, I became interested in *The Power of Now* by Eckhart Tolle. I felt at the time that his book helped me understand what I'd been trying to grasp in Zen for so long: the essence. His is a teaching of no teaching. Since it's similar to Joko's style, I connected easily with it. After about a year of listening daily to Eckhart's retreat talks, I found a sense of presence previously unattainable. I didn't know it then, but this was a glimpse into emptiness. I thought I was finding Nirvana and the fruits of all the years of practice. But it was just a beginning.

For this reason, I felt ready to move beyond the Zen sitting hall into different areas. When I relapsed, I swore off any kind of spiritual teaching. I thought it was all self-indulgent. I knew that my real base was in the 12 Steps, but I had not been successful in tapping into their true potential. After all, what good is spiritual teaching if you can't even stay sober? As I reestablished my Zen practice and clarified its meaning with *The Power of Now*, I saw more clearly that there were indeed spiritual teachers and teachings that could be useful to me in my recovery.

But I had no idea how thin my newfound sense of enlightenment really was, or how deep these Tibetan teachings could get. The Tibetans are not known for keeping it simple—*The Power of Now* is about as simple as it gets. And it fits right in with Zen. After all, Buddhism is about being present and mindful, right? But Tibetan Buddhism offers many methods that, on the surface, appear to conflict. After practicing with the Tibetan methods for a while, I learned that they facilitate mindful awareness in a deeper, faster way.

I began a self-guided study program called Discovering Buddhism after visiting the local FPMT office. I visited FPMT and left with an armload of books and CDs and a plan to get busy spreading new roots into this strange, exotic form of Buddhism. I studied the materials and did the requisite personal retreats at a nearby center in the woods.

My introduction was very different from the years of staring silently at a blank wall. The lamas, Tibetan teachers, talked about things that confused and upset me—hell realms, guru devotion, emptiness, bodhicitta (compassion), dependent origination, purification, and Tantra. It was all compellingly weird. And I had to learn more.

After a ten-day *lamrim*, a graduated path to enlightenment through intensive retreat, at Vajrapani Institute in the Santa Cruz Mountains, I returned at the request of the director to record teachings for Lama Zopa Rinpoche. I'd heard a lot about this amazing bodhisattva—that he was clairvoyant, didn't sleep, could teach an entire room on multiple levels simultaneously, would stop on the roadside to bless millions of bugs on his travels, and so on. I had to find out if any of these claims were true.

On the first night of our retreat, in a packed room of 150 people who were all obviously old-school California hippie Buddhists, I listened to Lama Zopa for the first time. I sent him secret thought messages to test if he really was clairvoyant. In my mind, I asked him to talk about one of my biggest problems: the leftover drug hallucinations. The acid and weed had left permanent tracks in my mind, and I needed help with this problem. No Western doctor or medication so far had had the slightest effect. But I waited all night, and Lama Zopa didn't seem to have received the message.

The next day, he came back and started teaching. My jaw hit the ground when he said he wanted to talk about hallucinations! I thought, "No freakin' way!" Was this funny little man in yellow robes going to answer my mental inquiry of the previous evening? He did, but not in the way I expected. In true Buddhist style, he answered the *real* question, which only becomes clear after a lot of cushion time.

Since then, I've taken teachings with Lama Zopa Rinpoche many times and will never miss the opportunity to connect with him. Although it's rumored that Lama Zopa has more power than he lets on, just this little bit made me a devotee. It takes what it takes, and coming from where I come from, a little magical demonstration is just what it took for me.

Everything in Tibetan Buddhism is elaborate. The *gompas*— meditation halls—are filled with colorful cloth draped everywhere, dozens of *thangkas*—paintings of deities—statues, water bowls, candles, and food offerings. The teachings always begin with homage to the lineage teachers; a setting of intention that the teachings will be of benefit to all sentient beings; taking refuge in the Buddha, the Dharma, and the sangha, as well as the guru if it's a Tantra teaching; and the offering of mandala—a symbolic offering of all objects of attachment—to the enlightened beings.

I tried very hard to establish myself in service at various Buddhist centers, as I've learned to do in the 12-Step world. I have to admit, supporting Buddhist teachers is not as easy as making coffee or setting up chairs for a bunch of addicts. It took me a while to figure out how I could be of service to various lamas.

As I've learned in the 12-Step community, service is key. Whenever I show up to teachings, I try to offer service. But more often than not, the opportunity finds me. I've walked in and found the organizers frustrated with their audio setup and wound up doing all the recording for the retreat. Another time on retreat in Spain, I ended up working security detail the whole time. We had the job of protecting the lama from too many students who wanted private interviews. The European practitioners kept asking me, "How did you get to do that?" I said, "Oh, I'm an addict. This is how we do it."

I mention this because it's a productive way of transferring what I've learned in recovery: show up early, be of service, connect while you're there, and stay late. This does not come naturally for me as an addict, but doing it for years in 12-Step communities has served me well in a variety of capacities, from giving talks in college to presentations to a room full of bloodthirsty television salespeople in New York.

One aspect that was difficult in my transition from Zen to Tibetan Buddhism was the sheer volume, variety, and complexity of the teachings. The rituals themselves can be long and elaborate, depending on where you go. Since I'm an addict who hates being in the dark on any topic, I did some fast research to bring myself up to speed. The biggest help in this area was Dr. Robert Thurman. He has some excellent books, DVDs, and free podcasts available. He covers everything you ever need to know about Tibet and Tibetan Buddhism.

I studied Bob's materials and frantically read everything I could. I attended teachings from most of the major schools, took empowerments (tantric initiations that prepare the practitioner for that path of practice) and began my own personal practice. Like I said, an addict like me doesn't like being the guy who doesn't know who's who and what's what, so I studied very hard. The problem is, you can study this material for many, many lifetimes and still not cover it all. It was overwhelming, but it forced me to stay in the moment, which is the ultimate point of spiritual teachings.

My Root Teacher

Note that this is my spiritual path; other recovering addicts can greatly benefit from just the basic teachings of Buddhism and the practices associated with each of the 12 Steps. The idea is to find a spiritual practice that will keep you sober and help you be happy in recovery.

The *guru*—Sanskrit for "teacher," *lama* in Tibetan—is the one in whom we trust completely to take us down the path to enlightenment. He or she is called your *root guru* or *root lama*. You can have more than one. But the Tibetans say it's important to find the qualified teacher who can lead you all the way to enlightenment. When I first heard this, I had some issues with the idea. Trust has never been my strong point. I was reminded of the seventies with the Symbionese Liberation Army and the Charles Manson acid murder cult. Later, there was Jonestown and the purple Kool-Aid suicide cult. It went on and on, all the way to Waco and David Koresh. And because I had the fear of the devil in my brain since *The Exorcist*, I wasn't keen on turning myself over to anything or anyone. I'd done the 12 Steps and worked out some higher power issues, but trusting anyone called a guru was out of the question. Until my sponsor told me something.

While sitting on my couch during a visit for his thirty-second sobriety birthday, my sponsor, whom I've known since the early nineties, told me that I needed to find a guru. He's never been a mainstream recovery guy and has always intrigued me with ideas of Indian saints and different traditions. He's gone everywhere from Cuba to Egypt on his quest to deepen his own recovery. And he was telling me to find a guru. I said, "John, I don't *do* gurus!" But since he was the one who had hounded me for a couple years to read *The Power of Now* and had been right about it, I strongly considered what he was saying. I told him, "All right, I'll take it under advisement." This was with no real intention of doing so, but with perpetual curiosity still driving my search for a new Buddhist teacher.

As I was looking for more Tibetan Buddhist DVDs, I came across one called *General Introduction to Dzogchen* by Namkhai Norbu Rinpoche. As I sat in my room watching the video, I was struck with the presence and clarity of this teacher. He described the essence of all Buddhist teachings: Sutra, Tantra, and finally Dzogchen (see chapter 5). I couldn't believe how easy he was to understand. This was the teacher I'd been looking for all my life, and I was in a hurry to make the connection. Little did I know that it would be more than a year before I could get some face-to-face time.

I listened by webcast and later attended in person as many retreats from Namkhai Norbu Rinpoche as possible. He is always sharp, to the point, rock solid, and crystal clear with a great sense of humor. He makes it all make sense, which is exactly what I needed to navigate through the vast teachings of Tibetan Buddhism.

I finally had the opportunity to meet Namkhai Norbu Rinpoche in Barcelona, Spain. As I walked up to him, hands folded, barely willing to look up, I remember having the experience of being connected to a very deep, spacious reality. He was also personable and warm. Meeting him verified what I already knew. I might have sounded like a dork with my American addict attitude, but I meant it when I told him, "Rinpoche, you're the man!" He was for me. And that's how this 12-Step Buddhist found his root teacher. The way my path has progressed from there has been pretty remarkable. I have relationships with a number of Tibetan lamas—all wonderful and different. And with this new ability to relax after I found my main teacher, I was able to go back to the Zendo—Zen practice center—to chill out.

Putting It All Together

As it stands now, I have a regular solo meditation and a daily power yoga practice.

In light of everything I've learned since the first edition came out, I've created a compassion-oriented recovery program for people who struggle with any form of problematic attachment or addiction: Compassionate Recovery. See the12stepbuddhist.com and compassionaterecovery.net for instructions on how to start your own meditation group for recovering people. Building from the original principles of what I then called 12-Step Sangha, the concepts have evolved into a universal, more secular approach that will reach more people without losing the power of the meditations.

On the site you'll find many formats for addressing specific areas of recovery, such as intimacy, honesty, PTSD, and others. The principles and formats for Compassionate Recovery meetings are dynamic and will be open to addition and modification over time.

In Compassionate Recovery meetings, we don't identify ourselves with any particular addiction, so as to not alienate anyone. This keeps the meeting from depending or relying on a traditional 12-Step style of sharing. To open our hearts, we sit silently for a few minutes to quiet our minds, and then the leader of the meeting reads a short topic from the spiritual literature of his choice—it doesn't have to be conference-approved literature. Then, we meditate and contemplate the topic for twenty minutes. Next, we go around the room and share in normal meeting style, except that the leader speaks last. In this format, being the leader is also a form of meditation in that you're listening, not talking. Remember, this is just one of the formats available. Compassionate Recovery is also open to contributions and ideas from members, so please feel free to contact me with suggestions.

I've found this to be an excellent integration between my 12-Step and Buddhist groups. You're invited to start your own meeting with any sized group of like-minded addicts. Later on you will find the steps section, which outlines many ways for you to find, define, redefine, reexamine, and dynamically create your own spiritual path. And in the upcoming book, *Compassionate Recovery*, you'll find an entire program devoted to healing attachment, addiction, and trauma based on different healing modalities.

Since compassion is the core of Buddhism, this program will fit right in no matter where you fall on the spectrum of attachment or addiction.

The Grim Face of Addiction

In the throes of my addiction, it was not uncommon to find me crouched in a public restroom stall, dried blood covering my hands, with the insides of my elbows too swollen to bend my arms. I believed that this was my place in the universe, living the only life I ever believed I deserved.

—*Maddie H.*

I want this book to be of educational value to non-addicts as well as addicts. Even though we addicts have firsthand knowledge of our own addictions, as well as close association with many addicts in and out of recovery, I think we need a bigger overview of the scope of the problem of addictions. For that reason, I include the following survey of scientific knowledge on the subject. For this edition, I have updated some of the previous statistics and have added new sections on discoveries made in the last ten years. May it be of benefit to all suffering addicts.

How Bad Is the Problem?

Why is a 12-Step book on spiritual recovery and Buddhist methodology concerned with statistics? Because the first step in any recovery program is to understand the nature of the problem. Those coming out of 12-Step programs know these hard facts, but I hope to encourage a similar awareness of the problem in Buddhist communities. They are open to working with the spiritual recovery of addicts but need to adapt their approach.

The problem of addiction is far worse than you can imagine. Here's an interesting number: the world's wealthiest country, the United States, holds 4 percent of the world's population but consumes two-thirds of its illegal drugs.[1] In this chapter, we'll examine the data from a variety of sources and perspectives. If you think you understand the nature of addiction, you'll be amazed at the depth and breadth of this astounding problem.

It's important for the Buddhist to understand the suffering of particular sentient beings called addicts. In the overall scheme, this suffering is what they call *samsara*—the infinite cycle of birth and death, based on ignorance of karma and our real condition. We stay stuck because we can't see reality right in front of our noses. In the reality of addiction, we say that we often don't see the elephant (addiction) in our living room. Funny, since Buddhism started in India where examples given about elephants abound.

On a daily basis, Buddhists encounter sentient beings who are definitely suffering, definitely don't want to suffer, want to be happy, but probably don't realize the extent of their misery. Buddhism holds out hope for them. But if those people are addicts, we need to change how we view and work to help them. Our first goal is to understand, so we may be of maximum service to those around us. There are more addicts around us than you think.

If you believe we're all in a web of interconnectivity, that on some level we're affected by each other in this global community, then it's not a stretch to consider that all this rampant addiction causes suffering that affects us all—even if it's not in our faces at the moment. And I don't just mean meth addicts on the street or alcoholics living under bridges, but those who smoke two packs a day or are fifty pounds overweight, workaholics who can't relate to their families, relationship junkies, chronic self-mutilators, gamblers, and sex-addicted porn surfers. This list reaches far and wide into every segment of our society.

What Is the Cost?

These are just a couple of ways to estimate the monetary cost, though not the spiritual or emotional devastation. According to the National Institute on Drug Abuse (NIDA), the total cost of addiction, including healthcare, criminal justice, and lost productivity, increased by 50 percent to $245.7 billion from 1985 to 1992. Between 1988 and 1995, over $57.3 billion was spent to buy drugs in the United States, according to the White House Office of National Drug Control Policy.[2] According to NIDA, the current data show that the cost of tobacco, alcohol, and illicit drugs in America is over $740 billion. In 2013, the data on prescription opiods came in at $78.5. As an addict, you probably don't care about these numbers. But just to frame the problem, it's important to realize that your addiction affects everyone.

Add to this the problem of vaping, smokeless tobacco, and fentanyl (a powerful synthetic opioid analgesic that is similar to morphine but is fifty to one hundred times more potent, according to the NIH). Maybe you or someone you know is addicted to steroids, ketamine, or Molly, or abuses prescription drugs like Adderall.

We have all lost people due to addiction and mental illness. My friend Mark, who read my book and gained one year of sobriety, told me he didn't want to go to meetings anymore because he didn't want to replace one addiction with another by getting addicted to meetings. Soon after, I learned that he drank himself to death, alone in Oklahoma somewhere. Another friend, Johnny, tried to connect with me for support so many times on Facebook, and now he's overdosed. His grandfather found him dead on the floor. I often play Disturbed's version of "The Sounds of Silence" and think of Johnny and all the addicts like him who don't make it. That could be you. That could be me.

Besides those close to us, we've also lost some of the rich and famous. There have been many, even in just the last few years: Robin Williams relapsed with twenty years sober and later killed himself, Prince died from an accidental overdose, Anthony Bourdain killed himself despite many years of sobriety, Dolores O'Riordan of the Cranberries drowned drunk in her bathtub, and the two rock singers Chester Bennington of Linkin Park and Soundgarden's Chris Cornell both committed suicide, possibly due to relapse. There are too many to name, but the point is that the problem of addiction is taking people we love.

We still need to do everything we can to help reduce and end the suffering.

How Many Are Addicted?

The numbers related to how many Americans are addicted are pretty consistent since the first edition. Estimates vary but hover around twenty-one million in the past few years. According to the surgeon general, "In 2015, 66.7 million people in the United States reported binge drinking in the past month and 27.1 million people were current users of illicit drugs or misused prescription drugs."[3]

Again, this is just based on the number of people entering treatment and doesn't necessarily include those involved in trauma-related attachments or process and behavior addictions. The main point is that the problem isn't going away. It's getting worse.

The surgeon general also reports, "Alcohol misuse contributes to 88,000 deaths in the United States each year; 1 in 10 deaths among working adults are due to alcohol misuse. In addition, in 2014 there were 47,055 drug overdose deaths including 28,647 people who died from a drug overdose involving some type of opioid, including prescription pain relievers and heroin—more than in any previous year on record."

The need for more and better tools is more important than ever. According to the Centers for Disease Control and Prevention:

> In 1997, more than 83 percent of all state prisoners (837,300) and more than 73 percent of all federal prisoners (64,000) reported past drug use. A third of state prisoners and a fifth of federal prisoners said they were using drugs at the time they committed the offense for which they were in prison. Data from 35 sites across the country on the drug use of adults who have been arrested show that . . . more than 60 percent test positive for at least one drug (arrestees are tested for cocaine, mari-

juana, methamphetamines, opiates, and PCP, among other drugs).[4]

If your house has ever been burglarized or your car stolen, chances are it was done by an addict.

You'll hear in 12-Step meetings that addicts affect at least ten people in their immediate vicinities. If this is fairly accurate, that would multiply the number of those affected by addicts to several times the nation's population. By this logic, every single person in the United States is affected by several addicts at least. And that statistic is only considering the effect from knowing addicts directly. When we consider the more remote costs, like your company's health insurance rates going up to cover addicts working elsewhere, the reach of the problem grows immensely. Addiction, its causes, and its effects are everywhere—not just under bridges, in jails, and in dark, hidden corners.

What Do the Numbers Mean?

The data suggests that those in 12-Step programs account for a very small fraction of the actual population of addicts. AA doesn't do surveys often, making longitudinal data nonexistent or hypothetical at best. In order to protect the anonymity of the members with criminal issues, Narcotics Anonymous doesn't traditionally keep any stats. The available data is limited, but we have at least an overview. Compare the NIDA figures above with numbers from AA's World Services. As of 2017, AA reports 2,087,840 members worldwide.[5] The number of sober AA members currently accounts for less than 5 percent of the more than 20 million people *that we know about* who need treatment in a given year.

In 12-Step terms, retreads are addicts who keep trying but just cannot seem to maintain sobriety. Some studies find that half of the addicts who receive treatment have had some prior substance abuse treatment. Among those, half had been in treatment in the previous year.[6] How can we help retreads get clean and *stay* clean? The answer among clinical studies seems to point to a multifaceted recovery approach. However, these programs leave out the spiritual piece that we use in the 12 Steps.

A small percentage of those who need treatment get it. Among those who get it, a large percentage don't stay in recovery. If you consider some of the data that say half of those in treatment have been in prior treatment in the public health system—not counting AA or NA—and that, of the more than twenty million addicts who are estimated to need treatment, under two million get it, that means a lot of addicts aren't getting the help they need, at least not from public health services.

Are 12-Step programs doing a better job? Not if you consider that the number of AA members, for example, hovers around a million in the U.S. at any given point during their periodic surveys. Regardless of how you slice the numbers, no one will argue that there is obviously a big discrepancy between the number who *need* and the number who *achieve* sobriety. We can do better; we have to do better.

This analysis is an effort to get an overview of how many addicts need treatment compared to how many are in 12-Step programs. AA is commonly said, mostly by its own members, to be the most successful treatment program in the world. There are those who argue unconvincingly against 12-Step programs. The courts consistently send people there for effective treatment, and some argue that this is unconstitutional because it's forcing religion on people. But for those who can do the work, 12-Step programs are effective in the short run—they can help get you clean. But *some people are sicker than others* and require more than a cookie-cutter approach to recovery.

Addiction Is a Brain Disease

One of the most useful things I was told when I first entered treatment was that I wasn't a bad person trying to become good. I was a sick person trying to get well. Counselors said that the process of recovering from addiction was as serious as recovering from heart surgery, and that while we had to take responsibility for our lives, addiction wasn't a moral issue. With this comforting news, the early stages of healing began for me.

Some critics of 12-Step programs and other treatment models are unable to grasp the disease concept of addiction. As I researched studies on the disease model, I was completely staggered by the amount of data on this topic.

Dr. Alan I. Leshner, former director of NIDA, wrote a series of articles that directly address the need to see addiction as a brain disease. He wrote in 2000:

The essence of addiction: uncontrollable, compulsive drug craving, seeking, and use, even in the face of negative health and social consequences. This is the crux of how the Institute of Medicine, the American Psychiatric Association, and the American Medical Association define addiction and how we all should use the term. It is really only this compulsive quality of addiction that matters in the long run to the addict and to his or her family and that should matter to society as a whole. Compulsive craving that overwhelms all other motivations is the root cause of the massive health and social problems associated with drug addiction. In updating our national discourse on drug abuse, we should keep in mind this simple definition: Addiction is a brain disease expressed in the form of compulsive behavior. Both developing and recovering from it depend on biology, behavior, and social context.[7]

In 2006 NIDA stated:

Drug addiction is a complex but treatable brain disease. It is characterized by compulsive drug craving, seeking, and use that persist even in the face of severe adverse consequences. For many people, drug addiction becomes chronic, with relapses possible even after long periods of abstinence. In fact, relapse to drug abuse occurs at rates similar to those for other well-characterized, chronic medical illnesses such as diabetes, hypertension, and asthma.

As a chronic, recurring illness, addiction may require repeated treatments to increase the intervals between relapses and diminish their intensity, until abstinence is achieved. Through treatment tailored to individual needs, people with drug addiction can recover and lead productive lives.[8]

And the Office of the Surgeon General reports as of 2019: "Well-supported scientific evidence shows that addiction to alcohol or drugs is a chronic brain disease that has potential for recurrence and recovery."[9]

To understand this better, we need to take a closer look at the brain.

The Brain

This will be a very rudimentary sketch of the human brain, just so we can have a framework to discuss the processes of addiction and trauma. It's radically oversimplified, but we need a few of these pieces in place in order to understand what happens in our addict brains. As always, this is meant to be a map to understand how doing Buddhist meditation practices with the 12 Steps can help us heal. We could study the brain forever, so let's just allow this little overview to give us some terms to discuss the processes of suffering and freedom from suffering.

In *The Body Keeps the Score*, psychiatrist Bessel van der Kolk explains:

The most important job of the brain is to ensure our survival, even under the most miserable conditions. Everything else is secondary. In order to do that, brains need to: (1) generate internal signals that register what our bodies need, such as food, rest, protection, sex, and shelter; (2) create a map of the world to point us where to go to satisfy those needs; (3) generate the necessary energy and actions to get us there; (4) warn us of dangers and opportunities along the way; and (5) adjust our actions based on the requirements of the moment.[10]

There are several parts of the brain that are relevant to understanding what the brain thinks it needs to survive and how that can feed into addiction, and they also relate heavily to how trauma affects us, which we'll get into a bit more in a moment.

The prefrontal cortex is in the front of the brain and is the part that manages our personality expression, decision-making, and complex thought processes. While this is where our decisions to do certain actions come from, it's not as simple as just deciding not to do them anymore.

The limbic system is in the middle of the brain and deals with emotions, memories, and stimulation. Within the limbic system is the amygdala, which according to van der Kolk is like "the brain's smoke detector" because its purpose is "to identify whether incoming input is relevant for our survival."[11] The amygdala is responsible for interpreting our emotional experience. It sends signals to the hypothalamus, which releases stress hormones such as cortisol and adrenaline to prepare us for survival. These hormones bump up our heart rate, blood pressure, and breathing rate. In a normal situation, once the threat subsides, the stress hormones diminish.

The brain stem is the communication system between the brain and the rest of the body, so when our brain senses danger, the brain stem is what makes us feel that in our body. The brain stem is part of what we call the reptilian brain, which manages our basic organ functions for survival—such as our lungs breathing, our heart beating, and how awake or sleepy we feel—and feeds into our compulsions.

The autonomic nervous system (ANS) also plays a part in managing the body's unconscious processes, like breathing, and it especially comes into play when the brain and body believe you're in danger. The ANS has two parts, sympathetic and parasympathetic. The sympathetic controls flee, freeze, or fight responses. Our parasympathetic system controls rest and digest functions. Here's where we can train ourselves to get into a safety sweet spot where we can heal. To be relaxed is a very good thing.

Executive Function

The brain is what manages our lives, and when it comes to decision-making, it all comes down to executive functioning in the brain. The eight key executive functions are impulse control, emotional control, flexible thinking, working memory, self-monitoring, planning and prioritizing, task initiation, and organization.

All that goes out the window in a trauma response. Fear takes over, and our flee-freeze-or-fight automatic software subroutines fire up. That's why talk therapy is not an effective cure for trauma. We have to get into the body with deep meditation and movement to create new narratives that will then move into our brains to retrain us to experience ourselves differently.

Now that we know about the parts of the brain, let's take a look at what happens to the brain during the stages of addiction.

Stages of Addiction

The addict is also physically different as the result of addiction. The new science does show that there are three main areas of the brain disrupted by addiction: the brain stem, the amygdala, and the cerebral cortex. The levels of some neurotransmitters (a type of chemical messenger in the brain) such as dopamine and serotonin are also impacted. During the stages of addiction, the chemicals and circuitry of the brain are affected, leading to dependence and withdrawal symptoms.

Depending on which source you're referencing, there are a number of stages of addiction. According to the *Psychopharmacology* journal, "Addiction involves progressive stages of drug binges and intoxication, withdrawal-negative affect, and ultimately compulsive drug use and abuse."[12] From the surgeon general's report:

Addiction can be described as a repeating cycle with three stages . . .

⊛ Binge/Intoxication, the stage at which an individual consumes an intoxicating substance and experiences its rewarding or pleasurable effects;

⊛ Withdrawal/Negative Affect, the stage at which an individual experiences a negative emotional state in the absence of the substance; and

⊛ Preoccupation/Anticipation, the stage at which one seeks substances again after a period of abstinence.[13]

There are also areas of genetic research that discuss the implications of the addict's DNA. That's beyond our scope here, but the data is available.[14]

The new science on epigenetics, the study of biological mechanisms that will switch genes on and off, is pointing to the existence of genes that contribute to addiction, but it hasn't proven anything yet. The science underscores the complexity of addiction in that individuals can have dormant genes that predispose them to addiction, but that many environmental and other intrinsic factors play significant roles in whether the "addict gene," if there is one, will get turned on or not and to what degree it will influence their addictive tendencies.

Another theory is that there are five, rather than three, stages of drug and alcohol addiction:

1. Experimentation: In this stage a person is just trying out the drug, person, or process.

2. Regular use: This could be seen as maintenance use, as the individual still functions in their roles at work, home, and the community. But use is definitely part of everyday life.

3. Risky use: Examples could be driving under the influence, getting high before work or important events, or using instead of working or going to school.

4. Dependence: This stage can look a lot like addiction. But those who abuse but are not fully addicted can stop if given sufficient reasons.

5. Addiction: Addiction means that when the person wants to stop, they can't. They make promises and fail to keep them. They enter

treatment only to relapse. They lose their ethics and morals, and they trade in everything they once valued for the drugs of choice.[15]

Regardless of how detailed we break down the stages of addiction, the brain is responding to the use of the substance or interaction with the person or process more and more with each stage. As drugs are used over time, parts of the brain such as the basal ganglia (which is responsible for motivation and which houses the reward circuit) and the extended amygdala (which plays a role in stressful feelings such as anxiety and irritability) become less sensitive to the stimulation that the drugs provide, hijacking the reward system to first create dependency and then as temporary relief from the discomfort of withdrawal.

When there's trauma, all the brain processes of addiction are also woven in with the trauma response.

Trauma and Addiction

We're going to talk about trauma, its relationship to addiction, and some of the complications of trauma that can also be related to addiction. This is a complex, scientific, medical topic. I am not a doctor. But I am trained as a research psychologist and will summarize what we now know about these topics and their relevance to your recovery in the context of being a 12-Step Buddhist, or however you would like to define or not define yourself.

Trauma is defined as:

> the unique individual experience of a [single] event, a series of events, or a set of enduring conditions, in which: the individual's ability to integrate his or her emotional experiences is overwhelmed (i.e., the ability to stay present, understand what is happening, tolerate the feelings, or comprehend the horror), or the individual experiences (subjectively) a threat to life, bodily integrity, or sanity.[16]

Whether you've read this book before or are reading it for the first time, I want you to know that I wasn't aware of the findings on trauma at the time of the first writing. But I was aware of the practices of Buddhism, the 12 Steps, and modern psychology. Note that the "individual's ability to *integrate* his or her experience is overwhelmed." This entire book is about integration. All the steps and teachings of Buddhism are about integration. If we take the brain science on trauma, on addiction, and on the practices of meditation and put that knowledge all in one place, can you imagine the healing power we could have? More on that in my next book, *Compassionate Recovery*, I promise.

What I want to say first about trauma is that it plays a big role in addiction and will play an equally important role in recovery. And just as addiction affects nearly every person in the country, it's pretty hard to be a human being on the planet without being traumatized.

One source states that "70% of adults in the U.S. have experienced some type of traumatic event at least once in their lives. This equates to approximately 223.4 million people."[17] This resource also says that 44.7 million people in the United States currently struggle or have struggled with PTSD, post-traumatic stress disorder. Another site says that "an estimated 1 out of 9 women will get PTSD at some time in their lives. Women are about twice as likely as men to develop PTSD."[18]

That's a lot of trauma. And one of the biggest responses to trauma is, you guessed it, addiction. Professor of psychiatry and clinical psychologist Lisa Najavits writes,

One big reason some people develop addiction is that they've lived through serious trauma. It's been called *deadly logic*: it makes sense to reach out for something to try to feel better. It's also called *self-medication, numbing the pain*, or *using to escape*. The addictive behavior feels like a solution for trauma problems, at least for a while. Some people with severe trauma and addiction say they made a decision to keep using because it was the only way

they could get relief from emotional pain. Other vulner-
abilities add to the impact as well, such as homelessness,
poverty, mental health problems, discrimination, and
social isolation.[19]

Najavits goes on to say, "It can take years to see the connection
between trauma and addiction. Often, the addiction is visible first and
the trauma history is recognized only later."

This is a key point to my own recovery and why I practice the tools
of Buddhism and compassion in my recovery. We just don't see how
traumatized we might be unless we do long-term, committed, deep
work that addresses issues such as trauma. For a lot of people, even
those with years of sobriety, this is a big hole in recovery. The results
can be catastrophic.

Not everyone who is traumatized develops complications like
PTSD or addictions. And not everyone who becomes addicted was
traumatized. But trauma is seen in the literature as a major contributing factor to substance abuse. In my opinion, based on my experience,
and according to what I've heard from thousands of people in recovery
spanning over three decades, most of us were traumatized as children.
We continued to traumatize ourselves with our addictions. And even
though we get sober and work the 12 Steps, we continue to suffer from
the effects of traumas that we were victims of. We also suffer from the
compounding of trauma on top of trauma that happens with us. We
unknowingly traumatize ourselves both in our addictions and in our
recovery. So what causes trauma? It's not all from childhood, but let's
take a look at the most important research ever done on the topic:
the Adverse Childhood Experiences (ACEs) study, conducted by the
Centers for Disease Control (CDC). Over seventeen thousand people
participated in this study from 1995 to 1997, and it is one of the most
influential studies on trauma that has ever been done. The original
study shows 8,315 citations, meaning that's how many times researchers have referred to just that one study. More studies continue to this
day as part of the ongoing research on child abuse and its effects.

The ACEs results link childhood trauma with a person's tendency to experience the following challenges, among others, throughout their lives:

⊛ alcoholism and alcohol abuse
⊛ depression
⊛ health-related quality of life
⊛ illicit drug use
⊛ poor work performance
⊛ financial stress
⊛ risk for intimate partner violence
⊛ multiple sexual partners
⊛ sexually transmitted diseases
⊛ smoking
⊛ suicide attempts
⊛ unintended pregnancies
⊛ early initiation of smoking
⊛ early initiation of sexual activity
⊛ adolescent pregnancy
⊛ risk for sexual violence
⊛ poor academic achievement

It can be interesting to look at the types of topics that were surveyed in the ACEs study (all of which refer to the respondent's first eighteen years of life)—I know for me, taking the test clarified that I did in fact experience traumas as a child. I have an ACEs score of 8, which means that the chances of me becoming an addict, experiencing depression, and becoming suicidal are way off the charts. To put it in context, people with an ACEs score of 0 have almost no probability of these things. For every bump of one digit, the likelihood increases two to four times. Most of the charts end with 4+ as the cutoff to maximum risk. And unfortunately, the issues do get more serious with age if left untreated. For that reason, I'm listing them below. Caution: Reading the following definitions will likely cause an emotional response in your body that you don't experience as a memory but which is most likely a response to your own adverse childhood experiences. Please remember to use your support system and healthy tools when dealing with this material. I do.

ACEs are classfied into three primary groups, each with several sub-classifications as follows:[20]

Abuse

⊛ **Emotional abuse:** A parent, stepparent, or adult living in your home swore at you, insulted you, put you down, or acted in a way that made you afraid that you might be physically hurt.

⊛ **Physical abuse:** A parent, stepparent, or adult living in your home pushed, grabbed, slapped, threw something at you, or hit you so hard that you had marks or were injured.

⊛ **Sexual abuse:** An adult, relative, family friend, or stranger who was at least 5 years older than you ever touched or fondled your body in a sexual way, made you touch his/her body in a sexual way, attempted to have any type of sexual intercourse with you.

Household Challenges

⊛ **Mother treated violently:** Your mother or stepmother was pushed, grabbed, slapped, had something thrown at her, kicked, bitten, hit with a fist, hit with something hard, repeatedly hit for over at least a few minutes, or ever threatened or hurt by a knife or gun by your father (or stepfather) or mother's boyfriend.

⊛ **Substance abuse in the household:** A household member was a problem drinker or alcoholic or a household member used street drugs.

⊛ **Mental illness in the household:** A household member was depressed or mentally ill or a household member attempted suicide.

⊛ **Parental separation or divorce:** Your parents were ever separated or divorced.

⊛ **Incarcerated household member:** A household member went to prison.

Neglect

⊛ **Emotional neglect:** Someone in your family helped you feel important or special, you felt loved, people in your family looked out for each other and felt close to each other, and your family was a source of strength and support.*

⊛ **Physical neglect:** There was someone to take care of you, protect you, and take you to the doctor if you needed it,* you didn't have enough to eat, your parents were too drunk or too high to take care of you, and you had to wear dirty clothes.

*Items were reverse-scored to reflect the framing of the question.

Let me ask you this: As you read over these questions that were given to people in the ACEs study, how do you feel in your body? The body "keeps the score," as Dr. van der Kolk says in his book. When we're traumatized, the memories, according to psychotherapist Janina Fisher, are encoded as bodily and mental states. But when we have flashbacks—unwanted memories—they're not experienced necessarily as memories. They come back to us in the shape of depression, fear, panic attacks, self-loathing, fear of abandonment, anger, aggression, and the sense that we can't be still. Is any of this ringing a bell for you?

I have to admit that when I study and write about trauma, it pushes a lot of buttons for me. Here's one that stands out for me. From Maren A. Masino, expert on sensorimotor psychotherapy, "Other symptoms develop as valiant attempts to cope with the triggering." One is "caretaking of others to combat a sense of worthlessness."[21] Wow. That one hits home for me.

If you're getting a response to reading this, there's a reason.

When people are traumatized, our brains become damaged. Brain science tells us so much about the internal mechanisms and areas of the brain, chemicals released, and so on, but to delve into it with any depth would take a whole book, and frankly, you're better off reading some of the work in the resources section to get a better handle on the deep details. For the purposes of taking a brief look to understand it in the scope of addiction, I'll try to summarize how trauma changes the brain and has a lasting effect on our addiction recovery.

This is my interpretation of what happens when we're traumatized: When we experience a traumatic event or series of events, our ANS goes into the sympathetic branch of high-alert reactivity otherwise known as fight, flight, or freeze, also referred to as immobilization. We get signals to our brain's alarm center, which is also the center for emotional memory. Dr. Jim Hopper discusses how society's perception of this framework insinuates that if we're attacked, we're supposed to fight first, then run away—or if we can't fight, freeze until we can run or the threat passes. But in reality, from an evolutionary standpoint our systems are designed to freeze first, until we can flee. If we do fight, it's just to buy time enough to flee. This insinuation is a difficult problem for those who experience traumas such as sexual assault because they shame themselves—and are shamed by others—if they *didn't* do anything to fight off their attacker. It's therefore important to understand the social underpinnings even in the way the science is described. If a traumatic event is happening to us, our decision-making processes are shut down and our instincts fire off automatically. Our brain and body are doing what they believe is necessary to keep us alive. We need to be sensitive with ourselves and each other when considering what options we may have had when traumatized.

The part of our brain that processes speech, logic, sequences, and analysis shuts down. The part of our brain that says "Run!" goes off, and in that period of trauma, the experience goes deep into the body and remains. If we were animals in the wild, we'd fall on the ground and start spazzing out, and that would release the trauma. But because we're humans, we might not release it from our bodies. If we don't get to release it properly or if we're subjected to the trauma constantly, the experience gets buried. And it will come up in all kinds of sideways feelings and behaviors. None of the time sequences will work. So we'll experience the trauma as if it's happening in the now, even if it happened decades ago. This is one of the symptoms of PTSD.

PTSD and Complex PTSD

According to the International Classification of Diseases, PTSD (post-traumatic stress disorder) is:

> . . . a syndrome that develops following exposure to an extremely threatening or horrific event or series of events that is characterized by all of the following: 1) re-experiencing the traumatic event or events in the present in the form of vivid intrusive memories, flashbacks, or nightmares, which are typically accompanied by strong or overwhelming emotions . . . 2) avoidance of thoughts and memories of the event or events, or avoidance of activities, situations, or people reminiscent of the event or events; and 3) persistent perceptions of heightened current threat. . . . The symptoms persist for at least several weeks and cause significant impairment in personal, family, social, educational, occupational or other important areas of functioning.[22]

And complex PTSD is:

> . . . a disorder that may develop following exposure to an event or series of events of an extreme and prolonged or repetitive nature that is experienced as extremely threatening or horrific and from which escape is difficult or impossible (e.g., torture, slavery, genocide campaigns, prolonged domestic violence, repeated childhood sexual or physical abuse). The disorder is characterized by the

core symptoms of PTSD. . . . In addition, complex PTSD is characterized by 1) severe and pervasive problems in affect regulation; 2) persistent beliefs about oneself as diminished, defeated or worthless, accompanied by deep and pervasive feelings of shame, guilt or failure related to the stressor; and 3) persistent difficulties in sustaining relationships and in feeling close to others. The disturbance causes significant impairment in personal, family, social, educational, occupational or other important areas of functioning.[23]

Most of us in recovery don't have to stretch our imaginations too far to identify with PTSD or complex PTSD symptoms. I've never met an addict who didn't have problems regulating emotions or who didn't suffer from feelings of worthlessness or shame. Guilt and failure are second nature to many of us. And if you want to talk about the number-one cause of relapse, besides money, you won't get much disagreement that significant impairment in personal, family, and other relationships is more common than not amongst addicts.

What I'm saying is that, in my opinion, many addicts suffer from the effects of trauma at various levels, maybe at the level of PTSD or complex PTSD. Further, the 12 Steps are not equipped to deal with the deep, lasting brain damage caused by trauma. Buddhism may not say it specifically, but the true healing power of compassion that the Dharma teaches is a critical—if not the most important—skill or quality that we can develop. And it can be developed with practice. The brain science on compassion techniques shows that the results are proportionate to the practice. The more we practice compassion and mindfulness, the better we get at it. Go figure.

Hyperarousal and Trauma Bonding

While many of us may be able to relate to the descriptions of PTSD and complex PTSD, there are even more ways that trauma can affect our lives. As we know now, when we're in fight-or-flight, we literally lose our minds. And when trauma is left unhealed, the body remains in a state of ongoing stress as if the threats are still occurring. This manifests in two ways, hypoarousal and hyperarousal.

Hypoarousal is the state of being below baseline, having less energy, even feeling emotional numbness. Hyperarousal is something like a manic phase. We might feel too hyper to think straight, be prone to talking fast, have racing thoughts, or feel super creative and like we can accomplish anything. We might have a lot of sex or engage in some high-risk activities, good or bad but nonetheless very stimulating. This keeps us on a kind of hyperarousal high. The problem is that this is also a state of increased adrenaline and other neurochemicals that are meant to be released as stress responses. These chemicals at moderate levels help us focus, but at increased levels—such as in a stress response to trauma—impair functioning of the part of the brain that lets us regulate emotion, think things through, plan, and analyze.

When we become addicted to the hyperarousal of interactions with an abuser, it's called trauma bonding, otherwise known as Stockholm syndrome. Freud called this the repetition *compulsion* and thought of it as an unconscious way to gain control over a past situation.

The phenomenon of the trauma bond is indicative of the brain's propensity to become addicted to someone who is *the source* of suffering. In AA we'd say that some of us are addicted to drama. This is one way of looking at it. We get hooked on the brain chemicals of stress to the point that we're bored, depressed, even suicidal in the absence of hyperarousal and the rush of dopamine and oxytocin that comes from toxic relationships and high-risk behavior.

Our society can tend to judge people who seem to be experiencing trauma bonding, as if they should know better, but be careful not to fall into this judgment. Trauma bonding is a powerful brain addiction that is as dangerous as any chemical but is much more complex. See the resources section for help with this issue. I mention it here because many addicts can relate to being addicted to someone who mistreats us. It's a real thing, and there are real solutions. Trust me, I've experienced this and have written about it in other books.

Self-Compassion for Our Trauma and Addiction

With what we know about trauma now, doesn't it make sense that some of the strategies we would use to deal with the extreme, unexplainable sensations in our minds and bodies would be to use and abuse substances, processes, and relationships? We can have compassion for ourselves for having taken this path even as we want to change our path.

The change in the brain circuitry that sends thinking offline and lets survival instinct take over is referred to in the trauma literature as a bottom-up approach, because the lower or earlier evolutionary parts of the brain, such as the reptilian brain, are online in a hurry to keep us alive when a threat occurs. A top-down approach is when we can think a problem through with our prefrontal cortex, where all the information processing happens. But in trauma—and when we relive it—we lose executive function.

The part of our brain that remembers trauma cannot process timelines, words, or thoughts. It's all about feeling. This fear response that's buried in our brains and bodies can be triggered in a split second without any warning, sending us into an emotional cascade that we have no idea how to manage—no matter how long we're sober or how many times we've worked the steps. The good news is, the trauma responses can be released. Much of what we already do in *The 12-Step Buddhist* deals with this. But it's very good to know that going in. The best way to heal fear is to create a sense of safety. There are therapies designed to do just that.

The other thing that happens in trauma, especially in the case of a sexual assault, is disempowerment. To heal from this disempowerment, we need to keep in mind the tools of self-empowerment. Whatever we can do to build our own strength in ourselves, and to encourage choices and good decisions when dealing with other traumatized people whom we are very likely to meet in recovery, is going to be a good thing.

Disconnection is another big part of the trauma experience. We might check out, leave the room, or leave our bodies mentally. We will feel like we are not valid, not valued, and not respected. Ask any addict, and they will tell you in a heartbeat that alienation—or that gut-wrenching sense of being alone—is like a dark plague that runs through the center of our beings. To be connected is the solution. To allow others to feel connected is the healing. Being connected to a group, a sangha, a community, or even just one person like a sponsor, therapist, or sober coach is an amazing step in the right direction.

Take that step. Help others take that step. That's Buddhist. That's recovery. It's compassion, and it's healing. Keep going.

Our behaviors and emotional responses are what we had to do to cope. Our incorrect development led us to have problems with regulating our emotions and controlling our behaviors. That caused social problems, which caused more trauma. Our coping mechanisms helped us survive for a while, even into adulthood. But eventually many of them, such as our addictions, wind up hurting us.

It's vital to our understanding and healing to realize that our responses to stress and trauma are mostly outside of our control. Like our addiction as a brain disease, our trauma responses manifest to ensure our survival. Remember, that's the brain's whole job—to keep us alive. And like addiction, our trauma responses, even though we didn't cause them, leave us with a choice to interrupt the process or keep doing damage.

Sobriety, Masimo says, brings more challenges to the traumatized person, not fewer. It would have been nice if we knew this on day one of sobriety so we could actively and consciously participate in our own recovery knowing something of the scope and depth of the work ahead of us. But that's what we're trying to do here, namely, lay out a road map for the people just coming into sobriety. Then you don't have to wind up curled in a ball, deep into the Funnel with years of sobriety and step work yet with no clue how you got there. Masimo uses the term "post-traumatic flooding" to describe how we can become overwhelmed and risk relapse even if we're working a program. In her opinion—and, as you know, I agree—treatment must address the relationship between the trauma and the addictive behavior, even if the behavior is different than the original drugs of choice. Some of these symptoms may include self-injury or starvation, suicidal thoughts, feelings of helplessness, and high-risk behavior as well as the typical addictive behaviors. These things are part of our makeup before we enter treatment, and they must be dealt with far beyond abstinence from drugs and alcohol if we are to become, as AA says, practically and usefully whole.

When we're traumatized, the effects of the trauma increase as the number of incidents go up, which is called dose response. Traumatized kids don't develop correctly. The more times we were abused, neglected, mistreated, abandoned, ignored, mocked, beat up, the more problems we will have up to and including early death. That's the bad news.

The good news is that the practices outlined in this book are also dose related. If you work through the steps, meditations, and practices that I cover in upcoming pages, your brain can and will change for the better. I can't guarantee results, but it works for me and many thousands of people who have read this book and have done the practices. This means if you do them more often, you'll get more and better results. It's called neuroplasticity—training the brain to experience life differently and let go of the trauma response. Check out my book *Compassionate Recovery* for a deeper discussion on that.

We have a saying in AA: "You can't think yourself into right living, but you can live yourself into right thinking." It's about how we can retrain ourselves to act in the world. Bring the body, and the mind will follow. This isn't to say that thought processes and verbal therapies have no effect. It's obvious that we need to talk about things to bring them to the surface and somehow begin to weave a meaningful narrative in our lives. It's to acknowledge that some things make no sense—like being raped or brutalized by a caregiver—and never will, and this part of the brain can't just think itself better from trauma. The good news is that we can learn to have compassion for our experiencer, the one who suffers. We might not ever be able to understand why we were hurt or how something inexplicable could happen to us. But we can learn to bring compassion to any person, place, or experience.

Take a nice deep breath, and as you exhale, just relax in knowing that. There is a solution, no matter how bad things are. The Buddha was a wise one. I don't think he would have told us about the Truth of Suffering if he didn't have a solution.

Treatments for Trauma to Aid Recovery

Many of the treatments that are being used these days for trauma therapy are very different than the typical talk therapy sessions. Among these are psychodrama, the acting out of emotional scenarios, as well as the plethora of mindfulness-based techniques such as mindfulness-based stress reduction (MBSR) therapy. As I mentioned earlier, dialectical behavior therapy (DBT) is another that takes mindfulness and nonviolent communication into account as well as self-regulation, self-soothing, and owning one's experience. Yoga, as you know, is a big one for me. Other tools that are being studied are martial arts, tai chi, and other somatic—body-based—therapies, such as sensorimotor therapy to help reset the parasympathetic part of the autonomic nervous system.

You know from my writing that I've been calling for a multifaceted, comprehensive, and integrated approach to healing from addictions since the beginning of my work. I must have known intuitively that this was the key to healing because, as I said earlier, we just didn't have the science in 2009 that we do now to support these ideas. In my opinion—and yes, I'm biased—the practices of integrating the 12 Steps, Buddhism, and these other tools like yoga are the holy grail of addiction recovery.

That said, one problem in the science right now is establishing the most effective combinations of treatments to ensure the best, longest-lasting results. There's a lot being done, and with the big explosion of neuroscience and mindfulness, everybody and their brother is becoming an expert meditation instructor/clinician/brain advocate. This is a good thing. My advice is to try different combinations and durations of various methods as you go along. Keep journals of your progress. Talk about it on social media and in meetings. Hell, write books on it! We need this in the discussion to help everyone find combinations that work.

There is definitely a need for collaboration among treatment professionals, therapists, and spiritual teachers. I feel that a revolution in recovery is underway and that if you look back on it twenty years from now, you'll see that the trends we're now seeing are going to change the ways in which we look at our experiences, not only as addicts but also as traumatized humans on a path to free ourselves and each other from suffering. Dang, if that's not Buddhist, I don't know what is.

One important goal of treatment for trauma that relates specifically to the work in this book is to learn to regulate our emotional state into an ideal window of tolerance between hyper- and hypoarousal.

According to van der Kolk, stress hormones—such as adrenaline, which gives us the ability to run or fight—in traumatized people are triggered more easily and spike to highs not found in the untraumatized. They also linger, which makes that feeling of being stressed last longer. And the long-term effects of stress cause memory and attention problems, irritability, sleep disorders, and other health issues. He also says that denial plays a part in chronic stress in those with a history of trauma.

As an addict, I know all about denial. In the early stages of recovery, it's the first thing that has to go. "The delusion [that we are like normal people] has to be smashed," says AA. But beyond the denial of drugs and alcohol is the denial of stress. If we can't admit we're having a trauma response, our bodies stay in stress mode. Stress mode can lead us to acting out, falling into depression, expressing rage, switching addictions, and heading straight into the Funnel. The persistent stress signals to our body also tax our organs, leading to illness.

If we don't know that some or a lot of what we experience is a response to trauma, then we may be in denial. Just like any addiction, we need to break our denial to get into the solution. One thing we can do is have compassion for ourselves and the experience we're having. It's easy for us addicts to beat ourselves up. Trust me, I've done enough of it over the years. How many times have we said something like, "But I'm x years sober—I'm not supposed to be feeling this way!"

Well that is exactly why I do the work that I do and write these books. Because the 12 Steps alone and the culture of 12-Step groups don't address these kinds of issues. Buddhism alone can, but it doesn't have the addiction recovery training and focus, and it most assuredly doesn't have the knowledge of brain trauma behind it. No, we are in a new day, my friends. We're in a place where we need to integrate everything we know, not just in little pockets here and there, but in a way that brings mass healing to this wounded, addicted world that we live in. The answer to all of this is in this book, and the work to come on Compassionate Recovery.

Fortunately, there are some therapists who agree with me too.

In regard to psychotherapy neurobiological findings can contribute decisively in the design of an appropriate treatment strategy. . . . The question emerges how can traditional approaches of CBT and psychodynamic therapy that are based on understanding and insight efficiently cope with the challenge of treating PTSD sufferers? Bessel A. Van der Kolk, a pioneer in the field of PTSD treatment concludes that "Neither CBT protocols nor psychodynamic therapeutic techniques pay sufficient attention to the experience and interpretation of disturbed physical sensations and preprogrammed physical action patterns."

He pleads for the integration of techniques that address the abovementioned particularities and enable the reprogramming of automatic physical responses.[24]

According to Christine A. Courtois, PhD, who specializes in treating PTSD, the goals of treatment for PTSD are to

⊛ increase capacity to manage emotions
⊛ reduce PTSD symptoms and levels of hyperarousal
⊛ reestablish normal stress response: symptom remission . . .

- ⊗ decrease numbing/avoidance strategies
- ⊗ face rather than avoid trauma, process emotions, integrate traumatic memories
- ⊗ reduce comorbid/co-occurring problems
- ⊗ educate about and destigmatize PTSD[25]

The goals of treatment then are obvious wins for any addict looking at this list. In my experience, the ability to manage emotions has been the most challenging aspect of being sober all the years that I've been doing it. It's because I've always swung between the hyper- and hypoarousal extremes and have *rarely* been in that "window of tolerance," as Janina Fisher calls it. In fact, even now, at twenty-one years sober, I can say that I have a long way to go in terms of reducing PTSD symptoms and levels of hyperarousal.

But with my years and years of meditation and yoga practice, along with my active involvement in the 12-Step communities, going to therapy, taking meds, and taking care of my fitness, I feel like many of the symptoms have been reduced, drastically. The process of decreasing avoidance strategies is ongoing and more of a lifelong process.

Of the most interest to me is the practice of facing the trauma. That will be one of the main subjects of the next book. I will talk about a process that I've learned in the Compassion Cultivation Training through the Compassion Institute at the end of this book. Those practices, which are closely related to those that we do in the 12 Steps, are right in line with the trauma treatment goals. Hopefully what we're discussing in this chapter will help to educate everyone and destigmatize PTSD.

Radical Treatments for Trauma to Aid Recovery

As I mentioned in chapter 1, I'm also open-minded to the more radical treatments for trauma to aid in addiction recovery. I regularly use CBD and have tried ayahuasca-style plant-based medicine and shamanic healing. Psychedelics can produce a powerful perspective shift that, with the right intention, context, and support, can alter our views toward our addictions and help us let them go.

Bill Wilson, founder of AA, claimed that he used LSD to enhance spirituality. Michael Pollan's work is often quoted in recovery circles and among proponents of psychedelic therapy. He talks about how these drugs affect the brain and gives some insight as to why they work the way they do: "The psychedelic experience had given many of them an overview effect on the scenes of their own lives, making possible a shift in worldview and priorities that allowed them to let go of old habits, sometimes with remarkable ease."[26]

Another psychedelic used to treat addiction is ibogaine. According to the Global Ibogaine Therapy Alliance:

> Ibogaine is a naturally occurring psychoactive substance that has been demonstrated to interrupt substance use disorders, as well as possess other neurological and psychological benefits. . . . In the early 1960's, the Chilean psychologist Claudio Naranjo conducted 40 ibogaine sessions with his clients and was the first to scientifically describe the experience. He reported that ibogaine helped people to view difficult experiences in an objective way, and that it helped to facilitate closure of unresolved emotional conflicts.[27]

I can't say that I recommend that you or anyone else take any drug at all to enhance your spiritual practice or your recovery. But I know that for me, like CBD, where nothing else worked, these things have provided me support that later led to deeper understanding of myself and my sobriety.

Given what we know about the devastating impact of trauma on the human brain and its role in predisposing one to addiction, some radical approaches can possibly be integrated into a Compassionate Recovery plan that works for some people. If we can circumvent the reward processes of the brain with our mindfulness, lovingkindness, 12-Step integration, breathing practices, good nutrition, psychotherapy, and yes even psychedelics and CBD, we can teach our brains new ways of coping with stress, emotion, and the triggers that often lead to relapse.

Of course, traditional AA views would say that if we take 'shrooms or acid or a pot-based derivative like CBD, we're not *really* sober. But I want to keep emphasizing that there is no one-size-fits-all definition of addiction or recovery.

That said, I don't think it's as easy as just having a session or two of radical, psychedelic treatments, and then you're sober for life. Because it's not an escape. It's work—very, very hard work. This is one of the main reasons that I don't consider the use of these drugs as a relapse, if done under the guidance of shamans, therapists, and other healers for the purposes of having deeper psychic healing. And I think, as I always say, that we need to work a comprehensive, multifaceted treatment program such as the one that I work for my own recovery. Do some combination of things, and change them up as needed. Be most consistent on the ones that work best. But don't hope for a magic recovery or enlightenment pill. The cost of admission to the temple of healing is a lifetime of commitment and work. We can pass through doorways of hope along the way, but it is a journey, not a destination.

In some ways I fear that if I share these things, you'll think I'm a failure as a Buddhist. But the reality is that there's only one perfect Buddhist: Buddha himself. These days, I'm on to some ways to take what we started in *The 12-Step Buddhist* further, to fill in the gaps in our understanding and to establish something new on the foundation that we've built together over the years through our practice, our dedication, and our sobriety.

The Argument that Addiction Is Not a Brain Disease

There are those who feel that it's not helpful to consider addiction a disease. Some of the reasons are based on disagreements over the clinical definition of disease. This argument can get complicated. Retired professor of psychiatry Lance Dodes puts it this way:

Compare addiction with true diseases. In addiction there is no infectious agent (as in tuberculosis), no pathological biological process (as in diabetes), and no biologically degenerative condition (as in Alzheimer's disease). The only "disease-like" aspect of addiction is that if people do not deal with it, their lives tend to get worse. That's true of lots of things in life that are not diseases; it doesn't tell us anything about the nature of the problem. (It's worthwhile to remember here that the current version of the disease concept, the "chronic brain disease" neurobiological idea, applies to rats but has been repeatedly shown to be inapplicable to humans.)[28]

But what Dr. Dodes and others like Marc Lewis, author of *The Biology of Desire: Why Addiction Is Not a Disease*, don't realize is that the technical definition from their point of view doesn't really matter to the suffering addict. NIDA and the majority of the treatment field of medical professionals still endorse the notion of addiction as a disease. In AA meetings and other groups, the idea of a disease is already firmly embedded. There's really no point, and it's not helpful, to go on a crusade to prove that addiction doesn't really meet the criteria.

The main problem with these arguments is the complexity of individuals and their addictions. It's not a case of whether a person is *either* a helpless victim of a disease *or* a fully volitional actor of their own design. We addicts are both. That's really the bottom line. We have a lot in common with those who have "real" diseases, but we also have the ability to arrest our illness. We can choose to heal. It's brutal, difficult, wrought with pitfalls, and takes lots of hard work and time. But as someone with twenty-one years of continuous sobriety as well as other forms of mental illness—depression, PTSD, hallucinogen-persisting perceptual disorder—I assure you that healing can happen.

Cancer patients can't just choose to get better. I don't know how effective positive thinking is in curing heart disease. But there are so many factors that go into the environmental, genetic, and behavioral choices of individuals. We contribute to our well-being, and our not-well-being. So I'll leave the arguments of doctors Dodes and Lewis to NIDA psychiatrist Nora Volkow and the treatment field. For me personally—and what I recommend to my readers—it's important to know that through the practices of meditation outlined in this and other works, we can come to new levels of awareness about what is in our control and what is not. I'm about self-empowerment over powerlessness.

How about you?

Addiction and Mental Illness

Addiction *is* a mental illness, as we have discussed. All you pure alcoholics—those who never touched a drug—please grab your phone now and call your sponsor. You're about to get what we call a resentment, particularly if you're one of those in 12 Steps who insists on calling yourself recovered—cured. Using that term is the kiss of death. As I mentioned, I don't agree that the alcoholic is a separate entity from the addict because my disease can take on many forms. I can never safely use x in any form, where x is any mind-altering substance, event, process, or person.

The physical effects of substance addiction are self-evident, but Dr. Volkow states that brain disruption is similar in people with addictions to processes and events to that of substance abusers. "Recent studies illustrate the similarity of addiction to some disorders that are not associated with drugs. For example, compulsive behavior and poor choices are hallmarks of obsessive-compulsive disorder and pathological gambling. These disorders, too, are characterized by disruption of the frontal brain's capacity for reason and control."[29]

Substance abuse is considered a mental illness by the American Psychiatric Association.[30] And, according to Dr. Volkow, "As many as 6 in 10 substance abusers also have at least one other mental disorder. Research increasingly supports the benefit of studying and treating co-occurring disorders together, with both medication and behavioral therapies."[31]

From the surgeon general, "According to the 2015 *National Survey on Drug Use and Health* (NSDUH), of the 20.8 million people aged 12 or older who had a substance use disorder during the past year, about 2.7 million (13 percent) had both an alcohol use and an illicit drug use disorder, and 41.2 percent also had a mental illness."[32]

The AA literature offers this advice when we feel resentful:

> Though we did not like their symptoms and the way these disturbed us, they, like ourselves, were sick too. We asked God to help us show them the same tolerance, pity, and patience that we would cheerfully grant a sick friend. When a person offended, we said to ourselves, "This is a sick man. How can I be helpful to him? God save me from being angry. Thy will be done." We avoid retaliation or argument. We wouldn't treat sick people that way.[33]

My hope in presenting this data is to show how sick the addict really is, that we as a society may be of benefit by easing the suffering and lessening the expense to our collective emotional and spiritual health.

Is Addiction a Choice?

No. Yes. Yes and no. The problem of addiction is a complex issue. It stems from and affects every aspect of an addict's life. From NIDA:

> Drug addiction shares many features with other chronic illnesses, including a tendency to run in families (heritability), an onset and course that is influenced by environmental conditions and behavior, and the ability to respond to appropriate treatment, which may include long-term lifestyle modification. Addiction is a chronic disease similar to other chronic diseases such as type II diabetes, cancer, and cardiovascular disease. Human studies of addictive behaviors have clearly implicated both environmental and genetic influences, as well as interactions

between the two. While genetics play a major role in defining who we are, the environment in which we are raised is just as influential.[34]

The first time I used was my choice, to a degree. I had the genes—my father was an alcoholic, my mother bipolar—and conditioning factors including a chaotic home life, improper modeling, lack of social support in the family, a school system not yet equipped for special education, and so on. But, as we say in the program, nobody put a gun to my head. When I see kids at the age I was when I started using, they look like tiny babies to me. My heart sinks to recall my experience as a kid on drugs. There's a reason why we have an age of consent for sex, tobacco, and alcohol. Kids don't have the life experience and judgment to fully understand the implications of an ill-informed decision with short-term relief but long-term consequences.

The Decision-Making Ability of the Addict: Our Brains Are Fried

Why do addicts have such a hard time stopping once they've started? In 2000, brain researchers at NIDA wrote:

> As for drug craving—the intense hunger that drives addicts to seek drugs despite the strong likelihood of adverse consequences—researchers have shown that it is related to widespread alterations in brain activity, but especially to changes in the nucleus accumbens area of the forebrain. An important type of craving experienced by addicts, called cue-induced craving, occurs in the presence of people, places, or things that they have previously associated with their drug taking. Brain imaging studies have shown that cue-induced craving is accompanied by heightened activity in the forebrain, the anterior cingulate, and the prefrontal cortex—key brain areas for mood and memory.[35]

Current NIDA Director Nora D. Volkow, MD, wrote in 2003:

Drugs exert persistent neurobiological effects that extend beyond the midbrain centers of pleasure and reward to disrupt the function of the brain's frontal cortex—the thinking region of the brain, where risks and benefits are weighed and decisions made.[36]

Once addicts become involved in the activity of addiction, they are, as Dr. Leshner states, "in a different state of being." The brain is actually changed. I remember sitting in my room, smoking weed, drinking wine, and feeling very alone. I used to listen to *Loveline*, a radio show with Dr. Drew (Pinsky) and Adam Carolla (whose run on the show ended in 2005, though the show is still running). From what Dr. Drew, an addictionologist, had been saying, I saw my pattern. I was the poster boy for the progression of drug addiction from pot to alcohol to meth. Addicts' brains are permanently altered from drug use. At the cellular level, we become, quite literally, different people. Those who smoked pot and/or took hallucinogens as teens, almost without fail, develop chronic, acute mood disturbances in their twenties and thirties. A lot of people are walking around with this repercussion driving their moods and daily choices.

This information really helped me decide to get clean and sober again and stay that way. It's tough to refute the science, especially when it relates to personal experience. I hope this is clear: addicts become very sick people. We are permanently altered from drug use.

Ouch. My brain hurts reviewing this data. Doesn't it make you feel just a little more compassionate toward addicts? How about toward the addict in you? So often we in recovery fight ourselves, loathe ourselves, and judge ourselves harshly. For most of us, it's really hard not to, considering the amount of suffering we've caused ourselves and others. Even when we work the 12 Steps over time, we often have difficulty letting go of the knot of self-hate buried deep within us. This book helps you loosen that knot.

The data certainly confirms what the AA literature has to say about the body of the addict. (Note: AA uses the term *alcoholic*. I'm taking the liberty of using the two terms interchangeably.) From the AA Basic Text, "The Doctor's Opinion":

The body of the *alcoholic* is quite as abnormal as his mind. It did not satisfy us to be told that we could not control our drinking just because we were maladjusted to life, that we were in full flight from reality, or were outright mental defectives. These things were true to some extent, in fact, to a considerable extent with some of us. But we are sure that our bodies were sickened as well. In our belief, any picture of the alcoholic which leaves out this physical factor is incomplete.

Treatment Is Complicated

No matter how well-meaning or educated or enlightened you are, if you are not an addict, you probably view addicts as bad people who should just not do that bad stuff anymore. According to the NIDA website:

No one chooses to be a drug addict or to develop heart disease. Sometimes people do choose behaviors that have undesirable effects. Personal responsibility and behavioral change are major components of any credible treatment program. Addiction, like heart disease, cancers, and type II diabetes, is a real and complex disease.[37]

No sane person claims that addicts are blameless for their addiction or its consequences. But the less integrated, even unidimensional, approaches used in 12-Step meetings, by therapists and by spiritual teachers, are not enough. If a therapist recommends 12 Steps and some 12-Step members are moderately open to therapy, there's a lot of power missing from what could be a seriously integrated model. The disease of addiction is multifaceted. The solution needs to be flexible, dynamic, interactive, and comprehensive.

"The clear and unambiguous message from 25 years of scientific research is that drug abuse and addiction are complex, dynamic processes. No aspect will be explained or resolved simply by choosing from a list of either/or options. There are no simple solutions."[38]

To Therapists

As a therapist, it's vital to understand the nature of addiction and to realize that no matter how much you actually know intellectually and scientifically, if you are not an addict, you can never say, "Me too." The we—as we say in the program—is why the 12-Step model works. Addicts are sensitive and finely tuned to the impressions non-addicts have of us. It's what we do. The tools and exercises in this book can be very helpful in getting deeper, and hopefully a little closer, to the actual experience of the addict. But, unlike many spiritual teachers, you at least understand addiction as a mental disorder.

My experiences in therapy were much more effective when the therapist took the time to read the same books I work from. I've used meditation with psychotherapy and recovery to my advantage. And if your client is in recovery, is in need of recovery, or has trouble with some of the spiritual language of the 12-Step model, please share this book. Try the exercises and meditations together. I think you'll find yourself connecting with your addicted clients more effectively.

In the past decade, many new therapies have emerged that integrate Buddhist principles such as mindfulness, lovingkindness, and self-compassion. A lot of therapists have an interest in Buddhism, and many clinicians have developed their own meditation practices, which they integrate with their clients' treatment plans. There are tons of retreats, apps, online courses, and weekend programs that offer extensive healing opportunities.

One psychologist who pioneered integration of Buddhist mindfulness principles is the late Alan Marlatt. Dr. Marlatt wrote many cutting-edge books on relapse prevention, among them, *Harm Reduction: Pragmatic*

Strategies for Managing High-Risk Behaviors. The harm reduction model has since become an integrated part of the approach to treatment and is widely used in Canada, where addiction is no longer a crime. If you've read the works of Dr. Gabor Maté you'll be familiar with this application.

In fact, mindfulness is so widely used as part of therapy now that in a recent conference on addiction, virtually every speaker mentioned the use of mindfulness in their programs. Mindfulness was designed in Buddhism with supports that helped the practitioner remain stable. These include ethical guidelines, stages of practice, and always the framework of Buddhism as a path to end suffering. The approaches used in therapies such as ACT, Acceptance and Commitment Therapy, can go so far as to say they're explicitly *not* Buddhist, even though Buddhists have been practicing in much the same way for thousands of years.

For this reason, I still think it's important that we do our research and understand the full context of where the practices come from. A qualified, safe teacher is indispensable for that. As always, it's good to integrate something like a mindful therapist with a Buddhist master and a 12-Step support program. This is especially true for those of us with a high ACEs score.

Unfortunately, the idea of mindfulness without proper support can be scary for traumatized addicts. That's why I advocate and am writing about the use of a strong community support group along with compassion meditations and group exercises as well as sharing and more traditional group processes. The fact is that for some people, sitting still creates anxiety, fear, and even panic. It's a necessary part of healing, but we now know that we also need to provide support for what comes up when we addicts get still and silent.

To Spiritual Teachers

Even if you're a well-meaning Buddhist teacher or concerned practitioner, you may be laboring under the erroneous impression that if addicts just practiced more, or better, or with the right teacher, they'd get free of addiction. One reason to present this brain research is that

I want well-meaning teachers to understand that, on a fundamental, physical level, addicts are different from non-addicts. Spiritual teachers will be more effective if this fact is accepted and their approach adjusted accordingly. We addicts need you, our teachers, to understand the nature of addiction, its causes and effects, and how it changes our response to your teachings: we understand some concepts—like attachment—quickly, others slowly, and some techniques, such as meditation, require more patience. But primarily, we have the addict personality, which is very tricky for anyone. We think differently, will present more challenges, and if treated intelligently, will make more progress than your average student.

Buddhism without 12 Steps—or something universal, inclusive, and trauma informed like Compassionate Recovery—can be dangerous for an addict. You'd know if you ever had a deeply philosophical, late-night conversation with a drunk Buddhist. The addict's mind becomes twisted trying to apply spiritual tools without the context and understanding of the nature of addiction that 12-Step recovery offers. I was on retreat once with a guy who had been a Buddhist practitioner and a practicing addict for decades. His attitude made me cringe. Without the steps, the humility, willingness, and self-honesty necessary in Buddhism are often just not there. The tools of Buddhism become another weapon of the narcissistic addict ego—as if the typical Dharma ego, a form of spiritual pride, isn't bad enough.

Once we're in recovery, we have a better chance to learn, understand, and apply tools from traditions outside the 12 Steps. But our addict minds are still fundamentally different than those of your typical Buddhist students, at least on the surface. That's really the point of trying to understand addiction through the Buddhist lens and Buddhism through the addict's eyes. Sure, if you meditate for thirty years, you may start to see that you're attached to your ego with all the severity of a crackhead and his pipe. But not always. Yet if you familiarize yourself with Buddhist principles, as this book tries to do, you can see that attachment is the root of suffering, and addiction is attachment gone wild.

Please consider this topic in your meditation and perhaps go to a few 12-Step or Compassionate Recovery meetings, undercover, to experience for yourself the magic in action.

The Spiritual Component

The upside is that spiritual principles defined in AA literature show that the purpose of the 12-Step program goes further than "to dispel the obsession to drink." The point is to "enable the sufferer to become happily and usefully whole." It also says, "We feel that elimination of our drinking is but a beginning. A much more important demonstration of our principles lies before us in our respective homes, occupations, and affairs."[39]

In the 12-Step program, members experience many difficulties in their homes, occupations, and affairs. Hundreds of times over the years, I've heard the desperation, hopelessness, confusion, and suffering that go along with being sober—and unhappy. All too often, speakers end their pitch with the resignation, "But I didn't take a drink today." The look on their face usually reveals that they know it's not enough.

The 12-Step program does afford the opportunity to move beyond such a static, rigid, and otherwise unhappy experience in sobriety, yet many are at a loss for how to make it happen within the confines of the program. The practice of Buddhism along with the 12 Steps is powerful and can help you work through these difficulties. It helped me after my relapse, and I credit my Buddhist practices as the reason for my current twenty-one years of sobriety and beyond. It is why I wrote this book.

At the time of the first edition, of all the physical treatments suggested by research, none included a spiritual component. I spoke with author and spiritual teacher Deepak Chopra on his radio show about this topic. Dr. Chopra told me that in all of his years working with addicts, "none of them found successful recovery without addressing the spiritual component. Ever."[40] This is certainly borne out by my own experience.

In some treatment modalities, such as cognitive behavioral therapy and groups like SMART Recovery, the spiritual side of recovery is not addressed or is even discounted. I believe now, more than ever, that the psychiatrist Carl Jung was right when he said that alcoholics and addicts need a spiritual experience to overcome their addictions. I realize that my lens is focused on spirituality, but I've been a spiritual person all of my life. Some people may not be, or they may just not have the taste for anything spiritual. If that's you, I would suggest that you try some of the non-spiritual approaches. If they work and you can find happiness and recovery, fantastic. But if you feel empty, like you don't want to live clean and sober or like you just don't have much feeling, please consider the spiritual approach. It works if you work it!

A Deeper Look at Treatment Goals

According to research, the goal of treatment is to "enable an individual to achieve lasting abstinence, but the immediate goals are to reduce drug abuse, improve the patient's ability to function, and minimize the medical and social complications of drug abuse and addiction."[41]

With the goal of maintaining sobriety, a more comprehensive approach addressed by 12-Step programs and one totally beyond the scope of most Buddhist organizations is necessary. It must reach those who can't otherwise be reached and help those who would likely relapse. Here are some facts to support this idea:

- No single treatment is appropriate for all individuals.
- Effective treatment attends to multiple needs of the individual, not just his drug addiction.
- An individual's treatment and services plan must be assessed often and modified to meet the person's changing needs.
- Counseling and other behavioral therapies are critical components of virtually all effective treatments for addiction.
- For certain types of disorders, medications are an important element of treatment, especially when combined with counseling and other behavioral therapies.
- Addicted or drug-abusing individuals with coexisting mental disorders should have both disorders treated in an integrated way.

❀ As is the case with other chronic, relapsing diseases, recovery from drug addiction can be a long-term process and typically requires multiple episodes of treatment, including "booster" sessions and other forms of continuing care.[42]

Let's look at these points individually in a little closer detail, with a bit of insight from both the 12-Step and the Buddhist points of view, as necessary. Otherwise, the government data can be a little dry and impenetrable.

No single treatment is appropriate for all individuals

Some people use the above facts as a claim that the 12 Steps aren't necessary. I disagree completely. I couldn't function without my involvement with the 12-Step community. I tried and failed, and know of countless others who've done the same. I've seen a lot of people fail over the years. To be fair, the sentiment that the 12-Step program is *all* we need is often used in the 12-Step community to foster a more limited approach, and that's not true either.

In the 12-Step literature, we're told that we "know only a little."[43] What this means to me is that the program is not just a good starting point and something to graduate from, but that it's a good foundation and something to build from. In meetings, we hear consistently from addicts who've tried everything before they realized that the 12-Step program is the only thing that ever worked. This gives the impression that doing the 12-Step program alone is enough. It isn't. It's a necessary, *but not sufficient*, route to happiness or late-stage recovery, as addiction expert Terry Gorski put it in a talk I heard in the old days.

The 12-Step community forgets that one of the reasons other methods fail is, when we're active in our addictions, we're unable to participate fully in treatment that might otherwise be helpful. Once we're sober and able to function for a day without our drug of choice, then we're in a position to take advantage of complementary treatment options in addition to the 12 Steps.

It's common in meetings to hear the room chuckle in agreement when someone shares past treatment failures. Counselors are referred to as "paid sponsors." Common sentiments are, "Therapy doesn't work," "If we take medications, we're not really sober," and, "Self-help books are a waste of time." This kind of uninformed talk is narrow-minded and limited at best, dangerous at worst.

I'm not saying I agree with the science-only, non-spiritual approach either. These government-funded programs have traditionally been required to keep religion out of their programming. But they confuse narrow-minded, faith-based initiatives with enlightening spiritual-oriented solutions, which they also tend to keep out of their programs. It makes sense to use as much integration with 12 Steps as possible while working with as wide a selection of professionals as one's resources will allow. The research finding that no single treatment method is sufficient for everyone supports the logic of an integrated approach to recovery.

Effective treatment attends to multiple needs of the individual

Again from the AA literature: "Of necessity, there will have to be discussion of matters medical, psychiatric, social, and religious."[44] But in the 12-Step community, we hear that these matters are outside issues and, therefore, to discuss them in meetings is against the 12 Traditions. Further, 12 Step moderators claim open conversation would threaten not only the purity of the message of recovery and the stability of the group, but also the very fabric of the 12-Step program's existence. Addicts can be extreme in their thinking. Or haven't you noticed?

Here, the *single-minded* purpose of the 12 Traditions is often more like *narrow-mindedness*. The purpose is a focused attempt to keep the recovery message pure. But recovering people must have a community that supports our need to address all aspects of addiction while maintaining sobriety and deepening spirituality. We can oversimplify the problem and the solution, rehash the same topics—gratitude, Step One, resentment, honesty—to the point of delirium. And we often miss the opportunity to collectively address issues vital to recovery.

I'm not suggesting that we go to our home group and insist on making the topic Medication or What My Therapist and I Talked about Today. Meetings work the way they work. But, you can discuss other topics—domestic violence, depression, single parenting, mental illness—if your group is open to it. Or you can have a private, unofficial meeting at someone's home or a community center. Even better, you can set up a new meeting without the limitations of regular meetings. Not as a substitute, but as an addition to your regular program.

An individual's treatment and services plan must be assessed and modified often to meet changing needs

I've found that in my own recovery plan, I need to mix it up to keep it relevant. Periodically, I might change meetings or even home groups, go on group or personal retreats, and try different service positions in and out of the 12-Step community. Use Buddhist methods to expand your program. I also suggest you use a management team—sponsor, spouse, family, friends, and sangha—to help you assess your needs.

In terms of non-spiritual methods you can add to your program, NIDA outlines several effective psychological treatments. Keep in mind that psychology, although it uses a different terminology, ultimately seeks some of the same goals as a spiritual approach. In fact, you can use all methods as spiritual methods if you have an integrated program. By the end of the book, you'll see how this works.

Those of us with personal experience can be more involved and more helpful in this arena. We can facilitate the 12 Steps and Buddhism as a way of life with addicts in these programs. How many Buddhists do you know who visit prisons, hospices, and other such facilities? I know of just a few, and it's to their credit, but they don't compare to the efforts of Christian organizations, for example. It would be fantastic if one day we had a lot of recovering addict Buddhist practitioners going to these facilities.

Since the first edition came out, I've received hundreds of emails from prisoners who've read *The 12-Step Buddhist*. The need for healing among those incarcerated is still high. I got an email from a man recently who read this book while still in prison, got sober, was released, and has maintained a sober life as a Buddhist in recovery. Amazing. That was one of many such stories that I've heard over the years.

Many prisons and jails allow 12-Step programs to hold meetings. I've met a lot of addicts who said their first exposure to recovery was in jail. It's harder to bring Buddhism into jails, but it is the legal right of all inmates in the United States to practice the religion of their choice.

Venerable Robina Courtin created and maintained the Liberation Prison Project, which offers spiritual help to prisoners by writing letters, being a friend, answering spiritual questions, sending Buddhist books, and giving instruction on basic practices. There are a lot of newer movements to bring healing to prisoners too, and the Lion's Roar Buddhism website has compiled a list of them to help people get involved. If you're on the Buddhist path and are interested in supporting the effort to bring Buddhism to prisoners, please visit one of these organizations:

The North American Vipassana Prison Trust is a ten-day Vipassana meditation program taught at correctional facilities in North America to help inmates of any religion incorporate meditation into their lives.

Prison Mindfulness Institute provides inmates, staff, and volunteers with nonsectarian training in mindfulness meditation, communication, and conflict resolution.

The Dharma Rain Prison Program offers meditation practices and Buddhist teachings to inmates and recently released individuals from state prisons in Oregon.

The Rangjung Prison Dharma Project focuses on meditation teachings that aim to hone clarity and insight in challenging environments for inmates at Rikers Island Correctional Facility, New York.

Ratna Peace Initiative provides mindfulness meditation instruction to male and female inmates in person and through correspondence to inmates in prisons throughout forty-eight states.

Zen Mountain Monastery National Buddhist Prison Sangha's program involves monastics and lay practitioners visiting New York State's prisons to lead group meditation practices, liturgy, Dharma talks, and meditation retreats.

This can be very rewarding. In my experience, when I feel that I've helped a person in a treatment center or institution find just a moment of calmness in an otherwise chaotic state of mind, there's really nothing comparable. If you're interested and willing, consider bringing a 12-Step meeting, meditation group, a Tibetan lama, or other Dharma teacher to an institution near you.

Counseling and behavioral therapies are critical components of virtually all effective treatments for addiction

This is really a very important piece to understand. Counseling is a critical component of *all* effective treatments. That statement doesn't say it *can* be, or it *might* be, or that if you really have to, go ahead. It says that therapies *are* critical. I've found that, if I have a good therapist, am very involved in my recovery community, my spiritual community, and the wider community, and combine these involvements with serious Buddhist practices, I do all right.

I'll take that one step further—I wouldn't be sober and writing about this if I didn't do *all* of the above. If more people took this approach, the numbers of recovering *and* happy people would grow phenomenally.

For certain types of disorders, medications are an important element of treatment, especially when combined with counseling and other behavioral therapies

As I've mentioned, taking medication with the guidance of a licensed physician who is willing to work on a recovering addict's multifaceted, comprehensive, and flexible treatment plan can be critical for some. We shouldn't refuse to take meds because people in 12-Step programs advise against it. *They're not qualified to make such recommendations.* But, on the other hand, don't regard meds as a cure. Combine meds with therapy and other tools, and give them plenty of time to work.

Addicted or drug-abusing individuals with coexisting mental disorders should have both disorders treated in an integrated way

Sound familiar? If six out of ten addicts have coexisting mental disorders, it makes sense to take a look at the *whole* problem and apply a *total* solution. Buddhism really is a total solution for the problems of the mind. But it's really, really hard to apply it if we're (a) not sober, (b) nuts, (c) not sober *and* nuts.

Unfortunately, most people in the 12-Step community don't want you to talk about mental illness openly. It makes them really uncomfortable. The literature talks about it from an outdated perspective. In order to be of service to the dually diagnosed, I recommend that we approach those sicker members with compassion.

As is the case with other chronic, relapsing diseases, recovery from drug addiction can be a long-term process and typically requires multiple episodes of treatment, including "booster" sessions and other forms of continuing care

Relapse is part of recovery. What a concept. In the program, you won't hear anyone agree with this. They'll tell you that if you do the program right, you don't ever have to use again—even if you want to. One thing that defines us as addicts is that we use even when we don't want to. While it's partly true that, if we're working a good 12-Step program, we don't have to relapse, it's also a bit of a backhanded slap to people for whom occasional, even chronic relapse is a reality. Here is what one member said to me:

> I was just too damn tired to keep doing the deal, so I quit
> going. Too tired to force myself out the door—told myself
> I'd go to the next meeting. The next one just didn't come.
> I was angry, resentful, hurt, and sad, so many emotions

that weren't being numbed. And I didn't believe I could handle or cope with having feelings.

And another:

Is it so impossible to believe that someone could "thoroughly follow the path" but run into problems that led to relapse? I think not. But in order to stay clean in the 12 Steps, I just keep my mouth shut in a meeting, talk about this only with my sponsor and one-to-one support system. There are always a few people that picked up one white chip [and] seem to find pleasure in negating the experience of people with relapse in their history.

I can't tell you how much of a pariah I've felt like in meetings after relapse. People literally turned their backs and walked away when I asked for help. I remember having six days sober at a noontime men's meeting. I shared, asking at meeting level for help. I cried and was really, really hurting. The next guy who talked went on as if I hadn't said a word. When the meeting ended, one guy out of about thirty-five came over to talk. That's how it usually goes. The old-timer doesn't know what to do with the guy who lapsed from long-term sobriety or won't get with the program. It's really sad. And it doesn't have to be that way.

Years later, I wish I could say the situation has changed. "New" or "newcomer" generally means you're in the first thirty days of recovery. But a person is considered new again even if they've been sober for long stretches at a time. If you go to any meeting and see how many newcomers introduce themselves, you can see for yourself who helps them after the meeting. Sometimes no one approaches them, and they stand there, awkwardly. Some meetings are more proactive about these situations. But for the chronic relapser, even the most service-oriented groups may not be open. This is because sober addicts just don't like to be confronted with the possibility of their own sobriety's mortality.

In Buddhism, we have direct methods to deal with our physical mortality. Practices like this will help when it comes to considering sobriety's mortality, because if addicts can deal with their own fears about death, they'll be in a better position to help sufferers of chronic relapse. In the 12 Steps and in Buddhism, we must face our own fears. As someone who practices both, I try to help addicts understand impermanence and Buddhists understand addiction, particularly as a powerful motivation to practice.

If we in the recovery world were about 100 percent more compassionate with each other and ourselves, we would help a lot more people feel welcome, wanted, and needed. But as it stands, we're pretty jaded. In my first ten years of sobriety, I was pretty judgmental about relapsers. I'd chastise them at podium level. Then I became one. Do you think that's karma?

As a Buddhist, I practice *tonglen*—exchanging self for others. It's a good way to open your heart to relapsers.

4

12-Step Programs:
What Works and What Doesn't

I just can't do AA. It's too pedagogical, sexist, monotheistic, and I have an addiction, I'm not diseased. Doesn't flow with me at all. I've looked into SMART recovery, and have a support network of friends who don't drink, plus other avenues of self-exploration, so I don't feel like I'm missing anything at all.

—*Beverly W.*

The 12 Steps work in my life. In my experience, there is nothing as *singularly* effective for recovering addicts as active involvement in a 12-Step community. If I had only one option to choose from among all of the available solutions, it would be the 12 Steps. But I'm glad there are more options.

My relationship to the 12-Step community has gone through many changes over the years. It went beyond my expectations in the beginning. Every meeting was mind-blowing. New insights into my addiction and a greater awareness of my condition were constant. For the first time in my life, I found a community of people who, while maybe they weren't *just* like me, had similar histories and the desire to stay sober.

Recovery got more complicated as the years went on. As a long-term spiritual practitioner with two periods of extended sobriety, along with mental illness and a relapse history, I'm forced to seek the highest teachings and to combine them with the 12 Steps, therapy, and other tools. Some of us, as they say, are sicker than others.

That's one reason why I wrote this book. Not many are equipped with enough tools to help those of us with such an amalgam of problems as mine. I've scratched and struggled for years to establish a solution that works. This book is the result of working through those problems so that others, including relapsers, can avoid some of the pain.

I've tried to integrate all kinds of meetings into the program: men's meetings, retreats, campouts, Alano clubs, hospitals, upper-middle-class suburban tightwad meetings, and inner-city midnight meetings. I've tried gay meetings and black meetings, not to mention sex, cocaine, emotions, codependency—you name it, I've tried it, but not always because the type of meeting reflected my own reality (for example, I'm not black or gay). But I have always looked for ways to cope and deepen my spiritual life.

I now feel connected to the program in a way I haven't felt since I started back in the mid-eighties. But it's the result of working a multi-dimensional program, weaving 12 Steps together with Buddhism in a dynamic, flexible way. Following are some points I've learned the hard way about 12-Step life.

The 12 Steps Speak the Language of the Addict, But...

The main reason why the 12 Steps work for me is because they speak to my addict in a language he can understand. All the spiritual teachings I've studied have their own beauty and truth, but they are not for addicts. Nothing in these traditions—so far—is oriented specifically to addicts.

I mentioned earlier that there is no substitute for the connection of one addict talking to another. 12-Step literature is written by, for, and about addicts. But I do criticize some of the language in the literature as well as the generic way that spirituality is discussed in meetings. There are many Judeo-Christian terms—He, Father, Creator—to discuss a Higher Power. This is a limitation, in my view. We're supposed to be able to choose our own conception.

I recently had a discussion with a young guy, two years sober, at a men's meeting where I tried to help him address his difficulty with this limitation of the program. He said, "Even though they say you can choose your own conception, they're really pointing you toward a Christian god." He relapsed soon after.

I want to help people like this to accept that the 12-Step model can work for them. There are ways to conceptualize and practice the program, even within meetings, that give addicts the freedom necessary to choose their own conceptions. I deal with this extensively in the section that lists the steps.

The 12 Steps Are Necessary but Not Sufficient

The 12 Steps are necessary for me to have a life. But I'm not the poster child for the 12-Step community. I have a history of difficulties with many aspects of the community. As a guy in Santa Cruz used to say, "Your mileage may vary." If you're doing fine, no problem. If you're not, this book will help.

I recognize the value of very deep connections to the recovering community. If you have some years of sobriety and feel you've outgrown the program and the connections to the recovering community because you've found something better, like a career, a relationship, an "alternative" to the 12 Steps, you may be in the Funnel, that dark place that precedes relapse. In my experience, this is a critical mistake that often ends in tragedy.

"So what's the problem?" you may ask. "Didn't you get sober to have a life?" We all do, but some of us get stagnant, maybe for different reasons. We might get sick of 12-Step group politics or what seems to be the rehashing of problems. Or we realize, but are afraid to say out loud, that we still need more than the typical 12-Step style has offered. Maybe we have an unquenched spiritual thirst, but think we've looked everywhere for those answers that the steps didn't cover. The steps can actually leave us with more questions than answers, depending on who and where we are on our paths.

The Trouble with 12-Step Programs

I had a smart newcomer a few months sober tell me recently that the steps aren't perfect, but people in the program act as if they are. There are others who come to my workshops, disappointed to hear me say that Buddhism isn't an alternative to the steps. There are a lot of objections that are valid, and of course, there is the denial and laziness that is part of addiction. It's often difficult to sort out the valid from the invalid objections.

One of the most cited criticisms I hear from people who want nothing to do with 12-Step programs is that it's narrow-minded. Critics before me have pointed out the one-sidedness that pervades the 12-Step community. I don't want to side with the knuckleheads who write books about how the 12 Steps are a cult or how the program failed them. I think most of these people never gave the program a shot before they judged it. But, if we open our hearts and our minds and really work the program, on the program, while utilizing Buddhist practices and therapeutic devices, we can save lives and heal suffering. The result: more happiness, less insanity.

Let's look at these as areas for improvement, rather than criticisms. With that spirit, I offer the following:

Those who make it in the program tend to be from the same demographic

According to the AA 2007 survey, most members are white, middle-aged men (average age forty-eight), sober over ten years. These are, mind you, the people who choose to fill out the periodic AA surveys, so the data is possibly skewed. They may be more likely to want to report their data than those with less success in recovery. Remember, at conferences and large speaker meetings, the sobriety countdowns are invariably weighted with newcomers and sprinkled with a few sporadic seasoned members collecting birthday coins.

But many who don't fit the typical demographic make a valid point when they say that the language of the program is archaic, written by middle-aged white men with strong Christian leanings. Looking at the stats from within as well as from outside the program, it looks like not much has changed since the 1930s.

In my own local community, there are about 95 percent whites in most meetings, irrespective of gender. That's not a blanket example of every meeting in the country, as the composition varies, although I'd guess that this sober stereotype is even more typical in rural areas. If you look at the larger, more popular meetings, the vast majority of them have a homogenous structure. The point is that, if you're similar to the people in the program, you'll identify more easily. The literature and the makeup of local meetings tend to communicate to an audience similar to its authors.

Outliers are cast aside, neglected, and overlooked;
anyone who doesn't toe the 12-Step party line is typically shunned

One of my professors liked to remind us often how the universe is normally distributed: everything everywhere clusters together in groups. No matter what kind of group, population, or trait is being measured, outliers are those few at the extreme high and low ends of the curve. Most people have an IQ of about 100. There are a few at 140 and a few at 80. The latter two are outliers. This applies to group dynamics. Let me explain how.

Statistics says that when we take random samples from a given population, the mean scores will form a bell curve. No matter how specific the population, as long as it's randomly selected, the average scores—on any trait, such as intelligence, extroversion, or agreeableness—will group together in the center, and what are called outliers will live on the extremes, in much smaller frequencies. That means the majority will share similar characteristics. Using such scores tells behavioral scientists where the group baseline on a given factor exists, such as in the previous example on IQ. Groups function in a way that creates sameness.

Similar members of a group that have a common purpose will band together to create the most efficient ways to achieve the group's goals. The needs of the individual are thus put to the side for the group's efficiency. The bottom line is that if you're too different, you don't make friends with all the members in the middle. That's how groups work.

The problem with this tendency in the 12-Step community is that it leaves people who don't fit in the middle, the outliers, feeling like they need to either conform to group thinking or leave the group. The

12-Step model works on the principle that since we're all on a sinking ship, we need each other. But we're not all equally suited by history and temperament to find our way into the center of the group—where it's conformed and feels safe.

A key component to success in the 12-Step group is sharing at meeting level. All groups have high and low talkers. High talkers talk a lot more than the low talkers. If you hang out in any meeting, you'll notice that the same people often speak. This makes participation hard for the low talkers.

When a quiet person opens up, it's often easy to see the depth there. The problem is that it's not a group norm in 12-Step meetings to encourage low talkers to talk more. They don't get much practice at it, and they wind up as background people; they've been going to meetings for years, but no one knows their names. Some meetings actually forbid volunteer sharing, in an effort to control the perception of wholesomeness of the group's purpose. Addicts, even though a subgroup of the general population, hang out with people who are alike. The 12-Step literature endorses being with people with whom we wouldn't normally mix, and it does happen in the more positive groups. But for some, they stay lonely.

We need to improve this situation by encouraging an equal power dynamic. Practicing principles of Buddhism would help bring the outliers into the inner sanctum. One way is to simply use an awareness meditation in the group to notice the suffering of others. Later I cover such methods in detail. Stay with me! It's amazing how much change is effected by a little awareness. I'll show you how.

An in-group, out-group mentality is prevalent

We admit at meetings that we're social misfits in the larger social context, but we're much less willing to admit that there's a group of social misfits within the group of social misfits. This needs to be improved. A little open-mindedness would help more people who otherwise slip through the cracks.

Something else we can learn from social psychology is that groups have a natural tendency to view nonmembers as less valuable than members. Us against the world is a dynamic of all groups. There are cliques in all of them, not just 12-Step or Buddhist groups. A unique feature of the 12-Step program is that our literature tells us we are "people who normally would not mix" with the rest of society.[1] But as a group, we still function as all sets of people do.

As homogenous as the program seems in terms of participation, alcoholism affects people from different social, economic, religious, and cultural backgrounds. The groups function differently when they are weighted with any of these demographics. For example, there is a gender bias in some groups in which women are not treated equally. When we enter the program, we feel the need to overlook our differences and identify similarities to bond with other addicts. Later, we stick with members who share our philosophy and interpretation. Even though our principles are high—trying to connect more than alienate—our actions remain limited. We glom together with those who are similar.

Buddhism has a lot to offer that will help participants see past these dynamics to better practice the ideals of the steps. For example, a simple understanding of karma and the first of the Four Noble Truths, the Truth of Suffering, will deepen our experience of what's already in the steps. A fresh perspective from Buddhism will make more addicts feel more welcome. Feel free to peek at the step for how that works.

The real reasons for relapse with long-term sobriety aren't discussed in meetings

People in meetings tend to oversimplify, minimize, and trivialize the complexity of causes that can lead to relapse. I've personally heard this statement more times than I can count: "The one reason why everybody relapses is because they stop going to meetings." As a researcher trained in statistical modeling, I can confidently state that there is no single cause for any phenomenon.

In the experimental methods used in the social sciences, there is no way to completely tease out the effects of coexisting causal variables. The more causes you isolate, the less applicable the results are to the wider population. Simply put, there is no one thing that causes one other thing. Every event has many causes and is related to many variables.

In Buddhism, we call it interdependence—the concept that nothing exists independently—and meditate on it as a spiritual practice. Everything—every person, thought, emotion, rock, tree, planet, universe, etc.—exists because of many causes. Buddhists say meditation on interdependence could lead you to an enlightened state. I like to keep this in mind when I hear oversimplifications and overgeneralizations. Buddhist practices have opened my mind to the idea that there is never just one reason for *anything*. It's ignorance to say there is.

It's human nature to put things in simple terms. We try to explain away troubling phenomena in simple language because it makes us feel better. Program people tell us, "Keep it simple, stupid." This is sage advice if given in the right context, but there is a difference between overcomplicating a simple issue and oversimplifying a complex one.

Research shows that addiction is complicated on many levels: its causes, its manifestations, its effects on individuals and the world. Common 12-Step thinking needs to be challenged. If we say, "Well, they stopped going to meetings, so they used," then it follows that if we just go to meetings, we won't use. But, there are individuals who go to meetings and still relapse or become emotionally unstable, depressed, and even suicidal. There are people in recovery who commit violent crimes and go to prison without ever missing a meeting.

Some of the reasons that I and others have relapsed are:

- ❀ Undiagnosed, untreated mental illness and the inability to find appropriate support for it in 12-Step groups.
- ❀ Inability to connect in the program, not being able to identify with others because of limited perspectives and participation of minority races, sexes, or religions.

⊛ Misunderstanding the progression of the disease even during abstinence. People with long-term sobriety are easily caught in the
Funnel.

⊛ Insufficient financial, emotional, and physical support for career
and educational development. (Programs like Vocational Rehabili-
tation exist but are limited.)

⊛ Childhood issues that aren't dealt with in therapy during early
sobriety. These issues tend to creep up later on, particularly in
relationships.

⊛ Confusion about what long-term sobriety should look like, and
unrealistic comparisons to the group norm or circuit speaker
mythology.

⊛ Failure to learn stress management, such as meditation, as a life
skill.

⊛ For those who do become interested in Buddhism, the inability to
understand issues that could cause emotional disturbance, such as
emptiness and meditation on death. Buddhists aren't ready for
addicts who become unstable when working with these
techniques.

⊛ Lack of reinforcement of the signs of relapse and inadequate support to manage the symptoms within the 12-Step group when they
arise. Members are chastised for falling off-track or out of the norm
of sober behavior.

People like me relapse daily. Buddhists, treatment providers, and
12-Step members will do a better job if they understand that many will
die if we don't increase our compassion, deepen our understanding of
the causes of relapse, and stretch our willingness to help everyone who
needs it. We can always use more tools.

I've found that practicing Buddhist principles in the context of my
recovery program has helped me in all of these areas. In Zen, I learned
a lot about mindfulness. From the Tibetans, I learned more about
compassion. Those techniques help me to feel connected to my fellow
addicts, problem people of the past, and everyone else. They help me

to learn forgiveness, to reduce the sense of me against the world. Other techniques, like meditation on emptiness, lead to less attachment. Remember, addiction is an extreme form of attachment gone wild, you could say. Anything that an addict can do to reduce attachment is a good thing.

We need these tools so that we can learn to look at ourselves and at each other more deeply and honestly. There are many practices that can help.

We wish we were normal

This is a common issue. Addicts want to be *normies*: non-addicts. When we clean up our act, get our lives together, have a few bucks in our pocket, and collect some time, we start to believe we are normal. We mouth the words, "I know I'm still sick," but no longer believe them. On the outside, we look so different than when we came in from the cold that it's kind of hard to believe we're *really* still sick.

Inside, memories of suffering have grown dim with time. People say they're grateful, recovering addicts—which is fine. But deep inside, a lot of us really wish we could just be like the normies. This is a function of the disease. We treat it in Step One, but it is pervasive throughout the life of recovering addicts. This desire may be dormant, but it is still present within each of us—despite how many meetings we attend, how many sponsees adore us, or our material success.

This is an area where Buddhists, other spiritual thinkers, and 12-Step critics make the point that it's counterproductive to constantly identify oneself as an addict. But, they—the normies—don't "get" addicts. So let me explain this to non-addicts.

We addicts need to stay in a constant state of surrender to the reality that we will never become non-addicts, physically or otherwise. We need to preserve acceptance of the solutions required to maintain and enhance a condition of spiritual growth.

What addicts often, and non-addicts more often, don't understand is that identifying oneself as an addict is a tool, not a total identity. We need to stay in touch with the inner addict, but we don't need to leave our self-esteem in the gutter. It's a tough track to negotiate. But it's important to balance awareness of the prevalence of the inner addict with the knowledge of the "Great Reality deep within us," as the literature states.[2]

Deepak Chopra said he would like to hear people in 12-Step meetings announce themselves like, "I'm Joe, a field of limitless potential."[3] It's definitely worth a try! Just as long as we surrender to the fact that unless we become some kind of super spiritually advanced mega-yogi, we're not going to be able to change our DNA. And when we think we can change our addict nature, we'd better check with our recovery management team before we try to prove it with a drink, fix, pill, person, donut, slot machine, social media, etc.

The limitless potential of the program is an untapped resource

In most 12-Step groups, we accept a lower standard of quality than we should. We ignore the limitless expansion that is truly possible for life in sobriety. I call this negligence the Just Don't Drink mentality. The literature is replete with support for my belief:

- ⊛ "Sobriety is not enough."[4]
- ⊛ "We are to grow in understanding and effectiveness."[5]
- ⊛ "God could and would if He were sought."[6]
- ⊛ "Self-examination, meditation, and prayer, when taken separately, can bring much relief and benefit, but when logically interwoven, provide an unshakeable foundation for living."[7]

The steps offer the possibility of incredible spiritual growth, far beyond the imagination of most of us. In order to make it through my second major term of sobriety, I had to uncover the root causes of my condition and apply many methods to address them. I've made a lot of progress, and there's always more work to do. It's my feeling that if I hadn't employed every tool at my disposal—primarily the 12 Steps, Buddhism, and therapy—I wouldn't be sane or sober at this point in my life. If you're interested in a little more sanity or a lot more sobriety, read on.

Buddhist Paths

I got clean and found Buddhism when I met my Lama 7 years ago. Tools I didn't know existed manifested in my life and I began to help others, and myself finally.

—Ali H.

Buddhism and the 12 Steps have several similarities, which is why they supplement each other so well. The reference table at the end of the chapter outlines the similarities as well as major differences between Buddhism and the 12 Steps. If it looks complicated, don't worry. A serious student could spend years in or out of a monastery contemplating any one Buddhist topic. But keep in mind, even the slightest consideration of one of these principles, applied to 1 percent of your life, will alter your course forever. I like the analogy of shining a laser beam into space. If you move it a billionth of a degree, by the time it reaches the stars, its trajectory will have been altered by many light-years. As we say in the program: meetings will screw up your drinking/using. A Buddhist interpretation would be that knowledge of karma and impermanence will help you become liberated and will shake up your view of life.

Next, I'll give an overview of the different types of Buddhism before I launch into practical methods in the 12-Step treatments.

Buddhism Overview

Let me preface this section by saying that I'm not a Buddhist scholar, an expert on the history of Buddhism, or a lineage holder. I'm an addict, and I use Buddhism to help me work a program. But I'm also a Buddhist, and I use the 12 Steps to help me practice Dharma as well. When I go to the various centers and Buddhist meditation groups, I'm usually the only recovering person there. After silent sitting practice, when we have our discussions, I regularly encourage open, honest sharing in a manner that I'm accustomed to from so many years of 12-Step meetings. It's a little odd for Buddhists to hear that level of self-disclosure, but they're getting used to me after all the years. In this way, I try to use the "desperation and willingness" that I feel as a recovering addict to help me be "willing to go to any lengths" to practice Dharma.

There are a lot of strange terms here, and I've defined some along the way. There is also a glossary in the back of the book. But keep in mind, there are many branches of Buddhism all over the world, each with its own idiosyncratic, traditional view and set of teachers. In some traditions, they spend a lot of time refuting each other, in the interest of deeper knowledge. In most, there are many volumes of works on all of these topics—108 from the Pali sutras alone. My Buddhism professor in college said that there were three hundred thousand pages in Chinese sutras, and that was only what remained after most were destroyed. In Tibetan Buddhism, the lamas have collected, translated, and organized every teaching they could find. There are *root texts*—original inspired works—and commentaries, and commentaries on the commentaries. It's all overwhelming, no matter where you begin.

But the great thing about having a Tibetan lama as a teacher is that they know how to sift through the essence of all these teachings because they've *practiced* the principles of the teachings. That's the only way to really understand any of this stuff. It is strange and wonderful, and if you have the interest in it, it's not a coincidence. If you don't, there's still a place to start and a way to apply it to your recovery.

The caveat is, don't get too frustrated if you can't "get your mind around it." The teachings of Buddha aren't something you can "get," but are principles that you have to practice to understand on an experiential level—exactly like the 12 Steps. We've all heard the newcomer who's glanced at the steps and said, "Oh yeah, I did those," because they look understandable. But there's a massive difference between intellectual understanding and heart experience over time. So try to relax and, if something jumps out at you and you want to know more, let me know or do your own research. The right answers will come. Let this section serve as a cursory overview. Much of it will be applied in the steps. Stay with me now!

I hope this book helps shift your consciousness in a way that is beneficial for you and all beings. If it does and you want more, then you'll want to find a lineage holder—a teacher in a succession dating back to the Buddha—as your teacher on the path. There are many amazing Buddhist teachers in the world. You'll find one who is right for you. This seemed overwhelming to me at one point. Twenty years ago, I would have told you that there weren't any good teachers, that everybody was on an ego trip. Now I've got many fine teachers and even more exquisite teachings to draw from. It's limitless, actually. Remember what 12-Step literature says before the ninth step, "We will intuitively know how to handle situations which used to baffle us."[1]

The aim of this section is to give you an introduction to Buddhist teachings with examples of how they've worked in my life, in the context of recovery. There are many schools of Buddhism throughout the world, the full range of which is beyond the scope of this work. I will give you an overview, and you can take it from there. There's a lot to learn and apply. As my old sponsor used to say, "It's not a fifty-yard dash; it's a marathon." He was talking about recovery, but this applies to Buddhism as well. My advice is to relax, take in what you can. You'll be amazed at the change in your understanding of yourself, and it will happen much sooner than you think.

I'd also like to say that to me, Buddhism is better than the best dope. I can't get enough. I know that sounds like an addiction. A guy in my first term of sobriety, Hugo, told me that if I was going to be obsessive, I might as well apply it to something that would be of good use. What could be a better way than to use that energy to save all beings from suffering and to help them find happiness? Some call this the bodhisattva syndrome, claiming it's unrealistic. It may be the view of some Theravada Buddhists. But this Solitary Realizer view is not relevant to the spiritual path for addicts. As a 12-Step Buddhist, I really do try to nurture the desire to help all suffering beings. One day at a time. Of course, we do the best we can.

The Buddha was an originator or, as Lama Surya Das says, a social activist. He encouraged his students to draw from their own experience rather than following through blind faith. This should appeal to addicts on a number of levels, particularly in choosing your own conception of a power greater than your fear-based, addict self.

Is There a God in Buddhism?

According to scholar on Tibet and Buddhism Robert Thurman, "Buddhism is a teaching that is not based on, or a reform of, any religion existing in ancient Indian culture. Nor was it based on a revelation received from any sort of deity. The Buddha flatly rejected the contemporary Indian form of the religious belief in an omnipotent world Creator. He did not 'believe in God' as Westerners understand God. To many Westerners, he would appear an atheist (although he did accept the presence of non-omnipotent, superhuman beings he called 'gods'). He did not even consider belief or faith an end in itself, as many religious people do. He encouraged people to question authority and use their power of reason, and not to accept irrational tradition. In his personal quest of truth, he was often quite irreligious."[2] I struggled with this concept for years, but I learned some interesting and effective ways to use Buddhist views when it comes to a Higher Power.

The Step before the Step

Before we go into too much detail about specific Buddhist teachings, let me offer some thoughts to help you with some of the hard issues. First, we should practice to understand that Buddhist teachings are vast, profound, and impenetrable. Take the Zen vow: "Sentient Beings are Numberless. I Vow to Save Them All." Interesting, isn't it? When I first heard that, I was struck instantly and deeply, in a place beyond the thinking mind. But what good does that do me as an addict if I can't stay clean or keep my hand off the poker machine? How does this kind of Zen vow help me as an addict? This was always an issue for me—translating Buddhism into recovery. Here's how.

Think about the vow. It doesn't say, "I might occasionally try a little bit to help somebody sometime." It says, "I vow to save them all." It sounds just like something an addict would say. We like to go beyond limitations. It's part of our makeup. We might word it differently: "What? You say that's impossible? Well, I'm not going to let that stop me." Translating Buddhism into recovery and vice versa can be a subtle act, but it has had huge implications in my recovery.

We ask newcomers in the program to "go to any lengths." We've all gone to unbelievable lengths in pursuit of our drug of choice. So for me, as an addict, I heard this and thought, "Yeah, beings are numberless. And hell yes, I'm going to save them all."

Second, what really matters is how it works in your life. His Holiness the Dalai Lama says that if you can't apply your spiritual practice when you're having problems, it's not of much use. Sometimes when I get a resentment, which is the number one offender for us addicts, I think, "How can I best serve this being?" The vow to save them all means even the knucklehead driving 24 mph in front of me in a 25 mph zone. This really allows me to do as it says in Step Ten: Pause when agitated. As a 12-Step Buddhist I might say, "Hold on a minute, ego. That's one of the beings I've got to save. So chill!"

As we say in the program, there is a solution. But we may not like it. I feel that no matter how much knowledge I collect, how long I sit in meditation, how many fancy terms I know, what famous lamas I've learned from, if I can't be a kind person, then I'm full of it as a Buddhist and as a recovering addict. My main teacher, Namkhai Norbu Rinpoche, says that if you're getting angry all the time, then the teachings for you are just a theory. In the program, we say that the spiritual life is not a theory. We must live it. When I ask myself this question before allowing my anger to fester, I am living the practice of Buddhism and the 12 Steps.

In my workshops, I pass on a Tibetan analogy. The lamas say that you can teach a parrot to recite mantras, but he's not going to understand, apply, and realize the fruit of the teaching—because he's a parrot! Being a parrot in the 12-Step program may impress the newcomers, but those with knowledge and experience know when you're faking it. We can all relate to being in a meeting, listening to the latest ninety-day wonder quoting the book and giving advice to newer newcomers; this is because that person hasn't had time to integrate the 12 Steps but has been to enough meetings to parrot the words.

The same is true for Buddhist teachings. Before we try selling our newfound ideas to everyone, we should probably write an inventory on our ability to apply the teachings to our life. My sponsor used to tell me that if you've heard a saying repeated in a meeting three times, then you can use it as your own. I'd add that, if we can see our own progress over time with any particular teaching, then we should share—not tell—it.

Oral Tradition

Most of the teachings I've received have been in the oral tradition: the written or spoken word from many qualified teachers in Zen and Tibetan traditions. I meet them face-to-face whenever possible. When not sitting in front of a teacher, I read, listen to audio, and watch videos.

The way the oral tradition works is a little different from taking a class at a university. It's not about writing down everything the teacher says in case it comes up on a quiz. Buddhist teachings are meant to be taken in, felt deeply, processed via meditation, and then applied to daily life.

This is very similar to listening to people share at meetings. I often sit and listen in meetings *as practice*. As I "listen for the similarities, not the differences," I feel I'm taking teachings from whoever is sharing. I'm being taught how their program works or doesn't for them. It's not necessarily a Dharma transmission, like listening to a teacher, but if I listen with my whole being, the meeting becomes a teaching environment. This way, I practice Dharma as part of meeting attendance. It's a good way to keep from becoming bored at meetings.

The Process

To know the Dharma, the practitioner takes teachings. Through a process of analyzing, discussing, meditating, and doing retreat on each point, we come to a place of deeper understanding or realization. We experience the teaching beyond thought. Then it can be applied to situations. For me, it's like working the steps in that growth has not been in a straight line.

In terms of analysis and discussion, there's a difference of degree in different forms of Buddhism. In my Zen tradition, there's little talk or mental work, in contrast to Tibetan Buddhism. In Zen, we don't work as much on verbal explanation, and the range of concepts is more limited. But there is an element of hearing, meditating, and realizing. There's just a lot more silence involved. I actually find this very refreshing now that I've been studying Tibetan Buddhism for a while. The silent Zen space is deeper and more meaningful when integrated with intense study, analysis, and ritual from my Tibetan practice.

Be careful not to get addicted to the silence though. Tibetan lamas warn of winding up in the god realm—blissed out for incalculable aeons—until good karma becomes exhausted and we wind up back at square one. Square one sucks. I was addicted to silence for a long time in Zen, and it was one of the factors that led to my eventual relapse. As an addict, I need to be free of attachments—especially attachments to states of mind. As recovering addicts, we need to be ever watchful of our addictive tendencies.

The Teachings

Buddhist cosmology is incomprehensibly detailed. You could spend lifetimes reading all of the Buddhist literature and learning practices, and countless aeons attaining realizations. This would involve learning many languages and gaining the expertise of a scholar. The best scholars in Buddhism are also devoted practitioners. They work with lineage teachers to make sure that the translation doesn't lose any meaning. They understand that names, dates, and terms, although important as respect to the lineage, aren't the essence of Buddhism, but are instead a way to organize the knowledge. Dr. Thurman is one of these people. He has humor, sensitivity, brilliance, and depth. It's because of him that I stopped feeling strange about Tibetan Buddhism, which was so different than Zen on the surface.

Briefly, the teachings of Shakyamuni Buddha originated about 2,600 years ago. Buddhas are infinite, and Shakyamuni is said to be one in a particular line of 1,002 Buddhas and is referred to as the Buddha of Our Time. His teachings were passed down orally and were not written for several hundred years after his death. According to world mythology scholar Joseph Campbell, at least one hundred years passed before there were even any images of the Buddha. Upon Shakyamuni Buddha's death, eighteen different schools of Buddhism emerged. They taught from different perspectives and argued amongst themselves about interpretations of his teachings. It reminds me how at one Alano club there are three daily men's meetings at noon. All three started because of resentments about the way things were being run in other meetings. Another similarity between Buddhists and addicts.

Buddhas can appear in three forms also known as the *trikaya* (three bodies): *nirmanakaya, sambhogakaya,* and *dharmakaya.* These represent the three doors of body, speech, and mind. The nirmanakaya Buddha is one who manifests in physical form, such as Shakyamuni Buddha. The sambhogakaya Buddha emanates from an energy level and only appears to advanced practitioners in visions during dreams and retreats. An example of a sambhogakaya Buddha from Tibetan Buddhism is Vajrasattva, who we'll discuss in Step Ten in a practice that I call the Tibetan Tenth Step. From John Reynolds: "Vajrasattva is not merely one Buddha in a long series of Buddhas, but he is the archetype of eternity, existing beyond profane space and time, dwelling at the center of the mandala of all existence."[3]

I learned how to do the Vajrasattva purification practice (see Step 10) on retreat with Venerable Robina. Now I do it daily if possible. It really has a purifying effect on my psyche, but it's taken a while to produce that effect. These techniques are eventually perfected with devotion and practice. When that happens, the total essence of the practice is fully understood by the practitioner. But as we say in the program, "First things first." We call it practice for a reason.

I like to take a little time in the morning to sit on my Adirondack in the backyard, looking up at the depth of the crystal-blue sky in summer, breathing it in and considering some aspect of the Dharma. It's similar to the meditation technique found in the recovery literature regarding the Prayer of St. Francis of Assisi. It has a pretty big influence on my day. When seriously considered, Buddhist topics cut through the normal activity of our minds and open us to a whole new level of experience and understanding beyond it.

The dharmakaya Buddha is the primordial Buddha, Samantabhadra, "all-pervasive, beyond all limitations and forms, beyond conceptions by the intellect or expression in words. The only proper description of the Dharmakaya is a profound silence."[4]

When I practice Zen nowadays, I feel like I'm dwelling in this space of dharmakaya as I sit in silence. It's quite excellent. My Tibetan studies have exponentially improved the benefits of practicing Zen. This calm state has been a long time coming in my recovery and something for which I am deeply grateful.

Sutra Teachers and Teachings

Buddhas present their teachings in these different forms and times. Sutra teachings occurred through the physical Buddha, while Tantra practitioners often report receiving *terma*: teachings through dreams. Those who get teachings this way are called *tertons*. They have existed throughout the history of Tibetan Buddhism, particularly the Nyingma, or "ancient school." This is not something that you'll hear about in sutra teachings, but it is an important distinction.

The teachings of Buddha Shakyamuni—the nirmanakaya Buddha in physical, human form—are called sutra teachings. *Sutra* means "thread" in Sanskrit. It refers to discourses in prose that were memorized and eventually written down in the Pali language of India. These were later translated into Tibetan and reorganized into what is referred to as a *lam-rim*, a text showing the graduated path to enlightenment.

The purpose of sutra teachings is to realize *shunyata*, which means "emptiness" in Sanskrit. The basic idea is that nothing in the phenomenal world exists on its own. Everything arises dependent on causes and conditions. If we look for the essence of a thing, it cannot be found. For example, take a minute to look for yourself. Are you a physical body? If you think so, which part, exactly, defines you? Limbs, senses, thoughts, memories, ideas? What part of your body is you? What part isn't? Can you point to the essence of you-ness that is present in your body? If you are your body, then what about your mind? What part of your mind defines you? Consider the Zen *koan*—riddle—"Who are you?"

These are the topics of sutra teachings in all schools of Buddhism. Zen, even though it is from Japan, is also a sutra tradition; its unique point is as a non-gradual path because enlightenment can happen at any time. The difference between Zen and Tibetan traditions on these subtle points is a little tricky, and I haven't met many teachers who are familiar enough with both schools to clarify the issue. As a practitioner of both, I've gained some insights.

While there are good teachers, a lot of so-called spiritual masters are not enlightened beings. They might think they are and want you to think they are, but they're just practitioners who may have had a brief glimpse of emptiness and think that's enlightenment. It's a step in the right direction but doesn't make them holy. Please be aware of this distinction. Just because someone calls himself by a Buddhist name, wears black, sits quietly on his cushion, and stares at you, it does not necessarily qualify him to be your spiritual leader. There are books that describe all ill manner of goings-on in some American Zen groups. As we say in 12-Step meetings, watch their feet. See if the teachers walk what they talk. As the lamas say, check up!

It's not up to me to tell you whom you'll be able to learn from. Personally, I think it takes a very seasoned practitioner who is also a qualified lineage holder. Having received the entire collection of teachings in their traditions, they then have the capacity and permission to redistribute these teachings themselves. Lineage holders have deep realizations—not just a glimpse of emptiness as many students do—and are approved by their teacher before becoming a teacher themselves.

Anybody can learn some terms, go to India, and claim to be a spiritual master. It was a trend in the sixties, and some of these people proved to have less going for them than they presented to the world. If you delve into what it takes to gain real knowledge and practice the essence of Buddhism, you can see the difference. It seems like everybody wants to be your teacher, but let's be reasonable. Not many of us are really willing to give up our egos to gain real understanding. Those who are so qualified have the highest of ethics as a natural result of spiritual realization.

This process of finding a teacher is similar in some ways to working steps with a sponsor. In other ways, it is entirely different. We choose a sponsor who has worked the program and has had a spiritual awakening, because we want what they have. After being with serious Buddhist teachers who really know something, I can share that I'm much more skeptical of 12-Step gurus who *think* they really know something! That said, I still need to learn from them and be in the program with them. In time, when you're firmly grounded in your 12-Step program, you might take teachings from people who are less than fully awakened but whose lessons are still of value. But in the beginning, please be careful. Not paranoid, just cautious. Apply the 12-Step credo, "Take what you want and leave the rest," when exploring Buddhist or other teachers. A real teacher won't mind.

Eventually, it makes sense to settle in with someone whom you've checked out for a while and trust. It takes time to know if a spiritual teacher is really trustworthy, and it's an important thing, especially for us addicts, not to get too carried away too soon. Stay in meetings, keep in contact with your sponsor, keep your service commitments. Take your practice seriously, but stay in your 12-Step program. Don't move to Guyana with your guru in your first year of sobriety. I can't overemphasize this point enough. Sobriety comes first. It's a long way back from relapse hell.

Buddhism Basics—Terminology

There are 84,000 gateways for entering the Dharma:

⊛ **21,000** belong to the *vinaya*, a code of ethics for monks, expounded as antidotes to the poisons of greed and attachment.
⊛ **21,000** belong to the sutras and are expounded as antidotes to hatred and anger.
⊛ **21,000** belong to the Abhidharma and are expounded as antidotes to delusion and confusion.
⊛ **21,000** are expounded as antidotes to all three of these poisons, which are the root passions.[5]

The sutra path is said to be the path of renunciation. Through *shila*, ethical behavior, we stop harmful actions, which stops further harm from happening to us in the future. Venerable Robina sums it up like this: "Keep your hands to yourself, and zip your lip!" After a really, really, really long time, you wind up with an even karma scoresheet, and only then can we realize emptiness and see the absolute truth.

Because teachings weren't written down for several hundred years, everything in Buddhism is grouped by numbers and expressed in verses that are easy to memorize. I figure that I have my steps memorized, so this is right in line with my program. Verses and groups of numbered ideas are easier to remember and pass down. There are a lot of these. Here are a couple of examples.

The Four Noble Truths

The most widely known numbered idea in Buddhism is the Four Noble Truths—the basis of sutra teachings. They're called Noble because not everybody is going to understand them. These are teachings for those with the capacity to hear, to practice, and to realize the value—the Noble Sons and Daughters of the Buddha. Here they are in brief:

⊛ The Truth of Suffering: Nothing gives lasting happiness.
⊛ The Truth of the Cause of Suffering: Attachment and aversion keep us in *samsara*, the endless cycle of birth and death.

⊛ The Truth of the Cessation of Suffering: If suffering has a cause, so does happiness.

⊛ The Truth of the Path of Cessation of Suffering: The Eightfold Path decreases negative behaviors and increases positive ones to decrease suffering and increase happiness.

It's all very logical. I'll show you some methods of how to apply these to your recovery program. Donchuworry!

The Two Truths

⊛ Relative Truth: Everything is understandable in relation to something else: us vs. them, subject vs. object, dualistic thinking.

⊛ Absolute Truth: Truth is not affected by anything that happens inside time (i.e., cause and effect); no beginning, no end; the basic nature of the mind, dharmakaya.

Three Jewels

This is a fundamental topic in Sutra Buddhism and is infused in Tantra as well. The Three Jewels are:

⊛ Taking Refuge in the Buddha: The Buddha is seen as the doctor, who knows what the problem is and has a solution.

⊛ Taking Refuge in the Dharma: The Dharma is the truth, the spiritual teaching of the Buddha, and is seen as the medicine.

⊛ Taking Refuge in the Sangha: The sangha is the spiritual community that one practices with and is seen as the nurse who dispenses the spiritual medicine.

The Three Times

The past, present, and future. In the higher teachings, there is also the fourth time: beyond time.

The Four Immeasurables

⊛ Love: *maitri* in Sanskrit, *metta* in Pali—the intention and capacity to offer joy and happiness.

❀ Compassion: *bodhicitta*—the root of *com* means "with," and *passion* means "to suffer," therefore meaning "to suffer with."

❀ Joy: *mudita*, filled with peace and contentment for self and others; rejoice: to feel joy for and celebrate others' happiness.

❀ Equanimity: viewing others without attachment or discrimination. The Tibetans are fond of saying, "like a mother loves her only child."[6]

The Five Aggregates

❀ Form: The four great elements and the forms derived from the four great elements. In Tibetan Buddhism, the elements are taught to be air, water, fire, and earth, sometimes with a fifth element: space. The elements play a role in tantric practices, which deal with energy.

❀ Feeling: Senses born of eye contact, nose contact, tongue contact, body contact, and mind contact.

❀ Perception: Discernment of forms, sounds, odors, tastes, tactile objects, and mental phenomena.

❀ Volitional Formations: Conscious choice regarding forms, sounds, odors, tastes, tactile objects, and mental phenomena.

❀ Consciousness: Eye-consciousness, ear-consciousness, nose-consciousness, tongue-consciousness, body-consciousness, and mind-consciousness.[7]

The Six Paramitas

❀ Generosity: Giving material things, protection, love, Dharma.

❀ Discipline: Avoiding the ten non-virtuous actions, cultivating the ten virtuous actions.

❀ Patience: Not reacting to situations out of irritation, frustration, or fear.

❀ Exertion: Willingness to apply oneself (should sound familiar to 12-Steppers).

❀ Meditation: To meditate is to become familiar with. Common methods are *shamatha*, concentration or calm state, and *vipashyana*, body awareness or insight. Also, the meditation of non-meditation, where we practice non-dual awareness. Eckhart

Tolle teaches this way. In Tibetan Buddhism, it's called *Ati Yoga*, *Dzogchen*, and *Mahamudra*.

⊛ Transcendental Knowledge: The direct state of knowing in which all ideas of subject and object have disappeared. In sutra teachings this is referred to as realizing emptiness.[8]

Everything on the sutra path is based on arriving at an understanding of emptiness (shunyata) and compassion (bodhicitta, pronounced bod-hee-chee-ta). According to Namkhai Norbu, "In the sutra teachings we speak mainly of *shunyata*—the emptiness or absence of self-existence or self-nature of all phenomena. When you are explaining the sutra teachings, you must always explain *shunyata* and compassion. What is referred to by the term *shunyata* is absolute truth, or the absolute condition. Then there is also relative truth, and two different ways of experiencing the relative condition, depending on whether you have real knowledge and understanding or not."[9]

The sutra path is broken up into the *Hinayana*, lesser vehicle, and *Mahayana*, Great Vehicle. In the Hinayana, practitioners focus on working toward enlightenment for their own sake because they understand the Four Noble Truths. They realize the Truth of Suffering, which leads them to practice. This parallels the 12 Steps—newcomers have to learn not to pick up a drink or take a drug before they can be of service to others. It's about restraint and learning new habits to replace the addictive ones. The Mahayanist regards his or her spiritual path in terms of the entire cosmos of suffering beings. This is the bodhisattva path. The 12-Step similarity is that after we are well established in our program, we resolutely turn to helping others. The purpose of the bodhisattva is to free all realms of all suffering beings—every last one of them. The bodhisattva's *samaya*, commitment, is to remain—that is, not to go into full enlightenment—until there is no more suffering anywhere, ever again.

That's why it's called the Great Vehicle, because it's a nobler purpose than "saving your own ass," as we say in the program. Our very lives as travelers in samsara depend upon our constant thought of others.

Tantra Teachers and Teachings

According to Namkhai Norbu, *Tantra* means "continuing in our real state."[10] We use our energy to transform normal karmic vision into *pure vision*, the vision of enlightened beings. To understand what this means and how to apply it to recovery takes time and serious commitment.

When you mention Tantra, everybody nods because they've heard about it, but most people don't really understand what it is. In the seventies, a lot of people wrote books and did workshops on non-Buddhist Indian tantric practices, which were often just excuses for kinky sex. The bookstores are still full of these books. But those are not what Buddhist tantric practices are about. As an addict, one has to be careful with these powerful tantric practices. I'm well established in my recovery and can explore them. For newcomers, the disruption could cause a relapse, so be careful.

A very advanced practitioner who is not keeping the *vinaya*, monk vows, can utilize sexual experience as part of spiritual practice. But this is not the goal of Tantra. The goal is expedited enlightenment. With Tantra, it can happen in seven or ten lifetimes rather than many incalculable aeons, as in the sutra path. Tantra is the fast track, and because of this, it comes with risks. It's not something to take lightly and is particularly dangerous for the addict. If you're stable in recovery, well established in a regular meditation practice, and have both the interest and capacity to go deeper, you can find a qualified Vajra master (Tantra teacher).

Not everybody is ready for these teachings. Back in the day, some practitioners misunderstood the practices and the vows and acted in ways unhelpful for those in the public eye. This kind of bad press is not good for monasteries that depend on public support. For these and other reasons, the tantric path was traditionally kept secret in ancient Tibet.

We have the example of Lama Tsong Khapa, who started Ganden Monastery in 1410 and was the founder of the Gelugpa tradition to which the Dalai Lama belongs. Tsong Khapa believed that no one should practice Tantra until that person had completely purified himself. He said that "those who were not sufficiently prepared for tantric practice ran the risk of misunderstanding it and bringing great harm on themselves and others."[11]

On a practical level, there is a big difference between the sutra view—which says it's bad to have anger—and the Tantra view. The sutra view says that a moment of anger destroys three aeons of good merit in a flash, so we renounce anger. Worse actions, which are the result of anger, cause rebirth in what are called the hot, hot hells. The difference in Buddhism from the Christian version of hell is that in Buddhism, it is possible to get free of the hell realms. This is why lamas and practitioners dedicate the merits of practice to all suffering beings. They can't escape without help.

Tantra is the path of transformation. The tantric view is the same as sutra in its explanation of the problems but differs in method. It requires individuals to be of a high enough capacity to work with their subtle energies. In Tantra, we don't use antidotes or renounce anything. Through the practices of Deity Yoga, we learn to transform, rather than resist, what is referred to as our normal, impure karmic vision into the pure vision of the deity. Through elaborate visualizations and mantra recitation, we cultivate the essence of being in the realm of an enlightened being. Acting as if we are that enlightened being, we transform the energy of anger into a positive energy of compassion. Green Tara and Chenrezig are examples of such deities.

You may have seen the extremely colorful Tibetan thangka paintings of these deities. A deity in Tibetan Buddhism is a fully realized being that represents a manifestation of our true nature. It's far beyond the scope of this book, but I want you to be aware of this concept so you can pursue these teachings when and if you're ready. You'll know.

There are different levels of deity practice: outer, inner, and secret. In the outer level, we pray and make offerings to the deity in the form of a statue, thangka, or symbol. For those of a higher capacity, the practice of inner Tantra involves the generation and completion stages, wherein one imagines the deity in front of herself, in much detail, building the visualization gradually over time. Eventually, the practitioner merges with the deity and performs further mantras and visualizations. In a very powerful way, this kind of practice has enabled me to come to terms with my conception of a Higher Power in the 12 Steps.

It's important to note that this isn't the same thing as imagining oneself to be God in a Christian sense. These are very well thought out, step-by-step practices that incorporate aspects of Tibetan science, astrology, and medicine. The practices work with subtle levels of the energy that forms the basis of our body, speech, and mind. It's like doing a fourth step inventory on a continual basis until resentment is reduced to a memory and compassion is what we're left to work with.

There exist higher practices, which are considered secret. I will refer the reader to the teachers mentioned in this book for further exploration of those topics. But to quell any concerns, I'll just mention that *secret* really means our innermost Buddha nature, and it isn't anything weird. Secret practice also reflects a principle of spiritual anonymity, in that we don't need to babble on about our spiritual leanings to people who could care less. It's like how we move beyond what I call the Three-Year Syndrome in 12-Step recovery. That's when addicts have done some steps, think they know something, and try to act like they're everybody's sponsor. In secret or anonymous practice, we keep our Dharma egos *and* 12-Step egos in check. We don't share unless it's asked for and is in service to others.

Initiation and Empowerment

Tantric practices involve ritual, which can seem strange to Westerners, Buddhist or not. They seemed strange to me after sitting in a Zendo looking at a blank wall for fifteen years, but there is something magical and fun about tantric practices.

In order to practice Tantra, one needs to have the teaching and the empowerment, which comes by way of initiation from a qualified lama. If you open any Buddhist magazine, you'll see dozens of ads for these at centers all over the country. But the responsible teachers won't do initiations without giving a firm background in sutra, renunciation, and emptiness. There are books on tantric practices, but even if you study and understand the texts, you won't benefit without the actual empowerment or transmission of energy.

When you go to an empowerment, they don't always tell you what the practice commitment (samaya) is until later, if at all. Many people go for a blessing and aren't interested in the practice. For those who are interested in the practice of these rare and sacred teachings, you might have to dig a little deeper to find out more information. Remember, traditionally these practices weren't public and weren't written down.

The empowerment is generally a necessary prerequisite for the actual oral explanation of the practices. In the 12-Step program, we determine when we're qualified to enter. We say, "I'm a member because I say I am." But in this regard, Tantra is quite different from the 12 Steps. You don't get it unless the lama feels you're ready. They've been known to cancel initiations when the vibe of the room is off. In one of these that I went to, we were instructed to meditate and recite certain texts for many hours before the teacher would even let us in the room. This is a way of purifying to prepare to receive the subtle teachings.

You may go to an initiation with hundreds of people. But during the oral explanations that follow, there may be only a handful of students left. Why? Because many people collect initiations like baseball cards but don't do the practices. Some lamas feel that if people become connected to the empowerment, they will benefit and eventually come around, in this life or the next, to being a real practitioner. This attitude relies on an understanding of karma. Just as I described earlier about how beings in lower realms are connected to the path by blessings from practitioners, some would-be followers can become connected to the tantric teachings by contact with a lama.

For example, anyone who's been to a public talk by His Holiness the Dalai Lama can see many thousands in attendance. It's said that the reason so many people are interested in the Dalai Lama's teachings is that, in previous lives, he blessed millions of insects and animals. They became connected to him and now, in their fortunate human form, are able to practice Dharma.

The lamas do blessings on bugs and worms and crabs then set them free. I have a MySpace friend in China who is a Buddhist, and she says that they go to the market to buy live fish so they can liberate them. This is another way that higher-realm beings help those who cannot help themselves. In the program, we say, "God does for me what I cannot do for myself." In that regard, it's easy to imagine a higher being helping addicts. Maybe one of them helped us by inspiring the 12 Steps. Stranger things are taken as truth. If you consider the smallest details of science or religion, you might see that we can take some pretty weird stuff for granted. For example, your heart is beating. How is that so?

So that's why the lamas do these formerly secret empowerments and don't mind so much if every single person doesn't stick around for the explanation or even plan to do the practice for life.

Ati Yoga: Dzogchen, Mahamudra

Dzogchen is a popular marketing term in the billion-dollar Dharma business. One lama says that it's like Coca-Cola. Everybody recognizes the name. It is the highest of all teachings for students of the highest capacity. I am not a Dzogchen teacher and am not qualified to give much information about it, but I do want the reader to know it exists. I will refer you to the teachings of Namkhai Norbu Rinpoche, who is an exceptional scholar, practitioner, and author of many books.

If you are seriously interested and you work a pretty solid program, I encourage you to explore all of the teachings. You can always contact me with questions at the12Stepbuddhist.com. I will be happy to refer you to some resources. Below is the chart I mentioned at the beginning. Remember, a chart can't explain all of these topics, but let it serve as an overview of some of what we've discussed and some of what we'll treat in the steps. Anything that's left over, I encourage you to explore further on your own.

Similarities and Differences between Buddhism and the 12 Steps

Buddhism	12 Steps
Similarities	
Buddhism offers many practical methods.	The 12 Steps are practical methods.
Buddhism offers detailed outlines of every possible state of mind, with equally detailed practices to treat them.	The 12 Steps are tools that address many states of mind specific to the addict.
Sutric Buddhism offers antidotes to negative emotions.	The 12 Steps, particularly Step 10, advise restraint of negative emotions.
Outer Tantric Buddhism uses prayers and offerings to external deities for help and wisdom.	The 12 Steps teach reliance on a Power greater than ourselves.
Meditation is a key practice in all forms of Buddhism.	Meditation is part of the maintenance steps, but not widely emphasized or practiced.
Vajrayana/Tantric Buddhism teaches reliance on the guru. Other traditions, like Zen, emphasize the devotional aspect less; however, reliance on a qualified teacher is essential.	12-Step programs, not necessarily the literature, teach reliance on the sponsor, which leads to reliance on a Higher Power.
	Continued on next page

Buddhism	12 Steps
Differences	
Buddhism's main purpose is complete and perfect enlightenment or nirvana.	The main purpose of the 12 Steps is to find a Power greater than ourselves that will solve all problems. The notion of perfection is frowned upon.
In some forms of Buddhism, intellectual understanding through deep analysis is emphasized.	The 12-Step model is simple to understand but difficult to apply. It avoids heady intellectual knowledge. The point is not to think too much and to develop intuition through the steps.
The Buddha taught 84,000 to serve different capacities of individuals.	The 12-Step literature advises us to utilize many resources, but few participants take advantage of this advice.
Buddhism does not claim the existence of a Creator God.	12-Step programs refer to an individual's own conception, but still purport the existence of a Creator God.
Buddhism places *total* responsibility on the individual, as in renunciation of samsara.	The 12 Steps place responsibility for behavior on the individual but maintain heavy emphasis on reliance on God for help.
Tantric Buddhism uses specific methods for purification of negative karma.	The 12 Steps have no direct correlation to purification practices on their face. But working the steps can be viewed as purification similar to Buddhism's accumulation of merit by Right Action.

Introducing the Steps

Getting free from addiction can be an arduous undertaking. Placing my feet on the well-worn path of 12-step recovery was the most direct route I could find, even though I didn't even know it at the time. Today my life makes sense and I've found what I have always sought: a sense of peace and freedom.

—T. W. S., 2008

Before we delve into the principles and practices of each step, I'd like to share my perspective on this offering. Some people are billed as Buddhist teachers in that they write about Buddhism. It is very important to understand that there is a difference between teaching and/or sharing personal experience, and being a qualified lineage holder. I've made this point earlier, but I want to make it clear before you read the commentary, meditations, and practices later in this section and in the steps. What follows is in large part the story of my Buddhist experience and how its teachings and practices help keep me sober after my relapse. It is arranged into a program to help others with the same inclinations and needs, but it is my interpretation of Buddhism as an addict in 12-Step recovery. I'm not a designated lineage lama nor a Zen master. What is offered here is an introduction that I hope you will explore further with your Buddhist teachers, 12-Step friends, family, and recovery team, whomever they may be.

I'll use the same fashion common to 12-Step meetings to describe my experience with each step. The way we view spiritual tools changes with time and practice, and those in the 12 Steps are no exception. My understanding has developed over the years. Some things that worked in the beginning failed me later. Others are still applicable. Ways that I viewed the steps early on might make sense to newcomers, but for me, they lost their luster when I found myself in the Funnel. I'll share what's changed in light of my Buddhist practice and how you can develop your own integrated program.

The 12 Steps Adapted from the Original Steps of Alcoholics Anonymous

- ✸ Step 1: We admitted we were powerless over our addiction and our lives had become unmanageable.
- ✸ Step 2: We came to believe that a power greater than ourselves could restore us to sanity.
- ✸ Step 3: Made a decision to turn our will and our lives over to the care of our Higher Power as we understood our Higher Power.
- ✸ Step 4: We made a searching and fearless moral inventory of ourselves.
- ✸ Step 5: We admitted to our Higher Power, ourselves, and another human being the exact nature of our wrongs.
- ✸ Step 6: We're entirely ready to have our Higher Power remove these defects of character.
- ✸ Step 7: Humbly asked our Higher Power to remove our shortcomings.
- ✸ Step 8: Made a list of all persons we had harmed, and became willing to make amends to them all.
- ✸ Step 9: Made direct amends to such people whenever possible, except when to do so would injure them or others.
- ✸ Step 10: We continued to take personal inventory, and when we were wrong, promptly admitted it.
- ✸ Step 11: We sought through prayer and meditation to improve our conscious contact with our Higher Power, as we understood it, praying only for knowledge of our HP's will for us and the power to carry it out.

⊛ Step 12: Having had a spiritual awakening as the result of these steps, we tried to carry this message to the addict who still suffers and to practice these principles in all of our affairs.

The layout of the steps allows the reader to approach them from different angles. You can go through each step sequentially, at the beginner's level of the 12-Step Principles and Meditations. You can skip the next sections and proceed to the 12-Step Principles and Meditations in the next step. This way, you won't get overwhelmed with the deeper, more serious practices in each step. Or, you can go through the deeper levels only, all the way through the steps. You could just do the Aspects of Self parts, all the way through again. You could also go through each step in detail, one at a time, as written. It's important to do what you're ready for and interested in. In this way, I hope the book will serve as a manual for your long-term program—one you can keep throughout your recovery.

After sharing some personal experience, I'll discuss one or more principles from each step and offer a simple practice that doesn't involve much Buddhism but still draws on it, which will help deepen your understanding and application of that 12-Step principle. The principles for each of the steps can be interpreted in more than one way, so if you have a different concept of what the principle should be, that's fine. However, it could be useful to apply the methods just the same. I've found that many people in recovery don't think about the principles of each step. They're not clearly spelled out in the literature, so I've outlined ways to make them clear and applicable.

If you're not familiar with typical 12-Step jargon, that's OK too. The material should be clear to anyone. But it is more relevant to those actively working a 12-Step program. Remember, this is not a substitute for 12 Steps, but if you're not an addict, have never been to meetings, and don't understand the way recovering people talk, I recommend that you go to some meetings and pick up the *AA Big Book* as well as *Twelve Steps and Twelve Traditions*. I'm not trying to duplicate that work here but am offering ways to enhance it.

My intent is to present a deeper approach, utilizing some Buddhist ideas that are more common to Westerners, drawn from my experiences in Zen. When relevant, I'll bring in some Tibetan Buddhist concepts as they relate to the underlying principle of the step. Tibetan Buddhism can seem daunting, so I'll try to translate what I've learned into layman's terms for those of us in recovery. If these more analytical and esoteric methods seem difficult at first, it's OK. Just take what you want. The point is to provide various ways to integrate 12-Step recovery and Buddhism, no matter what your level of experience in either.

Last, I will present the integration of psychology, recovery, and Buddhism with what I call Aspects of Self. I recommend exploring the works by Dennis Genpo Merzel Roshi and Hal Stone. Google *big mind* for resources. I've modified these tools to address aspects relevant specifically to addiction and recovery. For further exploration of the aspects, you can do therapy in combination with this practice, or even to get you started if the process proves too daunting at first. The dialogue work is something that should be handled with care. It mustn't be used aggressively toward yourself or anyone else.

Fundamental to most practices are the following:

Basic Meditation—Applicable to All Steps

When you read through any of these meditations, be sure to take your time—as much as you need. Pause on each line, letting the meaning sink in. Be flexible in your practice. Use what you need, and do the best you can, but be consistent. Apply the method for a while. Do the practice every day for thirty days. We're not going to be perfect the first time we try. Commit to the practice of practicing. Commit to practicing in silence and stillness for a few minutes at least.

This is a meditation to focus your mind. In Zen and many forms of Tibetan Buddhism, this is where we begin—single-pointed concentration or *shamatha*. Good concentration isn't the end goal, but it is required for insight, to settle the mind. Practitioners spend years perfecting this technique, so remember: progress, not perfection.

Do a little *shamatha* prior to any spiritual work, before chairing a meeting or reading Dharma books, while waiting in the therapist's office or your sponsor's garage, before seeing the judge. If you're one of the people for whom sitting still and quietly is challenging, practice willingness. Be willing to experience stillness. I promise you that it is possible.

With any practice, if you get distracted or confused, spend a minute or two with *shamatha* to get your mind stable. It may take some time to get used to it. It's OK if you don't do it perfectly. Just commit yourself to doing the practice and do the best you can.

Shamatha Practice

Sit in a chair or on a bench or cushion for 5–7 minutes. The back is kept straight. Sit like a Buddha. If you're in a chair, uncross your legs and rest your feet on the floor. Keep your eyes open and down at about a 45-degree angle or so. Become totally still. Point your eyes on a single point in the space in front of you. Keep them still. Let your tongue be still, resting at the roof of your mouth, the tip just behind the front teeth. Breathe naturally. Relax your hands. Having palms up in your lap or on your knees is a good way to practice feeling open and surrendered.

As you breathe in, notice the point where the air hits your nostrils. Pay attention to that and nothing else. Focus your mind. When you can sustain it, move to the next step. While maintaining awareness of the point where the air enters your nose, silently count your breaths on the in-breath. Count up to four and then backwards down to one. The point is to stay mindful of your in- and out-breaths. If you drift off or lose your place, start again at one. That's the trick. To do this, you'll have to stay alert. As thoughts arise, come back to the breath. Be compassionate to yourself. Trust your awareness.

Buddhist Views

A really big aspect of Tibetan Buddhism is to meditate on compassion. Tibetans view meditation a little differently than Zen or Vipashyana practitioners. Vipashyana, which did not originate in Tibet, is actually a part of Tibetan Buddhist practice—particularly pre-tantric training. The different practices can be interwoven, but remember that we need to be smart and to practice sincerely, with all our hearts, in whatever tradition that we choose.

Integrating Psychology with Buddhism and Recovery

In college, I trained in several versions of group therapy, one of which was called Voice Dialogues, based on a book by Hal Stone. I tried the techniques with some friends in recovery. It was very eye-opening. The method is to have a facilitator address different components of the personality. We ask for the Controller, the Victim, the Inner Child, and other archetypes. The participant agrees to speak only from the particular "voice" called out by the facilitator.

Dennis Genpo Merzel Roshi revised this method to apply it to the spiritual path, Zen in particular. He wrote a book called *Big Mind, Big Heart*, which you can review for background. This updated method is better than it was without the Zen angle, but I modified the process again to deal specifically with addiction. I call this modified version of the Big Mind/Voice Dialogues approach Aspects of Self. In my 12-Step Buddhist workshops, we work each step with this method, and we'll do that here as well. You'll find it helpful to work with a friend, sponsor, therapist, or small group as well as alone. Stay tuned on the12stepbuddhist.com for more articles, guided meditations, podcasts, and exercises.

Step 1

We admitted we were powerless over our addiction and our lives had become unmanageable.

The first time I saw Step One on a wall hanging, I said, "Yep, that's me." I had no trouble understanding that I had a problem and I was powerless over it. My life had never been manageable. The problem had a name, other people had it, and there was a solution. The second time through sobriety, I did Step One on a deeper level. After having it in my blood for many years, I knew the step required more than an intellectual exercise. On December 4, 1997, I woke up burned out, disgusted, and sick. I *knew*, wrongly, that I would never get sober again. I had tried many times in the past couple of years.

That night, I just wandered into a meeting, quite by accident. For some strange reason, I just took a seat. I was so tired. I didn't use that night, and it looked like I had a day of sobriety going for me. So I got my head into Step One, where we have to be as desperate as the dying can be. I've been clean and sober ever since.

What's different for me this time is that I haven't risen above Step One. I remember asking my sponsor a few months before he died if he felt that, after thirty-three years of sobriety, it was important to be as desperate today as he was the day he came in. He said, "No. I need to be more desperate."

It's hard to maintain that desperation when the ego kicks in. The "I" gets a foothold, gains strength. I learned, at a pretty high price, that the smarter I get about my disease, the smarter my disease gets about me. My disease is progressive. You'll hear that around meetings, but to my knowledge, it's not written in the literature. When I'd heard it, I thought I understood. But then I really learned, from experience, how true it is. I hope that your experience has convinced you too.

Principle: Acceptance

One of the main principles behind Step One is acceptance. According to my sponsor, a spiritual principle is something that you can practice. So how do we practice acceptance? The practice of acceptance is to simply allow everything—our minds, emotions, other people, and situations—to be exactly as they are. We don't try to change anything. Whatever it is, practice leaving it *as it is*.

This is a profound practice. See how good you can get at it. Just say it all day long on the in-breath, "As it is," on the out-breath, "As it is." Try that for several years.

Powerlessness

In the early stages of recovery or pre-recovery, we look at acceptance of our own powerlessness to control our addiction and our inability to manage our lives as the result of addiction. Our job at that stage is to be honest enough to see the truth of our addiction on an obvious level. Then and only then can we accept the condition of being an addict. Here are some typical 12-Step examples of how we might be in denial about powerlessness and unmanageability:

> **I'm in control.**
> **It's not my fault.**
> **It's not that bad.**
> **I'll quit when I'm ready.**
> **If I can cut down, I'll be OK.**
> **This is all I know.**

I can stop when I really want to.

Others are worse than I am. They really need help.

I know that I have a problem, but I just don't care.

Step One asks us to get honest about our disease and the effect it has on our life. It's hard to lie to yourself after looking at the problem honestly. But it's tough for the addict to get that honest, and it's hard to feel there's any hope if the problem is out of our control. The principles are the admission of powerlessness, self-honesty, and acceptance.

Most addicts have some form of brain damage, mental illness, and/or emotional disturbance. We're not good at making rational decisions. But our addict is excellent at thinking for us. By taking an honest look at our powerlessness over the addiction and the resulting unmanageability, we begin the lifelong spiritual practices of self-honesty, admission, and acceptance.

Meditation on Acceptance

Before you begin, consider some of the things from your experience with Step One that you are powerless over. Reflect on experiences that led you to a position of unmanageability. Take out your written first step. If you've never done a first step, grab the step book from your 12-Step program and take a good look at it. Call your sponsor. Go to a meeting. Do some writing or at least a little reflecting. When you've considered your own experiences of powerlessness over your drug of choice and the ensuing unmanageability, begin the meditation on acceptance.

Always begin any spiritual practice or meditation with a couple of minutes of single-pointed shamata. Then, allow your mind to be totally relaxed. Spend a couple of minutes relaxing from the inside out. From being still, silent, and totally relaxed, bring up an example of powerlessness or one of the excuses from the list on the previous page. Keep it related to Step One. Recall a scene; see the images in your mind. Let yourself remember feelings you had at the time. Notice the physical experience in your body. Breathe naturally. The object of the meditation is your personal, inner experience of powerlessness. Don't resist. Notice what it feels like. Be present to your sense of personal powerlessness.

Bring up an example of how out-of-control your life became as the result of your addiction. Again, simply allow your mind to be as it is. Allow your body to be as it is. Allow the sense of powerlessness to be exactly as it is. Be present; be alert. Don't push. Just relax with yourself and be aware of your experience.

As the feelings around powerlessness come up, let them. Allow yourself to feel. Breathe naturally. See yourself in the situation, and allow it to be. Don't try to change anything. You can't fix the past, but you can be present with the results of the past as you experience them in the present. Breathe and say silently to yourself, "Powerless over _____." Breathing out, say, "As it is." Do this a few times, slowly, at a natural pace.

Buddhist Integration of Step 1

The 12-Step literature helps us understand that our disease is real. We don't have control over it or ourselves. We're powerless. The addict within us is doing what's necessary to survive, and we suffer from delusions about the reality of our situation. A delusion is something that we think is real but isn't. Delusions are critical in Buddhism.

According to Yangsi Rinpoche, "cyclic existence is perpetuated by our continual rebirth as a result of karma and delusions. Of the two, the delusions are the greater danger. If we are able to eliminate the delusions from our minds, our karmic seeds and imprints will not have the conditions to ripen, and thus will never bear fruit."[1]

How do we eliminate delusions from our minds? From a 12-Step perspective, this means admitting the problem. If we insist on saying, "No, I'm not delusional. Every one of my thoughts is one hundred percent true," then we're not flexible enough to change.

Buddhist Meditation on Acceptance

Begin with *shamatha*. Use it to create a calm, abiding state of mind. When you feel calmer, take another look at your powerlessness and unmanageability from a Buddhist perspective. Recall the situations and events of Step One in as vivid detail as possible.

This time, break down the experiences into the component parts of your consciousness. Thinking about situations or people with which you had difficulty during addiction, experience it in vivid detail through the eye-, ear-, nose-, tongue-, body-, and mind-consciousness of your inner addict, one by one. Allow yourself to experience addiction *and* acceptance in each.

For example, if gambling is your addiction, you can say to yourself, "I *see* myself at the gambling casino, about to place a bet. I can *smell* the smoke in the air, *hear* the sounds of the machines, *taste* the drinks from the bar. I can *feel* my body as I walk through the lobby, my feet on the floor, my hand clutching the chips as I approach the craps table. I *witness* my thoughts as they were when I was in my addiction. Racing. Excited. I feel my heart pulsing with the thrill of the addiction."

In this way, we're breaking down our experience like a Buddhist practitioner, but we're applying it specifically to our addiction and keeping it focused on Step One. We're practicing acceptance by allowing ourselves to recall the experience without getting overwhelmed. We practice meditation by observing our mind as we go over these details. In this manner, we begin to see and accept that much of what we experience is, in fact, delusion. This process allows us to clarify and eventually change our view and behavior, even though it starts by experiencing the delusions through the senses and practicing acceptance with our condition. It's a little bit like the 12-Step saying, "Surrender to win."

Suffering: The Buddhist Perspective

The First Noble Truth of the Buddha is the Truth of Suffering. We all suffer. Nothing that we think will make us happy lasts forever. Addicts understand this deeply, in their bones. When it comes to our drug of choice, consequences and suffering don't matter, because even a moment of relief is worth the aftermath. According to the First Noble Truth, we have desires and become attached to whatever we desire. But it's never enough. We always want something else stronger, newer, hotter, smarter, and more thrilling. The fix is always temporary.

We spend a lot of time fantasizing and preparing for the next fix. Our excitement increases when we think about how we're going to feel when we get that fix. In the underlying subtle consciousness of our addict's mind, something like this is being whispered: "Go get it. Don't let anything stand in your way. Once you get it, everything will be perfect." Sound familiar?

In the program, we call these thoughts old tapes. In recovery, these tapes continue to run, sometimes quietly, beneath the surface of awareness. You can hear it in others at meetings. While meditating, we notice them. As we practice, we become acutely aware of these processes at deeper and deeper levels.

Sometimes people misinterpret the Buddhist teaching about suffering. They think Buddhists are negative. "Why are Buddhists so obsessed with suffering?" my sponsor asked awhile ago. We're not overly preoccupied with negativity. The teaching is asking us to do Step One on our samsaric condition.

If the Buddha were your sponsor, he might say something like, "Admit that you are suffering. Look closely at the cycle of addiction in your life. Do you see that the cycle perpetuates more suffering? Do you feel that you can win this game of attachment and aversion, striving for what you want, pushing away what you don't want, yet never knowing peace? Do you think your life is really working like this?"

The Buddha asks us to recognize that we are suffering. Although Step One asks us to admit that we are powerless and that our lives are unmanageable in terms of addiction, I think the process of attachment and aversion that is present in all conscious beings is a hell of a lot more out of control in addicts.

Tibetan Buddhist Perspective: Practicing with Suffering, Powerlessness, and Acceptance

Another way of meditating on powerlessness and acceptance comes from the understanding of how each of us suffers. We can practice recovery from the Tibetan Buddhist view, a synthesis of the Four Noble Truths, to give us another perspective.

Through understanding our own suffering, we begin to understand the suffering of others. This, in turn, allows us to have compassion for ourselves and others. The goal is to have equanimity—equal regard for everybody. But it's easier to start with ourselves to generate a feeling of compassion, from which we expand compassion outward to other people. First, we need to understand the three types of suffering from the sutras:

- **The suffering of suffering:** This is the pure experience of physical and mental pain. Tibetan scholar Jeffrey Hopkins calls this simply "ouch pain."
- **The suffering of change:** This type of suffering occurs when what we think is the object of our happiness ceases to bring us happiness. In other words, the character of the object seems to change. But it's really our delusional condition that causes the suffering of change.

    We see our drug of choice as the cause of our happiness. After we overindulge it, the drug transforms itself into the cause of our suffering. According to Tibetan Buddhists, this is true for everything in our experience. That's samsara.

    We falsely attribute an inherent nature to objects that do not inherently have an existence outside of the causes and conditions that create them. In Buddhism, this means that the nature of something seems to be concrete, permanent, and unchanging, as well as contained within that object. Upon closer examination, we find this to be an illusion. This is called dependent origination. It's a big topic that can be explored in vast detail by reading scholarly commentaries. For our purposes, the point is that what we think will make us happy eventually changes and makes us unhappy. Our own view is the problem.

- **Pervasive suffering of being under the control of outside factors:** This type of suffering is due to an endless cycle of causes and effects. The cycle is pervasive because it leads us into realms that cause further suffering. This pervasive suffering continues throughout samsara, cyclic existence. Every day sentient beings are battered by the pervasive suffering of pain and change. As an addict, this one is easy to see.

So I'm powerless, like a bucket dropping down a well. I can't stop the fall. It hurts, and I'm used to it hurting. Yet, somehow through the process of Step One, I see that I'm an active participant. Prior to Step One, I could claim ignorance. But ignorance perpetuates attachment, grasping, and afflictions. After Step One, I must claim responsibility.

Knowing this, we practice compassion. I always start my meditation on compassion with myself, then my dogs, my partner, my son, my friends, etc., but it's easy to have compassion for those close to us. The Tibetans say that every sentient being has a seed of compassion, like a mother has for her only child. The practice is to expand compassion beyond us. Let's try it.

Meditation on Compassion as Powerless, Unmanageable Addicts

From a calm and relaxed place, reflect upon your own suffering as an addict. Notice how you've been powerless to stop the cycle of seeking, preparing, and using your drug of choice. Recall how you felt when you became remorseful over the condition of your life between binges. As we did in the previous meditation, become aware of the places in your body where you feel the sensations and perceptions of suffering due to powerlessness and unmanageability.

From this awareness of suffering, consider the possibility of being free of suffering by saying this to yourself a few times: "What if I could be free from suffering and from the root of suffering?"

Then go back to the body. Notice any changes. Be aware of your breath, the temperature of the air around you. Notice your limbs. Breathing in naturally, bring your compassion to the level of intention by saying to yourself a few times: "I want to be free from suffering and from the root of suffering."

Coming back to the body, breathe in slowly, relax. Breathe out, letting go of any tension. Be present to the feeling of suffering in your mind as an addict. Notice the tension around the powerlessness of the condition of suffering. Take your compassion to a higher level by saying: "I will become free of suffering, and the causes of suffering."

Come back to your physical experience. Be aware of the sounds around you. Notice your toes. You may end the meditation now, or you can continue by repeating the process with a twist:

Do the three levels of "What if . . . ?," "I want to . . . ," and "I will . . ." on one individual in your life. Use the image of someone it's easy to feel compassion for—maybe another addict.

Integration Practice

Do this practice for 5 minutes. You can gradually expand it to 25 minutes as your capacity for meditation and concentration develops.

Allow yourself to be with life as it is. Say quietly, "As it is." Breathe in slowly, fully. As it is. Breathe out slowly, go all the way out, let the air move out as you push a little bit to force the last bit gently. As it is. Be with the addict. Life as it is. Be with suffering, as it is.

Notice the breath. Notice the body. Scan the body, starting from the head. Notice any tension. Don't try to change anything. Just notice. Be present to your physical experience. Allow yourself to be with life as it is. As it is. Breathe in slowly, fully. As it is. Be with suffering, as it is.

Come down to the neck, then the shoulders. Notice any tension. Breathing out, letting go, just relax and notice your body, your experience, your life. Be present. Say, "Being present." Not trying to fix anything, notice any emotional pain. Gently, experience the sensation. See if you can find the single point of where the pain is. Can you? Move your awareness down to your toes, then eventually back up to your head. Do this in your own time, being gentle with yourself. Say to yourself that it's OK. Breathe in nice and long and deep. Then relax.

At the end of meditation, we can place our hands together and make an offering of this work for the benefit of all beings who suffer. Choose your own words. I say things like, "May this practice be a cause of liberation for all beings." Offer it up. You did good work.

Then, give yourself a treat that suits your recovery program. Also, go to a meeting. Give someone a hug. Look a newcomer in the eye. Be present to their suffering in the way that only another addict can.

Aspects of Self: The Addict

We'll refer to the voice of our addiction as the Addict. This practice is about learning to talk to your addict and about listening to what he or she has to say.

Find a quiet spot. At first, do this exercise in solitude. Later, once you've mastered the process, you can do it anywhere in your head. This meditation can be repeated as often as you feel it is helpful. However, talk to your sponsor or your therapist if you feel overwhelmed or notice any abrupt changes, particularly in your mood, appetite, sleep, or behavior toward others. Be sure to always stay connected with the program.

Begin with *shamatha*. Try to stay relaxed during this practice. If you're somewhere you can speak aloud, cool. Otherwise, answer silently to yourself or write your answers. It is helpful to do this with a partner, sponsor, therapist, or small group of recovering friends. I don't recommend doing it with non-recovering people because it might upset them. What's normal to us can seem pretty weird to non-addicts.

Take as much time as you need with each question. You'll remember the Five Aggregates from the Buddhism Basics section: form, feeling, perception, volition formations, and consciousness.

Really explore these as deeply and thoroughly as you can from the perspective of the Addict. You can pick one thing—*sound* for example. Try to notice how the room sounds to the Addict, and stay with it. See through the eyes of the Addict. The only rule is to stay *in the aspect* of the Addict until the end of the session. If you're wondering whether or not you're in the aspect, you or your partner can ask, "Is this the Addict?" This works for whichever aspect we're having the conversation with. Ready?

We're going to address the Controller. First, I'd like to ask permission for you to let me talk to the Addict. May I speak to the Addict?

Please shift your body position a little bit to get into the space of the Addict.

Whom am I speaking to? (You answer: "The Addict.")
What's your job?
What's your drug of choice?
Does anything else matter?
What about consequences?
What would happen to the Self without you?
Are you appreciated for all your skills?
What do you think of the idea of being powerless? Does that work for you?

Sit for just a minute in this space, allowing, noticing, being present to body, speech, and mind. When you're ready, just go back to normal awareness by shifting your body position. Relax.

Aspects of Self: The Sufferer

With this practice, I'm going to ask you to let yourself experience suffering on a deeper level. In the 12 Steps and in Buddhism, we have to deal with our pain. This is a way of working more deeply with Step One. Think of the whole exercise as a meditation, a way for you to become familiar with your suffering. Remember to stay in the aspect of the Sufferer. Answer to yourself in your head, aloud, on paper, with your sponsor, whatever works at the time. Ready?

I'd like to speak to the Controller. Controller, I'd like your permission to speak to the Sufferer. If it's OK, please say, "Yes."

Please shift your body position and allow yourself to settle into the state of the Sufferer.

Whom am I speaking to?
How are you feeling today?
What is your job?

What do you suffer from?

How long have you been suffering? Think back. Go back further.

Following the feelings in your body, go back as far as you can.

Is there a beginning to the suffering?

What's it like living with the Addict?

Does the Addict listen to you?

Does the Addict care about you or how much pain you feel?

Does anyone appreciate how much you suffer?

If you could say anything to the Addict, what would that be?

What would happen to you if the Addict disappeared?

Step 2

We came to believe that a power greater than ourselves
could restore us to sanity.

In 1984, when I first did Step Two, my sponsor asked me to write out a list of what I wanted for myself in a year's time. He said to put it away for a year. Inevitably, we find that whatever we think we want for ourselves has sold us short.

Drunk one night, I stood in the yard of a church coming off a speed binge. Crying and looking up at the white, twenty-foot wooden cross against a gray dawn sky, I wanted there to be a god and for that god to help me. Early the next morning, still stinking of alcohol, I went to see the pastor. He was well meaning, but my acceptance of Jesus Christ as my savior didn't help me through this crisis.

So, when my sponsor said to write out my definition of a Higher Power—it could be whatever I wanted it to be—I wrote that it was a man with a beard who loves me for who I am. I had no idea how to think of God and less of an idea what the difference was between what others called God and the 12-Step version of a Higher Power. I didn't grasp that Step Two wasn't about anyone else's concept but my own personal understanding that often changes.

At the time, I needed an alternative to the definition of God that I'd heard about all of my life—a fundamentalist view of a jealous, vengeful God. For my second step, I adopted a metaphysical Christian concept through study of *The Sermon on the Mount* by Emmet Fox. This worked for me for a long time, and then it didn't.

At one point, I fell into the trap of nihilism that I mentioned in the introduction. I became apathetic, godless, and without a program. A therapist was unable to help me beyond compassionate listening. I had a Zen teacher as well. Regardless of those factors, it seemed I was on my own. When I took LSD and meditated, I found no answers, only more confusion.

Things are very different now. But it's been the result of many years of sincerely seeking to understand how to relate Buddhist practice with 12-Step recovery. I didn't find any of these answers from my 12-Step fellowship, not even my beloved sponsor. I had to work this out for myself. As you do the exercises in Step Two, you'll see what I've come up with as a solution for a Higher Power that really works for me.

We say in the program that "we came, came to, and then came to believe." If you don't like your Higher Power, borrow somebody else's, or make the Group of Drunks—G.O.D.—your HP. My experience is that the concept doesn't have to be a constant. The notion of a Higher Power can be flexible and dynamic, responsive to changing conditions. What should be constant is the view that there is a Higher Power, even if the definition is dynamic. Over the years, I've gone through many such changes. Some days, the program itself had to be the HP. Overall, I like to use the 12-Step tradition of a group conscience that my sponsor taught me for my own recovery. He calls it the management team.

I need my recovery management team, which consists of a handful of people whose advice I am willing to follow. The deal I make with myself is, if I'm willing to ask my team for advice, then I need to be willing to take it. When seeking a spiritual solution, I need to have enough faith in whomever I'm asking to follow their advice—whether I like it or not.

Principle: Confidence

We need confidence that there is a power greater than the insanity of addiction. In the program, we define insanity as doing the same thing over and over yet expecting different results. The literature says, "The main problem of the addict centers in his/her mind, rather than the body."[1] In my experience, the torture of addiction is being stuck in the cycle of using, remorse, using. Without abstinence and a recovery program, there's no way out. We know this, but the insanity is participating in the addiction when we don't want to do it. We wind up in the wreckage, feeling like crap for doing it yet again. That's addiction. That's insanity.

It's very hard to feel hope when we're active in addiction. We admitted that our thoughts and behaviors were out of control with Step One. In Step Two, we look at ourselves with a new degree of self-honesty. To get in the mindset, we have to admit at least that we've acted insanely. Addiction is a mental illness. The 12-Step literature refers to addicts as "outright mental defectives in full flight from reality."[2] Yet, it's still hard for many to accept this.

First, we have to come to believe that there is a power greater than ourselves. It's often useful for me to think of a power greater than my addiction, my ego, my self-defense mechanisms, etc. Next, we admit to ourselves that we're insane and that we're going to put our trust in this power. If we still think we can do it ourselves, we have no chance of being restored to sanity. If we already have a working God concept, this isn't a big issue. But if we have a negative history with religion or are atheists, we may need to adjust our antennae. We can see the insanity of the disease, but it's hard to come to believe in a power that we don't trust, don't understand, or don't believe exists. As the 12 Steps say, we need a spiritual solution.

Why Is Addiction a Spiritual Problem?

If you've tried everything else and haven't been able to break the cycle of addiction, the program says you're in a position to accept spiritual—nonmaterial—help. Many people in recovery say they don't necessarily know what a Higher Power is, but they know what it isn't. This is called backwards negation. An example that I used to hear in meetings is: "We can only get to heaven by backing away from hell." We come to know a Higher Power by defining what it isn't. The point is that we put our trust in a power that is not of our own, or of any other human's, making. It sounds difficult—and it is—but following the steps toward recovery is an ongoing process.

If you hold out on this step, you won't have a good foundation for the rest of the program. My experience is that you won't make it through the gut-level honesty that's required in Step Four, the inventory or self-examination step. We really need to understand that we've "placed ourselves beyond human aid."[3] If the concept of a Higher Power is too religious, too weird, or just too much, the 12-Step literature says to think of it as the combined power of the program as a whole. Whatever form our HP takes, we need the willingness to surrender to the process.

Meditation on a Higher Power

Meditate on the collective energy of the meeting as a power greater than yourself and your disease. As always, feel free to modify to suit your needs. The next time you're at a meeting, try this visualization: Look around the room and imagine that everyone is pulling an old, wrecked car with a massive steel chain. You are the car, but this wreck is diseased, sitting in a room, sad, alone, and powerless. They're pulling you through one more day of sobriety. Change the visualization to match your inclination. Remember, it's about applying principles. We can change the details. For example, if you like the idea of being lifted off a raft floating in the ocean, use it!

Be careful not to overlook the power of this simple tool. As you listen to other people share their experiences, strengths, and hopes, look into their eyes. Hear the words coming from their hearts. Know that these people are addicts, just like you, and that they are helping you as they help themselves make it through another day of recovery. Just that thought—just the willingness to observe each person and the group— has power to heal. It's a spiritual tool.

Buddhist Integration of Step 2

Sanity

From a Buddhist perspective, we mistakenly view the self as a concrete, inherently existing, separate entity. To the extent that we hold on to this false sense of self, we are holding on to the cause of our own suffering. The solution to denial and ignorance—the causes of suffering—in Buddhism is to realize, to understand deeply, the principles of dependent arising, emptiness, interdependence, the Truth of Suffering, the cessation of suffering, and the path that leads to the cessation of suffering. According to Buddhism, we are victims of our own delusions. Buddhists call this ignorance, but as an addict, I call it insanity.

When addicts don't practice recovery, we're in denial about reality. We were ignorant of our condition of powerlessness. We tried to control the uncontrollable—our drug of choice. Insane. So for addicts, we need to see reality, the fact that we're addicts, and what it looks like in our lives. For Buddhists, we're in denial of our Buddha nature because we see our "I" as solid, unchanging, and permanent.

All sentient beings, addicts or not, are also in denial, called ignorance in Buddhism, of our true Buddha nature. So denial and ignorance are problems for everyone, whether we see it or not. The difference for addicts is that our ignorance/denial brings on the classic sufferings of death, jails, and institutions. Later in the steps, we see that breaking through the denial about our shortcomings is another level of spiritual honesty and courage that the steps demand from us; however, Buddhism says the ignorance of the oceans of suffering beings in samsara keeps us all suffering for infinite lives. Denial/ignorance of the Four Noble Truths is a primary example.

To understand the Four Noble Truths—suffering, the cause of suffering, cessation of suffering, and path to cessation of suffering—but to fail to change the way we live . . . to Buddhists, that is the same as an addict doing Step One but not following through to Steps Two through Twelve. Just knowing about the problem isn't enough.

Through our suffering from addiction, we have the advantage of seeing how deeply ignorance, delusion, and attachment affect us. But we need to work the steps to bring it into our hearts and our experience of recovery. Most Buddhists—unless they've really realized their condition through deep, extended practice, or suffered a catastrophic life event—don't have the same level of pain that addicts do, so an addict is at a unique advantage to make use of the tools of Buddhism and the 12 Steps.

If you're new to recovery or have been around awhile but are dealing with the deeper issues of long-term recovery, your suffering might not look like an opportunity for spiritual growth. But with practice, it gets better. Today, I see the benefits of my own suffering, which I thought was everybody else's fault, including God's. My teacher used to tell me, "You're lucky. You have to practice." It made me angry to hear that, but the pain was my motivation to work harder in recovery and in my Buddhist practices.

Faith and Confidence

Do not accept any of my words on faith,
Believing them just because I said them.
Be like an analyst buying gold, who cuts, burns,
And critically examines his products for authenticity.
Only accept what passes the test
By proving useful and beneficial in your life.[4]

Words of the Buddha

Some Buddhists use the word *faith*, others call it *confidence*. Either way we mean that, based on trial and error, we learn what works. We acquire a sense of trust in that particular method. In the oral tradition, we take teachings and gain confidence in them and in the teacher. The teachings described in Buddhism that relate to the establishment of faith or confidence use the analogy of a clay pot.

First is the faith of a pot that is turned upside down. This pot can't receive anything that is poured into it. Our application of this principle to recovery is that, if we think we know it all, that our way is best, that we're smarter than the people in the program, we're not going to learn anything.

Second, we have the pot with holes in it. This one will be able to gather whatever is poured into it, but only temporarily. In recovery, we may have denial, limited short-term memory due to burned-out brain cells, or just a bad attitude. We might hear the same thing over and over—in one ear and out the other.

Third is the pot that is right side up. It collects and retains all that it receives. This is what we need in order to develop confidence in a power greater than ourselves, however we describe it.

In recovery, we call this being teachable. It's easy to apply this Buddhist teaching of being a pot that is right-side up, open, and ready to receive by listening at meetings, to our sponsor, or reading the literature. Learn from the enthusiasm of the newcomer. We've all seen eager newcomers who go to three or four meetings a day, big book in hand, coming early, staying late, absorbing the message of recovery as if their lives depended on it. This newcomer zeal is the mindset of recovery and the application of Right View. These are the kinds of potheads you want to hang around with!

Higher Power

The 12 Steps clearly use the word *God* in places. This scares away some people who would otherwise benefit from the program. It's often said in meetings that our addiction was a power greater than ourselves. The idea that there has to be *something* to believe in that is greater than our addiction isn't too far out of reach for even the most agnostic. But many remain in this gray area for a long time. I think it's a dangerous place to stay for too long.

In my experience, there is a new genre of addict that is more spiritually savvy than the typical veterans of the program. They have parents who grew up in the sixties, seventies, and eighties. The people who wrote the original 12 Steps grew up at the turn of the century. There weren't many New Age vegan ex-hippies running around then.

The psycho-sexual-cultural-spiritual revolution of the sixties changed a lot of perceptions forever. The people who come to recovery these days may have had parents who took hallucinogens, joined communes, protested in anti-war marches, and practiced yoga, meditation, and other forms of non-Western, nontraditional spirituality.

We could be a little more flexible and understanding of this new, spiritual generation gap. We might help those new to recovery, and those who've been around but need a revision in their orientation, to feel more comfortable exploring their own unique conception of a Higher Power. Greater awareness in this area could save lives.

In Buddhism there are ways of viewing the idea of a Higher Power, and they lend themselves nicely to recovery. These Buddhist views on having an HP don't conflict with most of what is written in the 12 Steps, and it can allow non-Christians, the spiritually challenged, and even atheists a way to participate in the steps. If these are used at the outset of Step Two, they can be applied for the duration of one's recovery.

Karma

Karma is basically the law of cause and effect. I know from my statistical training that in the Western scientific view, the more specific you get about a cause, the less applicable the results. One of the reasons psychologists try so hard to support their conclusions with hard data is because we can't see mental events directly. We can't see the internal causes, only the behavioral results. Before Freud, Buddhism, with its own scientific method, had for thousands of years studied the causality of mental conditions.

When we talk about karma, Buddhism looks at the mind in terms of our continuity of consciousness. This is a meditation—a test of causality to see if we can find a beginning. We follow our thoughts from this one to the one that preceded it and the one that preceded that, ad infinitum. We can use this meditation as a tool to examine our internal world. Using this method, we can see that the mind is a process of cause and effect. Our mind and our experience are created by our karma, ". . . from beginningless time," as Lama Zopa says.

Karma, to me, is a spiritual law. I can't change it. I can choose to ignore it, but that doesn't change the outcome. In that sense, karma is a power greater than I am. *Karma* means "action." Action is cause. A cause has an effect. The law or principle of karma says that there is a cause for everything that exists. If there is no cause, there is no effect. In fact, the logic of karma can be seen to rule out the possibility of a Creator God, which is the cause but has no cause and is thereby exempt from the laws of karma. Aristotle called this the unmoved mover, but I'm not sure Aristotelian logic would stand up to Buddhist scrutiny. This topic can take up many volumes and lifetimes of study. See the works of Jeffrey Hopkins on emptiness if you want to open that can of worms.

The cause of suffering as addicts precedes our usage of the substance, event, process, or person. We exist in a state that we don't like and want to change, so we use our drug, in whatever form it takes. The result doesn't end suffering but causes more. This is how we apply the law of karma to our recovery in terms of our active addiction. We surrender to that fact. Karma—the law of cause and effect—is inescapable. We can continue to deepen and apply an understanding of karma to our program throughout our recovery.

Surrendering to karma as a Higher Power is, to me, a realistic alternative to a Judeo-Christian Creator God concept; however, I have to go beyond a cursory understanding of karma. I have to meditate on it, deeply and often. On the face of it, it's no more difficult to understand than the way we surrender to everyday physical laws, like gravity. Knowing that the result would be getting hurt, we choose not to jump off the roof with our eyes closed. This is surrender and an understanding of karma that is applicable to recovery.

Buddhist Meditation on Karma

This is a meditation on karma, using continuity of consciousness as the basis for understanding the chain of cause and effect. Begin with *shamatha* to get focused. Then, observe your thoughts. When one comes, try to remember the one that preceded it. Trace your thoughts back to the beginning of the day. Looking back on the past twenty-four hours, notice the succession of activities and the thoughts or feelings that preceded them. What did you do when you got up yesterday morning? What was the first thing you thought about?

Trace your consciousness in this way as far back as you can. Go back through the week, the recent year or so. Think of the major events that have happened in your life in the past few years. What decisions did you make that led up to these events? Think of your history as far back as you can. What was your first memory?

I was at a 12-Step meeting recently where the speaker said that his first experience was finding himself wet, naked, and bloody, getting slapped by a large man. He wished he could say that was the only time that he found himself in that condition. Most people can't remember what they had for dinner last night, let alone their first moments of life, but if we trace our experiences back in time, looking for the connections, we can get a deeper sense of cause and effect. A Zen master might ask you to show him the face you had before your father and mother were born. The realization of karma and continuity of consciousness is, at least in part, the aim of such a question.

When the Tibetan lamas teach this lesson, the point is to see that our consciousness is not one fixed point in time but a series of moments strung together without beginning. We normally operate as if we're a single, concrete entity that never changes. But if we point our finger out in front of us and turn in a 360-degree circle, we can see that our point of view seems fixed, while the world around us seems to be changing. The Tibetan method is gradual; the Zen is instantaneous, once you get it. Once you get it, you got it, but don't hold on to it! If you do, you never had it.

A practical reason for this kind of meditation is that whenever we feel emotionally upset, overly resentful, or depressed, it's useful to have a practice to see the unending flow of causes and conditions that make up our lives and the lives of everyone around us. I was upset recently with someone who was talking too long in a meeting. Then, I realized that he came with his baggage, making decisions based in his history, his suffering, his desire not to suffer—all in one unceasing flow of karma. It helped me have compassion and took the power out of my resentment. We're all in the boat of sober samsara together. As 12-Step Buddhists, we can help each other by understanding karma.

Life Just As It Is

The 12-Step literature instructs us to accept life on life's terms. But, do we know how to do that? I submit that this is a powerful spiritual practice and can be used as a Higher Power by those in recovery. Life just as it is, is exactly that, yet we constantly struggle against life as it is. Eckhart Tolle teaches that the now is all that really exists. "The now will never leave you," says Eckhart.[5] We're all familiar with the bumper-sticker wisdom that the past and future do not exist. In 12-Step meetings, we've heard a hundred times that tomorrow is a promissory note, yesterday is a cancelled check, and today is cash money. Therefore, any thoughts or actions based on regretting the past or worrying about the future could be seen as denying this basic reality of now, of life as it is.

Note: Denial of reality is one definition of insanity. If we are not living in the present moment, we are not living sanely. Conversely, to live in the now is one way to look at doing Step Two: practicing sanity. Being in the now is a big part of being mindful, and mindfulness is a big part, but not all, of practicing Buddhism.

Meditation on Being Present

Anytime, anywhere, ask yourself the following kinds of questions. After you ask, let the answer, or inability to come up with an answer, permeate your awareness.

Am I present?
Where are my feet?
What am I doing right now?
Where is my body?
Who am I talking to?
How are they feeling?
Am I present for my life?

Are You Sure There Isn't a God in Buddhism?

When people ask if there's a God in Buddhism, I say no. Yes. No and yes. If you ask if Buddhist enlightenment is the same as knowing God, then you're getting a little closer to the right question, if "knowing God" means living by the principles of love and compassion. In this sense, Buddhism is similar to Christian mystical or metaphysical traditions, such as the ones that first inspired AA. But to say that God is Buddha and Buddha is Jesus and it's all the same thing, just different labels, is an oversimplification and a misapplication, as there are vital differences.

Yes, there are gods in god realms, but they're not what you'd think of as heaven from a Western view. As I said above, if we meditate on karma and follow the logic, we can find no beginning to cause and effect. God, as we think of it in a Western sense—as the cause of everything, in charge of everything, and responsible for everything—does not exist. It doesn't fit the law of karma, which explains that we are responsible for our lives. We're free. As my sponsor John C. often said, "With great freedom comes great responsibility."

In Buddhist cosmology, the god realm is where beings have higher capacity and powers than humans but are still prone to the laws of karma and therefore exist in samsara. In this sense, gods are pretty advanced, but are still not enlightened Buddhas. The notion of one Creator God who made everything and controls everything yet allows suffering does not exist in Buddhism. That's what made the Buddha such a radical in ancient India.

There are many expressions of God in Hinduism. Because gods are so much bigger and more powerful than humans, any contact with them inspires us to worship them. In the way a dog or a small child would look up to an adult, we superimpose our desire for someone to save us on these higher beings. Joko used to tell me, "No one is going to save you." That's a hard truth in Buddhism. Because of the law of karma, we have to save ourselves. But that doesn't mean we can't ask for a little help.

Deities

In Tibetan Buddhism, a deity is defined as a being who has gained total realization or enlightenment. There are infinite numbers of such beings. They are represented in male forms, such as Avalokiteshvara—the bodhisattva of compassion—and female forms, such as Green Tara, who brings swift action in response to prayers. In the tantric practices of Outer, Inner, Secret, and Most Secret Deity Yoga, we connect with the energy of one or more of these enlightened beings—through meditation, visualization, and mantra recitation—to defeat our delusions and ignorance and thus restore ourselves to sanity, or awareness of our real or Buddha nature. This is another way to practice Step Two as a 12-Step Buddhist.

These forms of Buddhism involve praying, making offerings, asking for help and guidance, taking blessings, chanting prayers and mantras, and visualizing one's self as the deity. Most of these tantric practices involve empowerment from a Tibetan Buddhist lama. The lama doesn't have to be from Tibet, as there are some ordained Westerners.

The Vajrayana practices can be daunting to those who think that Buddhism is just being mindful. Discussions of its rituals and deities, as well as its foreign terminology, take a bit of commitment to understand. I used to be concerned about this, but I've come to an understanding of how to apply this rich tradition to my recovery: we don't have to, and actually can't, get it all at once. As we say in the 12-Step program, "More will be revealed" if we're willing to go to any lengths to deepen our study and practice. Any lengths might mean learning a few new terms, just as you would with becoming a doctor.

We can begin in our understanding of this treasure of practices with a simple version using a figure we're all familiar with. It's so humbling and inspiring to do with a simple water bowl, flower, and incense offering in the morning. I'll describe how to do that ritual in a later step; for now we can keep it simple.

Tibetan Buddhist Deity Meditation: Outer Yoga

The Tibetans aren't the only practitioners of this kind of yoga, but I learned this from them. You'll find temples with massive statues in many Asian Buddhist countries. I heard about a place in Thailand, for example, where practitioners have been chanting the Heart Sutra for hundreds of years, nonstop, in front of a huge Buddha statue. The concept is simple: for our minds, our egos, we benefit from making offerings because it loosens our attachments to things of this world that we desire. The Buddha doesn't need anything. The Buddha is already enlightened.

Pick up any image of the Buddha that appeals to you. It can be as big as you want—an inch tall or several feet. Set up a little area for the statue or painting. It can be a spot on your bookshelf; maybe put a little Buddha where you keep your 12-Step books, anniversary coins, and so on. At the altar, you can do an offering practice by adding things like fresh flowers, incense, colored gemstones, light from candles, or Christmas lights. When I made my first little Buddhist altar, I offered a yellow dandelion from the grass at the retreat center. It's about intention, not price.

It's about letting go of attachment. So we offer whatever we would want for ourselves. We'll discuss offerings in more detail as we progress, but as addicts, we need something to loosen our grip on what we think we must have for ourselves. The practice of making outer offerings is a great way to get a sense of this loosening.

Tibetan Buddhist Deity Meditation: Inner Yoga

Sometimes it's helpful to make private offerings. Buddhists aren't proselytizers, and we don't want to make others uncomfortable. We can take the practice of making offerings inward, to a mental level. Here's how: To make an inner offering, when you see, hear, taste, touch, or smell something that is an object of your desire, before you gobble it up, offer it mentally. Simple and easy, this can be done any time in the privacy of your own mind. Say to yourself, "I imagine that this cookie is not one but an infinite number of cookies, all extremely delicious and satisfying. I imagine that the Buddha, totally enlightened, is sitting in the sky smiling. I imagine offering the Buddha all of these cookies that I want to eat." Then scarf it down. That is a beginning on inner yoga. Yes, it's that simple.

Remember, you're not worshipping the Buddha. The Buddha is not a god. The Buddha can't make you enlightened. But he can show you the path that leads to cessation of suffering, which involves letting go of attachments. Making offerings is a big practice in most Buddhist countries. But as I said, Deity Yoga goes much further than the outer and inner offerings. Find a lama to explore that topic with if you want to know more.

Meditation on Awareness of Basic Sanity

Notice your body. We exist in space. If we looked closely with a high-velocity, magnetron nanoscope, we'd see that we're mostly made up of space. Notice the space within you. Notice the temperature of your skin, the boundary of your body. Expand that boundary to the size of the room, the town, state, country—all the way through the entire universe. Notice the space in which you and all beings dwell. Be in that space, aware of your interconnectedness to all beings.

Breathing in, say silently, "I breathe with all beings." Breathing out, "I breathe with all beings."

> **All beings suffer. All beings want happiness.**
> **I breathe in with the same breath of all beings who suffer.**
> **I breathe with all beings who've ever lived, are now alive, and who will ever live.**
> **I breathe out love and goodness to all beings everywhere.**
> **This compassion and interconnectedness is Basic Sanity.**

Take note of that Basic Sanity. You can come back to this anytime, and when you do, you'll be practicing Step Two as a 12-Step Buddhist.

Aspects of Self: Basic Sanity

The 12-Step literature says that deep within every man, woman, and child is the knowledge of the Great Reality. It might be called the Functional Adult or the still, small voice within. Joko Beck says, "Life, just as it is, the only teacher." Chögyam Trungpa Rinpoche called it Basic Sanity. It's to Basic Sanity that I'd like to speak to next.

I'd like to speak to the Controller. Controller, I'd like permission to speak to Basic Sanity. Is that OK?

Please shift your body and get into the state of Basic Sanity.

Whom am I speaking to?

What do you do?

You know what to do, don't you? What's right and wrong, dangerous, safe?

How strong is your voice?

How hard is your job?

Do you feel that anyone listens to you?

How about the Addict?

Sit for a little while like this. Set your timer for 5 minutes.

Step 3

Made a decision to turn our will and our lives over to the care of our Higher Power as we understood our Higher Power.

The first time I considered turning my will and my life over to anything was scary for me. Cults and the lives of their victims had dominated the news in my adolescence. But the 12-Step community didn't raise any concerns that I was in danger of becoming a sober version of a Moonie. On the contrary, the people in the rooms were weird and interesting.

My sponsor described the principle of this step as a willingness to surrender. He said that our will meant our power of choice. The phrase *our lives* referred to all the various aspects of our lives. For example, this included our roles as worker, family member, parent, spouse, etc. We were to be willing to surrender our will—our choices—in all these areas to a Higher Power. This was the basis of Step Three as I learned it at that time.

I did this step in the usual way that you hear about in meetings. That early foundation in Step Three served me well for many years. To some degree, it's still part of my working knowledge of the third step— reliance on a power that is both greater than myself and my disease. But there are some major changes in my perspective since my relapse and subsequent recovery. The difference is mainly a shift of focus, from an outer God to an inner awareness.

In sobriety v.1.0, my understanding was that some God, out there somewhere, would come to my rescue. Even with the metaphysical view of Christ consciousness, I still felt unworthy of receiving help from any God. I think with the low self-esteem that most addicts suffer from, this is a pretty common challenge.

Our individual capacity for Step Three will vary, depending on our particular histories. We all have different traumas, from childhood abuse and/or the types of substances we used and to what extent. The resulting damage to our mental-emotional-spiritual apparatus affects our capacity to practice, live in, and apply Step Three. So we need to be flexible with ourselves and others. It's important to understand that while we need to be part of the 12-Step group, our individual spiritual journeys are unique to ourselves. The spiritual paradox is that it's a solo flight that we can't do alone.

We all know what it's like to be an addict who feels alone in a crowd. In the same way, we are alone in recovery but in the same boat with every other addict. While nobody can do the work of recovery *for* us, we don't have to do it without the support of others on the sober path. But in Buddhism, like recovery, we need to stay open to hearing the message from wherever it might come. Anyone—teacher, sponsor, or newcomer—can offer a new perspective. If we're open, we're constantly presented with the opportunity to see ourselves and our relationship to the world differently.

If I'm teachable, I process incoming information in a way that is unique to my journey. Being teachable means being present, which means being in Step Three. In practice, whether I phrase it as listening to the voice of God, my guardian angel, the Buddha, or Green Tara, the way I personally view myself and the world is unique. When the addict is sharing the teacher is teaching, and I see that as a reflection of my true self. In tantrism, this is called pure vision, a tool to become free of my deluded dualistic view.

It's like I'm in a dream, shouting to myself to wake up. This is the nature of what Buddha taught. Everything is unreal.[1] It's all a dream. The 12 Steps in general, and the third step in particular, offer a way to listen to a voice of clarity in the din of my committee, as we say in recovery. Buddhists might call the committee our samsaric mentality or impure vision.

The 12 Steps tell us that to recover, we need to put our thinking on a higher spiritual plane. When we do, our thinking will become more intuitive. But the addict's default mode, be it conscious or not, is one of fear, resentment, guilt, and other afflictive emotions. In order to elevate our thinking, we need to consider a mode of thinking that is higher than our low self-esteem. Only then will our thinking become aligned with our infinite potential. In Step Two, we began to consider this as a possibility, to get a little more willing.

In Step Three, we begin to move toward an integration of that willingness into a more concrete commitment. We have to follow up with Step Four, because if our mind is bogged down with character defects—what the famous AA speaker Chuck C. called the children of the ego—we can't operate on a spiritual plane. Buddhists would say that until we make such a commitment, we can't really begin to break free of the karmic delusions that keep us suffering.

When I returned to recovery, I felt that there was nobody to save or even guide me. I'd heard it all and nobody was in the position to educate me any differently. I was wrong, but it took a new level of surrender to see it.

Principle: Surrender

In the program we equate "turning it over" with doing an official third step once with a sponsor. Most recovering people, however, talk about a regular renewal of the commitment. Some members say a prayer several times a day or during times of stress.

The notion of surrender can be a little difficult to grasp. For me, it's dynamic in that it takes on new levels of meaning with the ebb and flow of my recovery process. I'll offer several day-to-day life practices that I use to keep the third step alive.

I encourage you to try these practices as they are, but be sure to modify the visualizations to suit your own circumstances. The following is drawn from a real experience I had on the Wind River in Washington State.

Meditation on Surrender

Do *shamatha*. Keep your eyes open or closed, but try to be alert. When you feel calmer, consider a scenario of *physical* surrender. This will help connect you with feelings similar to emotional and spiritual surrender. As you take yourself through this process, be mindful of the sensations in your body, the energy within you, and your thoughts.

Imagine that you are sitting along the edge of a river on a beautiful, clear day, surrounded by amazing, tall redwoods. The crystal blue sky is vast and deep. As you breathe in, you feel that the trees are breathing with you. As you observe the river, notice the ripples on the surface of the water, letting you know that there is a strong current running below. Sticking your toes in just a little, you become curious about how it would feel to wade in the water. But, after taking a step, you find yourself being pulled down and whisked away, completely out of control. Fear and panic strike you deeply as the rush of cold numbs your feet and legs. What will you do?

You call out, only to find that no one is there to help you. The thought of death comes into your awareness. Looking down the river, you notice that, as it bends, there is a tree branch and a little crop of rocks that connect back to shore. The current looks like it flows directly to this safe place, but right next to it is a rushing, turbulent run of white water. You have to make a choice: let yourself sink deeper into the cold or try to find the flow that will take you to safety. All at once, wisdom from meetings and teachings come rushing into your awareness: "Let go and let God," or "Pray like it all depends on God, and paddle like it all depends on you." Like the Heart Sutra says, "Gone, gone, gone to the other shore, realizing you had never left."

You are willing to trust that, with a lot of effort, you can work with the overpowering flow of the river to get to that safe place. There is no time for fear now. The only way to survive is to fully surrender to the present moment. Notice the water temperature, the sound of the rushing river, and the slippery algae on the rocks. Keep your awareness on what is happening right now. Guide yourself and let the river guide you to where you need to be.

You arrive and find that you are all right. Sitting on the rocks, let yourself feel the energy of this experience. It surges through your body. Become the gentleness of the mountain wind, the delicate warmth of the sun on your skin. Your heart fills with gratitude and surrender at the sight of your friend coming down the hill to find you safe. Be present to that.

Now come back to the room. Notice that the awareness before falling in the river is the same as being in the river. This is the same awareness of where you are now in this moment. There is no difference. This awareness is a Higher Power. Take it with you as you continue your day.

Buddhist Integration of Step 3

It's easy to integrate Buddhism with Step Three if we can equate the recovery principle of surrender with the Buddhist principle and practice of taking refuge. In a sense, they're the same thing. The only difference might be the object of refuge. In general, taking refuge means to find and accept shelter from dangerous conditions.

In the 12-Step process, we already take refuge in the steps, the group, our sponsor, and our Higher Power. We do this as we learn to "fully concede to our innermost selves"[2] that we are addicts, that we are powerless, that our behavior is insane, and that we need to find some kind of a Higher Power that will help us.

In Buddhism, we have several levels of refuge. As I mentioned in Step Two, many Buddhists take refuge in symbols of the Buddha, like statues and paintings. There are Buddhists who never consider another view and remain at this outer level of devotion to the external Buddha for life.

A deeper level is to see the Buddha as our own intrinsic, fully awakened nature, which needs to become functional in our daily life to be useful. We accept that we are Buddhas but realize that we don't have the full knowledge of our Buddha nature. For this reason, we turn to the teachings of the Awakened One to become fully aware of it. We learn that the real Buddha is really our own nature, and we use the external idea of a separate, individual Buddha as a guide. Just like with the 12 Steps, understanding deepens with experience.

The analogy used in teachings is that the Buddha is the doctor, the Dharma is the medicine, and the sangha is the nurse that dispenses the right medicine at the right time, just when we need it. The obvious 12-Step correlation is that the doctor could be our sponsor, group, and/ or our Higher Power; the medicine is the 12 Steps; and the nurse is our fellowship in recovery.

I've found that if I think of the 12-Step community this way after taking refuge as a Buddhist, the fellowship takes on a new purpose. Taking refuge has helped me understand something that a well-seasoned 12-Stepper said to me twenty years ago. I'd been complaining about how difficult it was to get along with addicts. He said, "Well, you better learn. If you can't get along with the people who understand your disease, you'll never make it *out there*."

In fact, when we practice Tantra, the students with whom we receive initiations are called our Vajra Brothers and Sisters. We will be with them until we are totally enlightened, and we need to treat them with the utmost respect. Transgressions against our tantric sangha are very negative. I think of my recovery group in the same way, but it took a lot of study and practice of Buddhism, and some mistakes and hurt feelings in recovery, to develop this understanding. When we begin to see recovery as 12-Step Buddhists do, it's hard to become stagnant. And, in my opinion, we'll never get sucked into the Funnel.

The practice of refuge means that we study Buddhist teachings with a qualified teacher. When we do, we become aware of our condition in samsara. We've talked about the most famous of the teachings, the Four Noble Truths: the Truth of Suffering, the Cause of Suffering, the Cessation of Suffering, and the Path that Leads to the Cessation of Suffering; these can help us begin to realize this awareness. There are many books on the subject by many great teachers. I recommend the Dalai Lama's book *The Four Noble Truths* and the DVD of the same name. Better yet, go to a live teaching.

As with any lessons, we take them over and over, growing at our own pace. Taking teachings is similar to going to meetings. I feel great in both. I hear it, get it, and love it. But as soon as I'm a few steps outside the door, I'm confronted with my own ego and delusions, and karmic and addictive visions and suffering. That's why I keep coming back to teachings, meetings, and this moment. This is how I keep my feet on the path.

Process vs. Event

My intent is to make you aware of a connection between the 12 Steps and Buddhism when we consider refuge and surrender. Neither taking refuge as a full-fledged Buddhist, complete with receiving a Buddhist name, nor surrendering to a Higher Power is a single event. They're long-term processes that rarely progress on a straight line. In my experience, the process of combining refuge and surrender as a 12-Step Buddhist has deepened and expedited my spiritual awareness. A useful way to practice 12-Step Buddhism is to meditate on life as it is, similar to what we did earlier.

Meditation on Life Just As It Is

Sit in your meditation position. Mine is on a zazen bench or in a chair at a meeting. Keep the back straight, eyes open and still. Notice the breath. Simply be aware of your breathing in and out. Being physically still helps the mind become still, but we don't want to make the mistake of using this as an escape. There is no escape. We just want to observe our life, not to shut off our thinking. But we don't follow our thoughts either. We simply observe and let them go. We're letting everything inside and out be just as it is.

When we notice that we're lost in thought or distracted with the external world, we don't try to stop it. We simply bring presence to the experience. We reside, as Lama Surya Das says, in the "Holy now, where we're wholly in it." To this now, we surrender. In this now, we take refuge.

We can do this as a formal practice for up to thirty minutes. When our timer goes off, we can say a refuge prayer of our choice or the third step prayer from the *AA Big Book*.

Joko Beck has her students recite the following precepts summarizing the essence of the Four Noble Truths at the end of Zen sitting practice. You might say it at the end of your sitting practice.

> **Caught in the self-centered dream, only suffering.**
> **Holding to self-centered thoughts, exactly the dream.**
> **Life, just as it is, the only teacher.**
> **Being just this moment, compassion's way.**

But we don't need to make meditation only a formal sitting practice. This practice can also be helpful in our informal setting. I've been doing this practice in meetings for many years—sometimes for a few moments and sometimes for a whole meeting.

Meditation on Awareness of Taking Refuge

With the awareness of your condition both as an addict and as a sufferer in samsara, you can do a simple practice of taking Buddhist, 12 Steps, or a combined refuge at any time. When you do this, you will be practicing Step Three as a 12-Step Buddhist. Find a calm place, get quiet, do some *shamatha*, and recite one of the following prayers out loud, three times. If you use a *mala*—Tibetan prayer beads (see the12stepbuddhist.com)—you can say the prayer, for example, seven, twenty-one, or even 108 times.

The AA third step prayer:

> God, I offer myself to Thee—to build with me and to do with me as Thou wilt. Relieve me of the bondage of self, that I may better do Thy will. Take away my difficulties, that victory over them may bear witness to those I would help of Thy Power, Thy Love, and Thy Way of Life. May I do Thy will always.[3]

The NA third step prayer:

Take my will and my life. Guide me in my recovery. Show me how to live.

Buddhist refuge prayer:

I take refuge in the Buddha.
I take refuge in the Dharma.
I take refuge in the sangha.

My own 12-Step Buddhist prayer for the third step:

To all the Buddhas and bodhisattvas of the past, present, and future, to Tara, the mother of all Buddhas, to Amitabha, the Buddha of infinite light, and to all my teachers: please guide me and help me to see the path of Dharma and recovery in all of my activities.

Aspects of Self: The Mind Seeks Refuge

May I speak to the Controller? How are you doing? May I speak to the Mind that Seeks Refuge?

Please shift body positions.

Who are you?
What are you seeking?
How long have you been a seeker?
What would happen to the Self if it weren't for you?
Will you ever find what you're looking for?
What happens if you do?

Sit for a while as the Mind that Seeks Refuge.

Step 4

We made a searching and fearless moral inventory of ourselves.

I want to reiterate that the 12-Step Buddhist approach is not a substitute for full involvement in a 12-Step program. This particular step is long, painful, ugly, and difficult—if done correctly. It can and will bring up a lot of stinky material. If it doesn't, you're not being totally honest with yourself.

For your own benefit and spiritual sanity, I am assuming that you're involved in a recovery program and have a sponsor and a home group. For this reason, we don't need to repeat the typical 12-Step literature. The purpose here is to delve deeper into spiritual recovery, freshen our outlook, and expand our sense of connectedness with ourselves, our Higher Power, and others—in and out of the 12-Step rooms.

You can find a lot of ways to approach this step, from Hazelden books to NA pamphlets to weekend workshops at your local AA or NA office. Some people in the 12-Step world say that if you do it right, you don't ever have to do another fourth step. Others say that if you do it right, you will do written inventories constantly. There are 12-Step traditionalists and New-Agers who argue about how this step should be done. I'll merely add that it's better to do it by the book first to get a good foundation before proceeding to more esoteric methods.

I focus on principles. I think that if we grasp the principle of a step, we can understand how to make it work for our recovery. This is what I've learned from both my sponsors and my Buddhist teachers. Progress is about learning principles that can be applied in daily life and a precise but flexible methodology that can be used throughout recovery.

The importance of Step Four shouldn't be underestimated. I've seen hundreds of people relapse after avoiding it for too long. It's a difficult step. It's normal after doing the third step to feel apprehension about a scary inventory.

When I got to the fourth step my first time, in 1985, I was feeling pretty spiritual. But I didn't know what a moral inventory had to do with enlightenment. I was looking for a spiritual rush, like the rock music and drugs had given me. But the veterans were talking about writing down resentments and admitting I was wrong.

My sense of foreboding was pretty heavy, but I knew I had to get it done. I didn't want to fall back into the mire of self-loathing that I had early on. But the last thing I wanted was to write about my secrets and share them with some old codger. I was, however, increasingly convinced that the 12 Steps were working for other people who were even crazier than I was. The identification that it is working is a real benefit of being in a 12-Step home group, particularly one comprised of people around the same age.

The experience of being in the group was the first time I'd ever felt connected to other human beings in my life. I had a sponsor and took a spiritual commitment in Step Three. It was the first taste of inner freedom I'd felt since before I started drinking and using. I knew that the people in recovery had some ineffable quality—and I wanted it.

The method prescribed by my sponsor for the first written inventory was to write about resentments, fears, and sex. Adding guilt to the list, he said, "If you're an addict, there's a lot you feel guilty about. I know that you have a conscience. Otherwise, you wouldn't even be here." I had a conscience all right, and I thought I was the only one. We call that terminal uniqueness. That's when addicts think we're so unique that it kills us.

I wrote about twenty pages for my first inventory. At twenty-three, I had plenty of resentment, fear, and a string of dysfunctional relationships behind me. The writing process was exhaustive and exhausting. But it did the trick at the time.

The Fourth Step and the Funnel

These days, I come across people who have long-term sobriety but are in spiritual bankruptcy, the Funnel, in complete disillusionment with the 12 Steps. It happens even though we've worked and followed the program. We try all of the recommended recovery advice that is supposed to help. But like our addictions, the effect of the 12 Steps can stop working for us, despite our best efforts. We wind up in a dark place, such as depression, or some new manifestation of our disease, such as switching addictions.

When you're in the Funnel and ask for help from the group, the hard-core veterans will ask, "When's the last time you've done a fourth step?" as if you'd never thought of it. It's called getting hit with a 12-Step frisbee. It means that some members can't go beyond the program outlined in the original book. They toss a saying at you like, "Just turn it over!" and walk away from you. We might say, "Well gee, Bob, I've written a dozen inventories and still want to slash my wrists. So what do I do now?"

The old-timers aren't entirely wrong. We do need to continue with self-examination. But I've found that there's a more effective way to address the deeper needs of long-term sobriety with an integration of therapy, 12-Step activity, and Buddhist practice. The whole idea of being a 12-Step Buddhist is about this continued self-examination. It is useful, however, to separate the step principle and isolate various aspects of the inventory process in light of some Buddhist techniques. One hot topic these days is integrating Buddhism with psychotherapy. I've been a veteran of this process for a long time.

In the early days, if you shared insight from any source other than a pure 12-Step view, it got slammed as psychobabble. These days, members are more open to it, depending on where you live or what group you go to. I've used therapy for most of the past twenty-plus years as part of recovery, but it wasn't until sobriety v.2.0 and deeper Buddhism that I was really able to make some headway. The ongoing self-examination process never stops. Whether I'm on the couch, in meetings, or on the cushion, I try to be in a constant state of self-examination, ready to do a spot-check inventory or just to check my motives.

Principle: Self-Examination

The AA literature says that resentment is the number one offender to our spiritual well-being and, therefore, to our sobriety. In Buddhism, we learn through meditations on various topics that anger is part of an illusion. The point of the fourth step is to get honest with ourselves through the principle of self-examination.

The NA literature says that people who don't do this step inevitably relapse.[1] The AA literature says "if our behavior continues to harm others, we are quite sure to drink."[2] Our survival skills have often led to destructive behaviors. If we don't look carefully at the ways we've hurt others, we can't get well and we won't make much progress on the spiritual path.

Meditation and Anger

I've meditated many times over the years when I was feeling full of rage. It's about as comfortable as sliding down a razor blade. Once I allowed the feelings to come to the surface in meditation, I was always confused about what to do with them. Until I learned about the Dharma from the Tibetan view, I had no recourse for my edginess in the context of getting still and silent. I had to use meditation and medication together for years to retrain my brain. In the recovery literature, they call this an entire psychic change.[3] For me, it happened slowly. I needed the meds to facilitate therapy, where I learned that I could experience turbulent emotions without speaking or acting on them. The point is that it can be done, even for those of us who've had serious trauma. I truly see myself as an example of "If I can do it, anyone can."

Meditation on Conscious Inventory Practice

To do an inventory means to get in touch with feelings and experiences beneath the surface. We can meditate with the intention of a conscious inventory practice. The NA literature says that we need to be quiet before we can be honest.[4] You can do this practice before, during, or after a therapy session or 12-Step meeting. Do this alone at home, out in your favorite spot, or with your sponsor. It's not a good idea to do it when you're really worked up and having a difficult time controlling your body, speech, and mind. Grab your fourth step notebook and show up at your meditation area or wherever you decide to do this practice.

Begin with *shamatha*. Next, do some focused writing. Stay in meditation mode without distractions. Respect the space of the work. Write about one single issue. Be concise. Focus on one resentment. You can do this many times, choosing to explore a fear or sexual issue. Write in the traditional 12-Step style: who you're angry at, exactly what they did to you. Explore the anger. Notice the feelings in your body. Bring your attention deep into your physical dimension. Be aware of the thoughts surrounding the resentment. Don't follow the thoughts. Just notice. Don't judge yourself. Let thoughts and feelings arise and dissolve naturally. Do this meditation for a few minutes. Try to go a little past your limits, but not too far.

Then, please go to a meeting and make coffee for everyone. Be the greeter. Set up the chairs. Work your program.

Buddhist Integration of Step 4

On a Zen winter retreat a while back, I had some issues with an individual, and I couldn't get over them in therapy or with my 12-Step sponsor. I had to take them to the cushion. For five days I sat, hour after hour. The constant thoughts rushed into my mind, parked, and stayed put, like a movie screen on pause. I focused on my breath, observed the thoughts and physical sensations accompanying this obsession.

Halfway through the retreat, I had no relief. "It's not about fixing it, not about relief," I could hear Joko say in my head. "Are the thoughts true?" "Whose thoughts are they?" Just notice. Allow this moment to be, just as it is.

I couldn't stand it. I grabbed my laptop and went to Starbucks and did a written inventory. I wrote nonstop for hours about my habits of body, speech, and mind in this particular situation. I saw that the pattern had been going on my whole life. The feelings that came up were of being powerless, terrified, isolated, and fatigued, to name a few.

What was different this time, from all the years of recovery and Buddhist practice, was that I could handle more intensity. I could let more of the underlying core issues arise. After writing, I checked in with my sponsor and a good friend on my management team. Then, I took it back to the cushion. The next time I had a break in the zendo sitting schedule, I went to a meeting. It went on like this until the end of the retreat.

> *"He was angry with me, he attacked me, he defeated me, he robbed me."*
> *—those who do dwell on such thoughts will never be free from hatred.*
> *"He was angry with me, he attacked me, he defeated me, he robbed me."*
> *—those who do not dwell on such thoughts will surely*
> *become free from hatred.*
> **Words of the Buddha[5]**

Much of Buddhism is about learning to deal with afflictive emotions and the delusions that cause them. Take this book as a guideline for your recovery and explore the teachings in-depth with a lama or other master. As a starting point, I translate into the language of recovery some teachings that I've taken to heart and applied in my life. I've always felt that the 12 Steps are spiritual teachings translated into the language that my addict mind can't argue with.

The Tibetans talk about needing the right qualifications to even become exposed to the profound Dharma teachings, one of which is a human rebirth. We have to meet a qualified teacher who embodies the teachings. We have to be intelligent enough to understand what is being taught. Then, we have to learn how to make ourselves ready to receive them. That's where we start. We become teachable; then we learn to apply the steps and other methods in our life.

Practicing Buddhism as a recovering person is, in fact, engaging in the principle of self-examination. If we consciously choose to integrate Buddhism with the inventory process, the results are *astrophenomical*.

Tibetan Teachings on Moral Ethics

Lama Yeshe said, "You must recognize that your real enemy, the thief who steals your happiness, is the inner thief, the one inside your mind— the one you have cherished since beginningless time. Therefore, make the strong determination to throw him out and never let him back in. But be careful how you approach this analysis. Don't feel emotional or guilty; simply recognize your situation with wisdom."[6]

Chuck C. said that when we live by our character defects, it's self-robbery. I'm not sure if Chuck knew Lama Yeshe or not, but I think they'd have gotten along just fine. So how do we as addicts learn to recognize our situation with wisdom? Yep. We work Step Four. The real wisdom of the fourth step is the part where we look at what we did to create the situation. How were we at fault? That, to an addict, is a ridiculous question. But in the Dharma, and in recovery, it is the question.

Remember, in Buddhism we are taught that life in samsara is an endless cycle of suffering and rebirth. The Tibetan Buddhists teach on practicing the perfections (Paramitas) of bodhisattvas as a way of bringing our body, speech, and mind to the Dharma. The Dharma is a path out of hell. When we practice Dharma, we are on the path. When we practice the principles of recovery, we are in recovery. When we're acting out of untreated addiction and/or afflictive emotions, we create negative karma, which leads to more suffering. In recovery, we call this relapse behavior.

According to the Buddhist teachings of renunciation, the path out of samsara is controlling our body, speech, and mind. Before we can control all of these aspects as 12-Step Buddhists, we have to do an inventory of our "grosser handicaps," as they say in AA. We can use the teachings of the lamrim, the graduated path to enlightenment, to clarify our character defects, Buddhist-style.

The causes of our principal defects are said in the teachings to be the Ten Root Delusions. It's outside the scope of this chapter or this book to deal with all of them, but I think we should address the principle of one delusion here. You guessed it: anger. We'll treat anger as an example of how Tibetan Buddhist teachings can be understood and applied to recovery as it pertains to the principle of self-examination.

The Mind of Anger

Yangsi Rinpoche said, "The second delusion, the mind of anger, arises in relation to those whom we have labeled the enemy, in relation to that which we have labeled bad, or in relation to that which we consider unpleasant . . . anger can arise out of ignorance, without any logical reason."[7]

According to the Mahayana teachings, the generation of bodhicitta (compassion) is absolutely critical to developing the mind of an enlightened Buddha. Relative bodhicitta is really the beginning stage. Absolute bodhicitta is totally developed. It is the mind of an enlightened Buddha.

To develop perfect compassion, we practice the Paramitas of the bodhisattva path. Remember, a practitioner on the bodhisattva path seeks enlightenment for all suffering beings. This ideal distinguishes the Mahayanists ("Great Vehicle," named so because we take everyone with us to enlightenment) from the Hinayanists ("Smaller Vehicle," enlightenment for one's own sake). There are many teachings available on these topics.

Lama Surya Das explains:

The ten Paramitas—the transformational practices that constitute the Bodhisattva Code—are far-reaching, well-rounded principles for living the truly good life, one of truth and integrity. Often the word *paramitas* is translated into English as "perfections," but this doesn't mean that we need to enact them perfectly in the sense of getting a perfect score on a math test, nor should we give in to the internal tyranny of perfectionism as we strive to cultivate and further develop them. These panacean virtues don't come with precise measurement criteria, although they definitely do become evident as they emerge. The perfection aspect refers to the fact that all ten paramitas, each perfectly complete in and of itself, together combine perfectly to create the total way of being a Bodhisattva, and that when we walk this way, we release our innate perfection.[8]

As the practice of the perfections relates to recovery and the fourth step, we'll deal with the perfection of moral ethics in general and with the mind of anger specifically through the perfection of patience. We can apply the practice of the perfections to any and all situations, wherever they occur.

From *The Jewel Ornament of Liberation* by Gampopa:

Even though you may have the practices of generosity and moral ethics, anger will develop if you do not have the practice of patience. If anger arises, then all the virtues which were previously accumulated through generosity, moral ethics, and so forth will be destroyed in an instant. The *Bodhisattva Basket* says: "That which is called anger will destroy the roots of virtues which had been accumulated for hundreds and thousands of kalpas."[9]

How long is a *kalpa*? According to Lama Zopa Rinpoche, if you take a handkerchief up to Mt. Hood and start rubbing, when you've rubbed it all to dust, that's a kalpa.[10]

The point for recovery is that anger, like our drug of choice, is something we're not qualified to handle in any form. The treatment for anger, in recovery and in Buddhism, is spiritual. Addicts know how destructive anger can be.

Here's an example of how to apply the teachings to the step. After you've done a spot-check (mini fourth step), you see that you resent your boss because he doesn't appreciate your genius. You're right, he's wrong. This assessment is about as far as we get without the help of a sponsor. To take it further, we have to look at our part.

We can use one of Geshe Langri Tangpa's tools from *The Eight Verses of Thought Training*. The Eight Verses are recited by the Dalai Lama every day as his way of reminding himself to practice the bodhisattva perfections. This one actually coincides with the fourth step very well because, if we do it, we're left looking at our part. The Zen version is to say, "Your greatest enemy is your greatest benefactor."

Eight Verses of Thought Training: Verse Six

When one, whom I have benefited with great hope, unreasonably hurts me very badly, may I view him as my supreme Teacher!

I know what you're thinking. What does this have to do with meditation or the fourth step? In terms of the fourth step, we know it's about dealing primarily with resentments. Practice of any of the Eight Verses, but particularly of this one, gives us a Buddhist approach to the antidote for our self-centered ego, which is not found in the 12-Step literature. Practices like this add a lot of punch to the standard recovery program and might make the difference in whether you stick around. They have for me.

That's fine, you say, but isn't Buddhism about being mindful and watching your breath? In part, yes. But Dharma practice is a lot more than sitting on a cushion. Gampopa, Longchenpa, and other great teachers taught that we have to put our mind to the Dharma as the path in all of our activities.[11]

Thinking about our lives as sufferers in samsara is practice. We go about our day, staying aware of our patterns of resentment, fear, and so on. This is actually a form of meditation. The 12-Step literature says "sometimes quickly, sometimes slowly, they [the promises] will always materialize if we work for them."[12] In much the same way as we work the steps to gain more understanding of our disease and our assets, we work with concepts in Buddhism until we realize our Buddha nature on a totally natural level. At that point, we begin to spontaneously act from our Buddha nature of absolute bodhicitta, rather than our ego. This is a big parallel to the 12 Steps. In both, we learn over time and with practice to apply the spiritual principles. This is what I call Applied Spirituality. As we learn to apply the steps, we begin to act like people in recovery. As we apply Buddhist principles, like the Eight Verses, we begin to act like Buddhists. But don't expect to fully get it all at once. No one did. Not even the Buddha.

To develop the "mind that recognizes wisdom," as Lama Yeshe put it, we practice awareness with our partner, boss, commuters. We change our thinking to "This person is my supreme teacher. What is she teaching me?" Maybe patience. Maybe compassion. You decide. It's your path. Your recovery.

Karma and the Fourth Step

"If you can't understand karma," says Venerable Robina, "you can't understand any of the rest of what Buddha taught."[13] Karma is the foundation of Buddhism. If we truly understand it, we'll know that every moment of our experience is the result of our own past actions — karmic seeds—ripening. This takes the notion of seeing our part to a whole new level.

Namkhai Norbu explains it well. He says that in the West, we understand karma easily, even if we don't use the term karma. When we watch movies, for example, we know full well that negative actions get negative results and positive actions get positive results.[14] We also understand karma when it comes to making money, being hard-working Americans—the old Protestant work ethic. But, like with all spiritual principles, there are levels of intellectual understanding, and levels of application into our experience.

The Buddha didn't invent karma. He just reported on it and explained it, based on his realization, further than the Hindu Brahmins had. Robina says that we begin to understand karma when we see that our negative actions, set in motion by negative intentions fueled by negative emotions, cause suffering. To avoid just my own suffering—not to mention the suffering of all sentient beings—I try to think about karma.

The process of doing an inventory, whether it's traditional 12-Step fashion or doing therapy, is all about meditation. Meditation means getting familiar with our minds. The main problem of the addict centers in his mind. The fourth step is about getting familiar with our minds. So the fourth step is a meditation. We'll take it deeper as we proceed through the rest of the steps.

Meditation on Awareness of Basic Courage

Begin with *shamatha*. As you breathe, notice your body. You are Basic Courage, and you have the gumption to be present to the experience of resentment and fear. If there is a sensation of anxiety, let it pass through you. Imagine the Resenter sitting in a room all alone, being resentful. You are aware of how the Resenter suffers. You can feel the tension in the body where the Resenter lives, but you are not overwhelmed by it. With awareness, you simply notice. Bring compassion to the experience. Don't try to change anything. Let the Resenter be who he is.

Shift your body just a little. Now, become more aware of how it is to be Basic Courage. Notice the thoughts, sensations, smells, and sounds of Basic Courage. Bring the present awareness of Basic Courage to the surface. Allow it. Nurture it. Say silently in your mind, "I am Basic Courage."

Say out loud, if you can, or silently, "May this Basic Courage be a path to freedom from suffering for all addicts."

Notice that Basic Courage, like Basic Sanity, is an Aspect of Self that is always available. You can come back to this at any time. Just take a long, deep breath. Let it out and say to yourself, "I am Basic Courage, and it's OK."

Aspects of Self: The Resenter

I'd like to speak to the Controller. Controller, I'd like permission to speak to the Resenter. Is that OK?

Please shift your body and get into the state of the Resenter.

Whom am I speaking to?
What are you resentful about?
Can you tell me your biggest resentment?
Whom do you protect with this resentment?
How strong is your voice?
How hard is your job?
Do you feel that anyone listens to you?

Aspects of Self: Fear

I'd like to speak to the Controller. Controller, I'd like permission to speak to Fear. Is that OK?

Please shift your body and get into the state of Fear.

Whom am I speaking to?
What are you afraid of?
How long have you been afraid?
Where in the body do you live?
What would happen to the Self if you weren't around?

Aspects of Self: Basic Courage

I'd like to speak to the Controller. Controller, I'd like permission to speak to Basic Courage. Is that OK?

Please shift your body and get into the state of Basic Courage.

Whom am I speaking to?
What is your job around here?
What would you like to say if everyone was listening?
Would a fourth step be possible without your voice?
Where in the body do you live?

What would happen to the Self if you weren't there to regulate the
     Resenter, Fear, and the other emotional aspects?
Would you like your voice to be stronger?
If you could ask Fear for a favor, what would it be?
The Resenter?

Sit for a while in the space of Basic Courage.

Step 5

*We admitted to our Higher Power, ourselves,
and another human being the exact nature of our wrongs.*

In meetings, we say that we're as sick as our secrets. When we say them out loud in front of God and everybody, we get a sense of relief and connectedness that is unique to 12-Step programs. But the principle of the fifth step is more than telling someone what we're ashamed of. As the NA literature says, it's not a mere reading of the fourth step.[1] The AA steps tell us "selfishness and self-centeredness is the root of our problem."[2] No matter how sincere we are, we can't see the truth about ourselves accurately without the honest feedback of another addict. For this reason, the fifth step is most effective when it's an interaction between one addict and another.

The original AA literature says that we can do the fifth step with a non-alcoholic, as long as we're careful whom we choose. There is a good application of this, for example in ongoing therapy, but I think if we don't do it with another addict, we're likely to miss out on its real benefit. It's critical that we share our secrets with someone who has firsthand knowledge of the spiritual malady of addiction. This, in my experience, is the primary requirement of someone to listen to our fifth step.

The listener should be one who knows what it feels like to be an addict and has done his or her own recovery work. If your lama, Zen master, or priest is also in recovery, he or she qualifies. But remember that the sponsor connection is on more of an equal footing, based on shared experiences, than the typical teacher-student relationship. But, in this regard, not all sponsors see it that way. Some can get pretty bossy or downright overbearing; it's a fine line to walk. A few addicts may need a more militant approach, such as that used by various factions of 12-Step groups. But in my experience, addicts respond better to sharing rather than telling. Doing a fifth step, it's important that both teller and listener are able to share. You'd be hard pressed to get your Buddhist teacher to share with you like an addict would. It's even harder, and probably unethical, for a therapist to share her or his difficulties in the clinical setting.

Therapy has a place in the overall process of practicing the principle of Step Five: self-honesty. But, since we're usually paying for therapy, the nature of the client-therapist relationship is different than that of the sponsor-sponsee. People in recovery often mockingly refer to therapists as paid sponsors. If our therapist is doing pure 12-Step work with us for money, this is definitely an issue. But if they are helping us with deeper aspects of our recovery in addition to our work with a sponsor, it can be a very powerful approach, but the distinction needs to be clear.

The person who hears your fifth step should have a perspective and a recovery experience beyond your own. This person is then able to guide you to the next level. The issue is, to see the precise nature of your wrongs, a sponsor needs to see his or her own. In addition to having uncovered the truth in their own journey through the steps, fifth-step listeners need to have come to terms with and accepted the exact nature of their own wrongdoings as addicts.

I don't know of many people outside of the 12 Steps who have this level of self-honesty. Buddhist teachers can help non-addicts see the nature of their delusions, but addicts are special cases that require different understanding, such as the topics in this book. If you give a copy of this book to your Buddhist teacher and sangha friends, then they will be better equipped to understand not only your recovery and its challenges but that of others who will undoubtedly cross their paths.

My First Fifth

I took my earliest fifth step in 1985 over at my sponsor's house. I read my confessions of fear, resentment, and wrongdoings to him on his front lawn. About the time I got to the really juicy part, I heard a snort. To my dismay, he had fallen asleep in the sunshine and was snoring restfully while I poured out my woes.

About six months later, I found a new sponsor, Johnny O. He was a meditator who'd been to spiritual retreats in the mountains, which impressed me. I knew he had the secret to conscious contact, so I sought him out. He told me that I had to have a certain amount of sobriety before he'd work with me, in case I wasn't going to stay sober. I was sold. When I had the right number of days, I called him up.

I read my fifth step to him later that year. He didn't fall asleep. I was grateful. After all, this was important stuff; we were talking about the monumental shortcomings of my life! I read and he listened until I was done. Then, he asked me the purpose of Step Five. I said something unintelligible, duly humiliated after laying myself out there.

He said that I obviously had misunderstood the intent of the step. Luckily, since he'd been paying attention, he had some advice for me. He told me that the exact nature of my wrongs was that I had no self-esteem. I had acted all of my life without it. To be honest, I had absolutely no idea what he meant. I didn't know what self-esteem was or how I'd managed to live to twenty-three without it, but I knew I'd better find some.

Taking It a Step Further

I went to some friends in recovery and had conversations about self-esteem. I found out from my friend Big Book Dave, who had gotten sober at fifteen and was nicknamed "Big Book" by fellow members, that he'd been listening to Dennis Waitley's tapes on being a winner. So I picked up the book and the tapes. Being a self-help aficionado since first reading Wayne Dyer's *Your Erroneous Zones* in sixth grade, I could tell that Dennis was on target with his teachings. It wasn't long before I began to spout win-win wisdom from the podium at my home group. Thankfully, most were patient with me.

The Psychology of Winning was full of inspirational tips. I found that it fit nicely with the philosophy of the 12 Steps and Emmet Fox. I found out later, in college, that there was a whole branch of study called cognitive-behavioral on this type of psychology. One of the main points is to use affirmations. Change your thinking. As one of Wayne Dyer's book titles suggests, *You'll See It When You Believe It*.

I remember reading about how the ego stands guard outside the subconscious, preventing us from getting the life-saving, positive messages inside our deeper minds. The method was simple: repetition. If we said it enough times, we'd believe it. And when we truly believed it, we'd see it materialize in our lives. Any reader of the well-known bestseller by Napoleon Hill, *Think and Grow Rich*, knows this strategy.

My problem was that no matter how many times I said an affirmation to myself, in the mirror or otherwise, I didn't believe it. And it didn't change my life too much in the long run. Big Book Dave fell off the wagon after some years of sobriety too and, to my knowledge, never returned. I still think the method makes sense, in part. Combining Buddhist methods with the 12 Steps is my way of using the power of positive thinking with the power of facing reality.

The point is, in my early years of recovery, I had no idea what it meant to find the exact nature of my wrongs or how to practice the principle of the fifth step correctly. I thought it meant that I should tell everything at every meeting. I made the common newcomer mistake of openly sharing my addict secrets with strangers everywhere: in line at the grocery store, with people at work, to the mailman. I'd speak openly of former drug use, family drama, you name it. I spoke like we did in meetings, in harsh, to-the-point language that was not, in hindsight, respectful of the "normies." Blowing their minds with our kind of disclosure is *not* the correct way to practice Step Five.

Although it was huge progress just being willing to look at my part in any resentment, I had to learn to stop blaming the world. The fifth step was a great way to get honest with another person who understood the disease and was on the 12-Step path. But low self-esteem wasn't really a deep enough explanation for the cause of my unhappiness. All the positive affirmations and motivational stories of Olympic gold medalists didn't get at the root of the problem. What I needed was a road map to the mind that would show me the *real* nature of my wrong-headed views. A navigational system, as my current sponsor calls it, is what would be required.

The Road Map

Anybody who has a destination needs a navigational system as a guide. When I was in Barcelona, Spain, we saw the church where Columbus had to break the news to the queen that he didn't find India on his famous mission, but he had stumbled across this other place that could be of interest. Maybe the map or method we use works fine, but we wind up somewhere we never planned on going.

We don't really know where we'll wind up with the 12 Steps as a spiritual path. The only guarantee is that it will be different. Father Tom, a 12-Step speaker, says, "First it gets real. Then it gets different. Then it gets real different." Ain't it the truth?

As I've mentioned, if you shined a laser beam into space and moved it just a millimeter, it wouldn't look any different from your perspective; but over time, because of that slight alteration in course, the beam would wind up many light-years away from its original target. Maybe that's what happened to Columbus. He got a little off-course and *whammo*, America! And maybe that's what happened to me with all the motivational thinking I did in the early years. It didn't cure my mind, but it changed my direction. That, in turn, helped me eventually develop the program I have today.

The 12 Steps are the correct navigation system for the addict, but it doesn't work if we don't practice it. The program needs to be integrated into *all of our affairs* in order to take us where we need to go. It's an ongoing process, and growth occurs on several levels at the same time. Step Five is a vital, but not singular, event in that progression. It's critical in the beginning but can have powerful benefits later on, when we get stuck.

Getting Unstuck

Being in "full flight from reality,"[3] we addicts are not big fans of true consciousness. It's one thing to admit some of our faults, quite another to continue to dig with the long-term goal of spiritual awakening. It takes more time and effort than we think. One old-timer says, "It takes five years for reality to sink in. It takes ten for self-honesty."

In recovery, staying stuck is called getting complacent. There may be an association between getting stuck in long-term sobriety and failing to treat the root of our problems as addicts—selfishness and self-centeredness, according to the 12-Step literature. It's interesting to consider the dilemma of these older members who get tired of their active involvement with the community. In the first years, it's said that we "come, then we come to, then we come to believe." When we stagnate, we may find ourselves doing a "go, go less, go away completely" style of recovery. I've seen this many times over the years. It certainly was the case with me. And it nearly cost me my life.

So what exactly happens to our original enthusiasm with the 12-Step way of life, and what can we do to keep it alive? I think Buddhism has the answer because it attributes most of our suffering to anger, attachment, and ignorance, and is effective in dealing with each of them.

Step Five is sometimes thought of as a confession of sins. In my experience, that's not the issue. If what we needed was a confession, we could just go talk to a priest and we wouldn't need the steps. The purpose of this step is to discover the exact nature of our wrongs—selfishness and self-centeredness. The acknowledgment of resentment, fear, etc., is just the beginning. These resentments are the result, not the cause, of self-centeredness. To grow and keep from stagnating, we need to treat what we call in the program "the disease of self."

Principle: Self-Honesty

The principle of Step Five is self-honesty. In meetings, you'll hear about cash-register honesty, but that's just the first part and would be an oversimplification if we stopped there. When we sober up, we learn to observe the basic laws of society as we regain our innate sense of right and wrong. But to practice rigorous self-honesty, we need to face our feelings and get *extraordinarily* honest with ourselves. Only then can we experience a profound connection to humanity. The sense of alienation diminishes along with the effects of low self-esteem. This self-honesty is the real affirmation, and it has legs.

The insanity that the program talks about is our dishonesty with ourselves.
Jack Sullivan

As we progress through the steps, over and over throughout our sober lives, we get to "peel back the layers of the onion," as we say in meetings. But even with the keen eye of a sharp sponsor who knows us well, we're limited in how many layers we can really reveal. I've found that using therapy is a very effective means of working on the deeper levels of self-deception.

As I've said earlier, having a long-term relationship with a good psychotherapist who understands the process of recovery through the 12 Steps and having my Buddhist practice has been an integral part of my recovery. In a sense, it's an ongoing fourth and fifth step. But my therapist is not an addict, and I need to be aware of what he doesn't know about recovery. I have the responsibility to educate him on how we do it in the program. Then, he can help me get past my own illusions. For example, I would go into a session with a negative, dark feeling. We would get to a point where I saw that the afflictive emotion of the moment and the memories associated with the feelings and behaviors in the past were not the *whole* picture of who I am or how I felt about others. I would share that addicts tend to think one-dimensionally, black or white. But then the mood could change and we would wind up on the other end of the extreme. Eventually, I learned to accept myself as a whole package without attaching absolutes on either side.

The goal in therapy, Buddhism, and in Step Five is to see oneself clearly and objectively.

Meditation on Self-Honesty

Begin with *shamatha*. After relaxing into this calm state, remain still and silent. Being fully present to this moment, think about the following terms in the context of your recovery and the fifth step. Self-centeredness. Selfishness. Ask yourself silently, "Are these the root of my problem? What is the root of the problem?" Follow the root all the way to its beginning. Allow yourself to sink into the experience of self-examination while being present, silent, and still. Where is the self? Who is at the core of this self-centeredness? Is it a feeling? A thought? A memory? Don't push; just let your attention be on the body sensations as you invite your attention toward these questions. Don't overanalyze. Just settle in.

Considering how you felt about yourself while active in your addiction, how do you feel now that you're in the process of recovery? What sensations in your body accompany this emotional state? Remembering the meditation from the fourth step, has the physical sensation accompanying resentment and fear subsided? Is it stronger? Where in your body do you feel this exactly? Ask, "Who am I? Am I my resentment? Am I my fears?"

Let the questions linger. Just notice the body, the breath, the energy moving through you. Practice being present with the experience of self-honesty.

If you find this type of practice difficult, know that I do too. We all do. So why do we do it? Remember, in Step One, we had to admit that we had a life-threatening illness. In Step Two, we admitted we couldn't get over it without spiritual help. In the third step, we made a decision to follow through with the practice of spiritual principles. In the fourth, we followed through on the commitment, and now that we have made it to Step Five, we are well on our way to "a new kind of happiness," as the AA literature states.[4] The fifth step, like all of them, has an element of discomfort associated with the process. But the willingness to let yourself feel the feelings, ask the questions, and sit silently and peacefully with the answers or the non-answers is a very important spiritual tool.

We say in the 12-Step program, "In case you're wondering if you're an addict, non-addicts don't wind up in these meetings." We can also say that people who aren't serious about recovery don't bother asking themselves the questions that the steps demand. Be appreciative and commend yourself for being willing to do this work. Others who don't have a lot of the troubles that we addicts do also have less of a motivation to pursue spiritual awakening.

Buddhist Integration of Step 5

Bodhisattvas on the path to total enlightenment are instructed to speak the Dharma with every word, to teach the Dharma not only with words but actions, and to embody the Dharma with our very being.

It has been said in Kevin Griffin's *One Breath at a Time* that the Buddhist principle of the fifth step is about Right Speech.[5] I agree. I can add that when I took my Buddhist refuge vows, I thought the one about not lying would be almost effortless to keep. But on the more subtle levels of self-deception, I have to keep a very watchful eye. Am I lying to myself? What's my motive? Am I acting for myself or for the benefit of others? These questions haunt my addict-centered ego as I try to actively apply self-honesty as a tool on my journey to full awakening. Here is where other addicts are vital and necessary in my life. But I must also defer to the Buddhist teachings because they peel back the layers in a way that works very well with the steps. The steps allow me to dig into the Buddhist teachings much more rigorously than the average student, and the teachings allow me to get much more out of the steps than the average addict.

When applying the teachings, I can draw from the 12-Step attitude of willingness to understand the exact nature of my wrongs at the level of the root delusions of anger, attachment, and ignorance. According to Buddhism, these misperceptions on the nature of reality and ourselves are the main reasons why we stay stuck in suffering.

I've found over the years that, if I only deal with the micro day-to-day issues as they come up, they just keep coming back, like brush fires in a windstorm. To really deal with anger, resentment, fear, and so on,

I've found that cutting it off at the root is more effective. What's the root? The teachings say it is ignorance of our Buddha nature.

The Buddhist teachings on ignorance are of great benefit in regard to self-honesty. Through them, I've gained an understanding that ignorance of my intrinsic Buddha nature is at the core of my troubles, not only as an addict, but also as a person. This is how I connect self-honesty in the fifth step with the honesty of knowing my true nature as a 12-Step Buddhist.

To explain, I'll turn to the Tibetan teachings on ignorance. By ignorance, Buddhism is pointing out that we retain a false sense of self. This sense of self is not concrete. It's not real. It is, as I said earlier, a dream. The meditations on emptiness aim to wake us up from this ignorance.

According to Geshe Rabten Rinpoche: "The first of the twelve links is ignorance, the root of all samsaric suffering. The Sanskrit term, *avidya* [Tibetan: *ma-rig-pa*], means 'not seeing' and implies an obscuration of mind."[6]

The process of doing the fifth step helps us begin to see through the veil of our own misperceptions. We start to chip away at the core beliefs that keep us imprisoned in low self-esteem, fear, depression, and so on. Practicing the fifth step, self-honesty, with the teachings on ignorance in mind, is very powerful.

Geshe Rabten continues, "Each of us is subject to our own conception of 'I.'"

In Buddhism, we can use the analytical meditations on emptiness (Madhyamika school) to deconstruct the false sense of "I."

Continuing with Geshe Rabten's teachings:

> It is important to contemplate whether or not this "I" really exists as it appears. If we search for it within ourselves, from the top of our head down to the soles of our feet, we'll come to the conclusion that neither our physical body nor any of its individual parts can serve as the "I" that under certain circumstances arises so strongly. . . . If we analyze our minds in the same way, we'll find that

the mind is nothing but a stream of different thoughts and mental factors and conclude that nothing in the mind is the "I" that we conceive either.[7]

In Zen practice, we simply sit in awareness as we practice no-self, or abandoning a sense of self, letting go of our fantasy of our "self," to realize emptiness. As a 12-Step Buddhist, we work with the fifth step to expedite our ability to see beyond the conception of our false "I." Through examination of our actions and feelings with the help of our sponsors, we can see how false beliefs about who we are contribute to the feelings and behaviors that we wrote down in Step Four. As noted, the level of self-disclosure that we're used to in meetings is not always well received in Buddhist groups. It helps to be mindful and respectful of this when sharing with your sangha. In a group like 12-Step Sangha (see 12stepsangha.com), we can share as openly as any other meeting. But in the privacy of our own minds, we can always use the same tools of the deconstruction meditation with an emphasis on resentments, as we did in the meditation on self-honesty above.

As Geshe Rabten says, "Actually, the situation is very subtle. We neither exist as simply as the ignorant mind supposes nor do we not exist, and gaining an understanding of the true nature of the self requires thorough training and sustained meditation practice."

Below is a meditation that I wrote to expand your sense of self beyond the limited vision of resentment and the fear-based self that was discovered and examined—with much courage I might add—in the fourth and fifth steps.

Meditation on the Vastness of Consciousness

Start with *shamatha*, even a few moments is helpful. Set your intention to be of maximum service to those around you. It can be as simple as saying, "I hope this meditation helps somebody." Think for a moment of your self, your problems, your fears, and your desires. Your life is a series of experiences, all connected in a beginningless stream. Notice where you are in space and time: the room, the neighborhood, the town. Pan out to a wider sense of your region: the state, the country, continent, planet, and solar system.

Think for a moment of how many people there are on the planet right now besides you. The number is about seven billion. Notice that for a moment. Say to yourself, "I am one of seven billion people—all of us have desires, fears, histories, memories, families, and thousands of thoughts per day." Notice your body. See yourself in this bigger context, as part of a human community with seven billion members, each with as much on his or her mind and in his or her heart as you have right now. At first, this may be overwhelming. Let it overwhelm you. Consider now the rest of the beings on the planet. How many creatures are there? How many animals, fish, insects, birds, and even single-celled beings living beneath the ground, or even inside other beings? How many are there? Trillions? Hundreds of trillions?

In the overwhelming awareness of how many beings exist in this moment, allow your ego to be less significant, less important, less in charge than a few minutes ago. Taking it a step further, think back through time, through the continuity of causes and effects of every one of these trillions upon trillions of sentient beings that exist right now. They all have some kind of parents, who had parents, who had parents, and so on. Think of all the beings who have ever lived in the past and all of their karma, all of their relatives, all of their experiences of birth and death and suffering. Notice how vast the universe is from this perspective.

Now, take it to the future. How many beings will come to exist in endless time? How far can your mind reach to comprehend this unfathomable power of infinite, sentient beings of the past, present, and future? Where do your resentments, fears, and concerns stand in the face of this vast awareness? You might think of these sheer numbers as a power greater than your single self or ego.

Meditation on Awareness of Truth

To practice awareness of truth as it relates to self-honesty and the fifth step, bring yourself into the calm state with a simple breathing meditation. Remember, calm is relative. As you sit, spend a few minutes noticing the balance between truth and lies, honesty and fiction, as it's come up for you during this work. Be patient with yourself. This is hard stuff. Notice within you the source of self-honesty that has allowed you to come this far. Now, go treat yourself in a healthy way to something nice, like a hot tub soak and a massage, a good movie, or tea with a friend.

Aspects of Self: The Liar

I'd like to speak to the Controller. Controller, I'd like permission to speak to the Liar. Is that OK?

Please shift your body and get into the state of the Liar.

Whom am I speaking to?
What is your job?
Do you value the truth?
How strong is your voice?
If you didn't speak so loudly, what would happen to the Self?
It takes a lot of work to keep the cover-up going!
Who are you most useful to?
Thank you for speaking. Your job is safe.

Step 6

We're entirely ready to have our Higher Power remove
these defects of character.

Some don't give Step Six due consideration. They lump it together with Step Seven. However, my sponsor believes that six and seven are the most misunderstood steps. I asked him recently, "Could you point out one reason to explain the phenomenon of relapse among members with long-term sobriety?" He said, "They forget six and seven."

Back in the eighties, after I left Johnny O.'s house having recited my fifth step, I went home, shell-shocked. His suggestion was to sit with the aftereffects of my reading. In Step Six, I was to contemplate my willingness to have the character defects that I wrote about removed, followed by the request for removal in Step Seven.

I asked Johnny what I needed to do for Step Six. He said, "When people have done the fourth and fifth steps correctly, they're entirely ready. That's Step Six, the state of readiness." Examining our character defects, as they're called in 12-Step language, or the Seven Deadly Sins from a Christian perspective, does put us into a state of willingness to have them removed. This feeling is compounded by having another person hear the facts about our behaviors, secrets, hidden resentment, and so on.

The AA literature leads us to believe that we'll feel pretty spiritual after taking the fifth step. It describes a spiritual experience something akin to walking with God down the road to freedom. "We feel that we are on the Broad Highway, walking hand in hand with the Spirit of the Universe."[1] I didn't get that feeling. In a sense, it was the same kind of disappointment I'd had after being "saved" by that Lutheran priest. Whatever was supposed to happen, didn't.

Sure, I was relieved and somewhat proud of myself for having made it over the hump of the fourth-step inventory, but the afterglow wasn't that strong. I knew I did my best, but there really was no big magic show.

I moved on to another sponsor, John C., known as "The Preacher" because of his overwhelming enthusiasm for God and the 12 Steps. He was Christian but never pushed it in meetings or our many conversations over the years. He was in love with recovery, after having a powerful "white light" experience in early sobriety. He spoke often of having a better relationship with God because of the steps.

John said that Steps Six and Seven could be summed up as, "God, you show me, I'll stop." The idea was that doing the steps to this point put one in a relationship with his Higher Power. John's prayer was, "Father, I have a problem. I don't know what the solution is, but you do. Please show me what I need to do or stop doing." If pride, for example, was causing difficulty, my job as a recovering addict was to be aware of it specifically. When it would pop up, instead of acting out old behavior patterns, I was to stop and say John's prayer, "You've shown me, now I'll stop."

Principle: Willingness

Step Six is about being aware of our character defects, being shown their impact on our lives. We need to be willing to experience those defects and their effect on us and the lives of those around us. To take a meditative approach to willingness, try the following exercise.

Meditation on Defects

Imagine each of the defects, one per session: anger, pride, greed, lust, gluttony, envy, or sloth. We'll start with one: lust. Begin with a few minutes of *shamatha*. Set your intention. Say something like this, out loud if you're alone: "I will become mindful of my character defects for the benefit of everyone I have harmed as the result of indulging in them." Imagine yourself in the last situation where you were lustful. Where were you? Were you alone? If not, who were you with? What were they wearing? What were you thinking? Notice the lustful thoughts. Were they focused on sex? Did you have a physical reaction? What was the room like? The weather? Was it warm or cold? Recall and notice as many details as you can from your last memory of being lustful. After you have a good feel of what it was like, shift your body.

Next change your focus to what a normal desire would be like. Think of a role model, maybe that's your teacher or sponsor. I used to think of my friend Bob, who reminded me of Mr. Miyagi from *The Karate Kid*. Put your role model in the situation you just reviewed. How would he act? Try to imagine yourself responding to the situation as he would. Feel how it would feel to have an appropriate level of desire. Notice the difference between the experiences of body, speech, and mind with appropriate desire compared to lust.

According to *The Twelve Steps for Christians*, "We work Step Six by being ready for God to bring change into our lives. Being ready doesn't seem like work, but it is—it's spiritual work."[2] Indeed, the *Twelve Steps and Twelve Traditions* book, called the 12 x 12, leans toward this Christian affiliation: "As they are humbled by the terrific beating administered by alcohol, the grace of God can enter them and expel their obsession. Here, their powerful instinct to live can cooperate fully with their Creator's desire to give them new life."[3]

For many years I approached the steps in this way. I used Zen meditation to be closer to God, my Higher Self, the Indwelling Christ, but the more I looked, the less I believed that God lived there. Depression, agitation, and anxiety were all I found. And no amount of prayer, counseling, Zen, or step work made them disappear. As a result, my faith in God and in the 12 Steps dwindled as the years wore on.

What happens when you have long-term sobriety, do everything they tell you to do, and still wind up feeling just as bad or worse than in early recovery? The Funnel. Step Six really is the turning point for me in terms of understanding how I can relate to the 12 Steps as a Buddhist. There is no magic wand in Buddhism that somebody waves to "strike us wonderful," as we say in recovery. No God is going to come down from heaven and render me as pure as the driven snow.[4]

I prayed, waited, worked hard, and didn't really get better. As I've told in my story, I wound up desperately seeking a chemical solution to my unease. The effort of combining LSD and meditation exacerbated my character defects. Through the relapse, I felt that God had truly deserted me or, worse, was never there in the first place. At best, I had a foggy memory of the conscious contact I had formed in early recovery and in my studies.

Work the Steps, or the Steps Will Work You

In the mid- to late nineties, I thought I was done with the steps, done with recovery, done with trying to improve myself. I surrendered surrendering. Gave up completely.

What I didn't realize until years later is that the process of the steps never stopped working me. As I see it, the point of Step Six is to become willing to let go. The earlier steps bring us to this awareness, but we tend to hold on, settling, as the 12 x 12 says, "for about as much perfection as is necessary to get by." The point for me is that I've never been in recovery for just a little taste of what it had to offer. I saw the words *spiritual awakening* and took it at full value. I wanted it, and I was willing to go to any lengths to get it. But I had no idea what that process would entail, or how much I'd have to willingly give up getting there. And, as I said, even when I thought I'd abandoned the process, it hadn't abandoned me.

I didn't realize until after years of sobriety to what extent our character defects—anger, pride, fear, jealousy, the whole list—remain. I thought meditating and working a program while going to college for a psychology degree would make me feel more spiritual. Instead, the meditation just amplified my awareness of the raw emotions and unresolved issues of the past. Therapy gave me an outlet to discuss issues as they came up, but the long-term solution just never played out there.

It would take a hard crash and a resumption of Buddhist teachings in a much more serious way than ever for me to make real progress.

The spiritual covenant that I made in Step Three—turning my life over to my Higher Power—was intact the whole time, even in relapse. Just because I resisted the experience of witnessing my character defects didn't mean the step wasn't working. On the contrary, the sixth step continued to work me in ways that I couldn't conceive. The defects unrelentingly came up, staring me and those around me right in the face.

Six and Seven as a Process

This is how I view Step Six today. It's a process that I can't back out of. I have to work it, or it will work me. I tried to fight, resist, and deny the process, but it did no good. Of course, in my experience, the 12 Steps are not enough. The idea in Steps Six and Seven that we can get ready and get well by saying some prayers is really tricky. We get ready all right, but it's not in our timeframe. We say in the program that it's in God's time. I'd say it happens when we're ready, really ready, to completely surrender to the solution—as all great spiritual seekers of the past have.

It's really a process that looks like an event. If I'm angry, the natural response is to think *you* caused my bad feelings because of your actions. But, according to the 12 Steps, we're mistaken when we blame others for our feelings. This is also in line with Buddhism, in that because of karma, we create our own condition.

We know from any study of physiology, biology, and chemistry that what looks like one action is really a confluence of factors, parts creating the illusion of a whole, just like my fingers typing on the keyboard seem like one activity while there are trillions of nerves, muscles, chemical processes, cognitive structures, intentions, memories, plans, and so on happening really fast. I think; therefore, I act. I act; therefore, I am. Who am I? Am I the activity, relationship, drunkenness, rage, fear, loneliness, depression?

We identify ourselves through our experiences on the mental and physical level. The mistake is that these are very low levels of understanding. Because of meditation and daily living practices, I started to understand more deeply some Buddhist topics like karma, suffering, and so on. This caused a fracture in the wall of my own self-perception. This wasn't a brand-new process, just a deeper one.

Like I said, when I got sober the first time, I didn't know myself very well but soon realized that I was living a life based on stressful emotions, reactionary mechanisms, and old habit patterns. And after immersing myself in steps for a while, I felt that there was more to me than that junkie scrambling through the garbage can in East San Jose in the middle of the night. I became a member of society and a spiritual being.

But the character defects were still there, which caused a lot of confusion. Subconscious questions pervaded my every waking moment: How can I be this when I act like *that*? What am I really, now that I'm in recovery? All that doubt wasn't dispelled by the many philosophies, theories, steps, and books. The real answers were outside my reach. I would find out later that Buddhism at least asked the right questions . . . as long as I was willing to do the work.

Buddhist Integration of Step 6

If the Seven Deadly Sins seem challenging, try fifty-one! Here are some as described by Thich Nhat Hanh. "When our feelings are stronger than our mindfulness, we suffer. . . . The basic unwholesome mental formations are greed, hatred, ignorance, pride, doubt, and [holding] views. The secondary unwholesome mental formations, arising from the basic ones, are anger, malice, hypocrisy, malevolence, jealousy, selfishness, deception, guile, unwholesome excitement, the wish to harm, immodesty, arrogance, dullness, agitation, lack of faith, indolence, carelessness, forgetfulness, distraction, and lack of attention. According to the Vijñanavada School . . . there are fifty-one kinds of mental formations."[5]

With the basic mindfulness of Buddhism, we can overcome these mental formations—things that are formed in the mind, by the mind, and in the service of the ego—through simply being aware of them. In Buddhism, you have lifetimes to deal with them, but I didn't have time to wait. My defects, defilements, passions, afflictions were strong and needed to be brought under control. I used medication for several years as a way of buying some time, allowing for insights and acceptance with meditation. But at some point, I had to let go of the meds and get into more serious Buddhist practice.

I'm not downplaying mindfulness meditation. It's a big part of my daily practice. If you ask most people to define Buddhism, they'll say mindfulness. But mindfulness is just one teaching out of thousands. That said, I do think that if we become truly aware at exceedingly deep levels, and that awareness is tempered with wisdom or enough knowledge about ourselves and how our minds function, eventually mindfulness meditation could melt the defects. But sober addicts really don't have a lot of time to sit around waiting to become holy. There are pressing life problems, brain dysfunction, financial stresses, and all the rest. The wolves are always snapping at our heels, so to speak. For this reason, we addicts need an immediate solution that can help us keep our lips zipped and our hands to ourselves. From the Buddhist view, this doesn't involve waiting for God to take them away for us. Truly, I have never seen or ever heard of that happening.

I think we get degrees of relief and are able to get a handle on our emotions if we do a lot of hard work in the 12 Steps. But, to eradicate character defects, it takes stronger medicine. For me, it took doing some challenging work in an effort to deepen my spiritual experience. That is why we're on the path. It isn't about just not using anymore. Real recovery is about a deep and effective spiritual transformation. I found out that the real spiritual life is not what I thought it was. It's really about looking at what I don't want to know, about how I've used substances and addiction to *avoid* feeling anything most of my life.

Step Six and Impermanence

One thing that we all avoid is the fact that we're going to die someday, but as Buddhist author Stephen Batchelor reminds, we don't know when. Maybe this thought will shock you, but you and I *are* going to die. Wait, you knew that? Well, we all know that, but do we know it in a way that is deep and useful and life changing? How can we possibly apply a meditation on death as part of Step Six?

As we say in the program, it's simple but not easy. To apply Buddhism to Step Six, we get willing, then we get honest, then we get grateful. We meditate on our own impermanence, which includes the inevitability of our own death, the preciousness of being born human, and the law of karma. If understood in Buddhist terms, it means that we will be reborn endlessly in a cycle of birth, death, and all the suffering in between. Samsara.

If you think these topics are morbid or unspiritual, maybe Buddhism isn't right for you, but I've found that when I'm truly willing to go to any lengths to understand the teachings, I learn about my self, become more appreciative of every moment of my life, and am generally less inclined to overreact based on character defects. I think of this as a state of humility.

Buddhism is a science of mind. It is about examining our condition as human beings. The purpose is total enlightenment. That's right, a complete spiritual awakening. But you'll find that most people in recovery don't believe in this concept. In the NA literature, it even states that spiritual perfection will never happen. What they consider perfection is not what Buddhism considers enlightenment. There's a difference. And, say the Buddhists, our innate perfection already exists, we just need to wake up and smell what the Buddha's cookin'. I love how Robina puts it: "Buddhism is logical. Think it through." We are all going to die eventually, and as my dad used to say, "There's no two ways about it." So, if you're feeling brave, join me for a meditation on death.

Meditation on Death

Begin with setting your intention. In recovery, we talk a lot about checking our motives. Here's a way to do it: Say, "When I do this practice, may it bring benefit to all who suffer." Then do some *shamatha* and mentally run through the following:

I was born; I will die. So how should I live my life in between? I know that my defects of character are born of afflictive emotions, which spring from ignorance of my true, enlightened nature. To get closer to awakening, I need to understand that this life is impermanent. The moment of my death will come.

In the words of one teacher:

> As death approaches, you collapse into your bed and no longer have the strength to get up. Even when you see food and drink, you feel no desire for it. Tormented by the sensations of dying, you feel more and more depressed, and all your courage and confidence evaporate. You experience forebodings and hallucinations of what awaits you. Your time has come for the great moving on. Your family and friends gather around you, but there is nothing they can do to delay your departure—you are going through the suffering of death by yourself, all alone. Nor is there any way for you to take your possessions with you, however limitless they might be. You cannot bring yourself to let go of them, but you know you cannot keep them either. Remorse overtakes you as you remember the negative actions that you have done. When you think of the sufferings of the lower realms, you are terrified. Death is suddenly here. Dread takes hold of you. The perceptions of life slip away, and slowly you grow colder.[6]

Knowing that I will die, but not knowing when, I promise myself that I will do my best to grow spiritually, to not waste time on resentments, fears, jealousy, and the like. Let this meditation be a reminder to be grateful for every precious moment of life.

Aspects of Self: Pride

I'd like to speak to the Controller. Controller, I'd like permission to speak to Pride. Is that OK?

Please shift your body and get into the state of Pride.

Whom am I speaking to?

How are you?

What do you do for the Self?

How strong is your voice?

Who's your best friend?

Do you feel that anyone listens to you?

How about the Addict?

Aspects of Self: Pride in Reverse

I'd like to speak to the Controller. Controller, I'd like permission to speak to Pride in Reverse. Is that OK?

Please shift your body and get into the state of Pride in Reverse.

How are you feeling?

What is your job?

How are you the flip side of Pride?

Does it matter if you or Pride is in control?

Step 7

Humbly asked our Higher Power to remove our shortcomings.

The object of the seventh step is to gain humility—understanding the truth about oneself. On the face of it, the difference between Buddhism and the 12 Steps is the definition of that truth and what to do about it. The steps say that we're on a journey to understand our relationship with God. Buddhism says that we're totally enlightened Buddhas who are asleep at the wheel. Step Seven is a profound and vital spiritual tool and is easy to underappreciate. Adversity teaches us who we are. The process of the seventh step shows us who we are by showing us what we're not—namely, the character defects that seemed to define us. While the steps lead us to discover new meaning in our lives through our relation to God, Buddhism sees that thinking as a false duality that still keeps us from seeing the full truth—the real humility. The teachings of the Buddha, in whatever form they take, lead us to discover, beneath all the delusion, that we are perfectly complete from the beginning.

The programs tell us that if we don't find humility, we're not going to get very far in our recovery. From the AA 12 x 12, " . . . attainment of greater humility is the foundation principle of each of AA's 12 Steps. For without some degree of humility, no alcoholic can stay sober at all. . . . Unless they develop much more of this precious quality than may be required just for sobriety, they still haven't much chance of becoming truly happy."

Step Seven is an event the first time it's done, but this step is an ongoing process. We have to be truthful to stay on this path. It's a lot of work, but the benefits outweigh the difficulties. My first Step Seven was really combined with Step Six, just a few minutes after doing Step Five. At that point, I was made acutely aware, in front of my sponsor and my Higher Power—or my hazy concept of one at that time—of how disgusted I was with my life. But I was about as ready and willing as a young man could be. I made my prayer request, straight out of the book, for God to make me better. I asked him to take away all of my character defects. Then I waited to see what happened. If I only knew.

My sponsor said, "Do your seventh step prayer as sincerely as you can. Then you better duck." We have no idea at first how acute the awareness of our shortcomings will become. It's part of the commitment and the process to be willing to walk down that road, feeling all the emotions while sober.

In a meeting a long time ago, a man came up to me in response to some difficulties I'd been sharing. He drew me a diagram on the blackboard of the schoolroom we were in, showing how as we progress toward "the light," the forces of darkness struggle to keep us down in their realm. The process of being in Steps Six and Seven is one of struggle—acute awareness of negativities on one hand, and the opportunity to walk the path of wakefulness on the other. In fact, the road gets very narrow at this point for those of us who choose to do this work.

When we first enter recovery, we're able to get away with old behaviors, ignorant about the underlying defects that keep us trapped in our addict view of us against the world. But the more we work the program, the more spiritual progress we make, and with that progress comes the greater awareness of our limitations. It's tempting then to fall back into old ideas and to let those forces suck us back down. That's what the sponsor meant when he said, if you do six and seven correctly, duck. But we must maintain our faith and keep our feet on the path, no matter what it looks like in the process, even if that means years of depression, anxiety, or whatever. We will get to the other side to truly walk in the "sunlight of the spirit," as the steps put it.

If I'd really known this on a deeper level, I might not have relapsed. The relapse for me was actually part of the process of six and seven: the magnification of the disease of addiction as it lived in me, even with multiple years of recovery. In fact, the disease may have reared its head so strongly because of the hard work I'd been doing. My advice is to keep going, no matter how you feel. Stay humble; stay in the truth.

Principle: Humility

A principle, as I understand it, has to be something that can be practiced. While many of the steps have various interpretations about their underlying principles, everyone's pretty unanimous that the principle of Step Seven is humility. The practice of this principle comes into play once all of the steps are learned and internalized. To isolate the function of Step Seven, I've laid out a chart that shows the graduated increase in severity of normal traits in Column One into full-blown addict shortcomings/defects in Column Two. The solution, or practice of humility, is summarized in Column Three. The practice of humility from a non-Buddhist perspective is simple: when we become aware of our negative behavioral traits, we try to put a cap on it. For now, we'll limit the defects to the well-known Seven Deadly Sins.

For pride, the Buddhist way to practice humility is to work on making yourself lower than the other person. For example, a guy pulled up after running a stop sign and yelled at me for going in front of him, even though I'd had the right of way. I started to get defensive and argue with him about how right I was. I know that the core of this reaction for me is pride. I can feel it in my chest as I get more and more worked up. In this situation, the last thing my addict wants is to concede. After all, I'm right! The practice of humility would have me say to the guy, "You're right, I shouldn't have pulled out. Is there anything else?" Remember, it's progress not perfection. This is an example of acting in a way that's contrary to my habitual reaction. Without a 12-Step program or my Buddhist perspective, this incident could have ended badly.

Normal Trait	Character Defects	Practice
Self-confidence	Pride	Make oneself lower
Self-preservation/ care	Greed	Generosity
Honest desire	Lust	Offer service to others
Anger	Rage	Patience
Hunger	Gluttony	Moderation
Acknowledging the success of others	Envy	Rejoicing
Resting when needed	Sloth	Exertion

There is a practice for generosity as well. I will often catch myself rushing through the door of places like Starbucks. I want my coffee, and I want it now. Do not try getting in line in front of me! The practice is to stop and open the door for the person a couple of steps behind me, letting them go first. I practice this with my dogs as well. When I come home on a typical cold, wet Portland night, the first thing I want is to get inside and get warm and dry. My dogs have other ideas. They're ready to run. So we go for a walk and they get to relieve themselves before I do.

With lust, and this is a really tough one, I have to practice constantly. Addicts get in more trouble with lust than any other defect, except maybe resentment. I got involved with a newcomer girl in the mid-eighties, which created quite a stink in my home group. Our son is twenty-one at the time of this writing. Like most addicts, I don't just like anything that I want; I gotta have it and can't stop obsessing about it (or her) until I do. Then, it's on to the next lustful obsession. In the news recently there have been articles about the growing problem of sexual addiction, Internet porn, and so on. Once again, we can practice the contrary behavior. Although lust isn't limited to sex, let me give an example on the intimate side. When making love to your partner, try to please him/her first. Give them all of the love that you know they need and want. The principle is, "What I want from you, I give to you." This can apply to just about anything the two of you want and need from each other.

You can come up with your own examples and practices for the rest of these and other troublesome character defects in your life. Just remember the basic principle is humility—knowing the truth about yourself—and acting in a manner contrary to the defect. It's never safe for us addicts to indulge in our character defects. The best way to be humble is to know the truth and to take the spiritual action that is the opposite of the defect.

Meditation on Humility: Rejoicing

Begin with *shamatha*. From a calm space, notice how you view yourself. Are you OK, in your own eyes? When you think about your character defects, do you over-identify with them? This kind of meditation can work with any shortcoming. Let's focus on envy as an example. Bring to mind a situation where you were very envious of someone else's success. Did a coworker get a promotion that you wanted? Did your friend in high school go out with the one who you had a crush on? Whichever example comes up for you is the right one to work on. Focus on the experience of body, speech, and mind as you mentally relive the situation. Bring yourself into the time, place, and feeling of envy.

Notice, but don't follow, the thoughts. Whenever you have a strong taste of envy in your heart, take a long, slow in-breath. As you let it out, visualize releasing the envy in the form of green smoke coming out through your nose, your mouth, your ears. Feel the envy seeping out of your every pore. Let it all wash out of you. Just relax and let the entire experience of envy flow through you and out of you. When you're ready, just notice where you are now: the smells in the room, the air temperature, etc. Be present to all you are now, in this moment.

Is envy the truth of who you are? Or are you a person who some-times feels envy? Notice the place within where feelings of love and happiness grow. See a ball of white light in the center of your body. Let it grow warmer with every breath. Let the light represent peace and inner happiness. Relax into it. Now recall the person you were envious of. See them with the thing you wanted for yourself. Send a little bit of that light from within you their way. Send more and more with every breath. Allow this person to feel for themselves what you want for your-self and what you love. Give them all that you desire. See them smiling, in a state of total peace. Enjoy this moment of happiness with them. See him or her with the person or job or item that you want, and notice the glow of joy on their face as they go about their life. Feel the light in your body. Be happy for them. This is rejoicing. You can do rejoicing meditation anytime.

Relationship with a Higher Power

My sponsor was big on forming a relationship to a Higher Power. Step Six is "God, you show me," and Step Seven is "I'll stop." The NA litera-ture emphasizes this point of forming a relationship to a Higher Power as well. "We ask for help because we cannot do it alone. . . . We have to get out of the way and let God do God's work. . . . Humbly asking for the removal of our shortcomings means we are giving complete license to that loving Power to work in our lives."[1] The concept of an actual give-and-take relationship with God is pervasive in 12-Step pro-grams. From Al-Anon, the program for friends and family of alcoholics: "We learned to accept our part in our relationship with our Higher Power. . . . By accepting that God can do for us what we cannot do for ourselves, we begin to achieve the humility that is necessary for change to take place. . . . We need the assistance of a Higher Power."[2]

I worked with this idea for many years, thinking it was how the 12 Steps were supposed to work. I had a hard time, but I believed what the old-timers said about the program being the last house on the block. I didn't want to go back to the way life was pre-recovery, so I always tried to stick it out. Even when life made no sense, at least I was still sober. In this regard, I felt that my commitment was as solid as anyone else's, no matter how dark it got.

In the program, we take the commitment to the spiritual journey made in Step Three much further with Step Seven. In the beginning, we surrender to the fact that we're addicts, can't do it alone, and need a spiritual solution. But at this point, we have to get down on our hands and knees and ask "our Creator" to remove our shortcomings. I asked God, as humbly as I could. And I asked, and asked, and asked as the years wore on. The problem was, they don't get easily removed that way. At least they didn't for me.

I continued to have problems with anger, anxiety, depression, and the other afflictions we've talked about throughout my first ten years. I've discussed many of these in my personal history. You have your own that you can identify with. The point is that my continued lack of progress on these issues made me feel less worthy of God's love. And the more confused I got about that, the more depressed I became. I continued to pray, meditate, and use affirmations, trying to find the humility that the program was describing. But my ego had other plans.

Buddhist Integration of Step 7

Another way Buddhists look at character defects is as *kleshas*. This is not the place to detail all the afflictions individually. In fact, there are complete systems of Buddhist teachings that do just that. But so you're familiar with some of the terminology, *klesha* is the Sanskrit word for "defilement" or "passion." Some of these are: desire, hate, delusion, pride, false views (belief in an ego, eternalism, or nihilism, denial of the law of karma, persistence in these false views, and belief they can lead to liberation), doubt, rigidity, excitability, shamelessness, lack of conscience.[3] Another term for these is *nivaranas*: obstructions, hindrances, desire, ill will, sloth, restlessness, doubt.[4]

To study these with a qualified Buddhist teacher would take the seventh step to a deeper place. But in many systems, be it Sutra, Tantra, Mahamudra, Dzogchen, or Zen, there is the notion that, if we cut the delusions out at their root, we will clear away all obstacles and realize total enlightenment. The end goal of all of these systems is just that: total enlightenment, full Buddhahood. This is a very different aim than the 12-Step literature that states, "It doesn't matter that we will not attain a state of perfection or complete humility in our lifetime. The ability to contemplate this grand vision and meditate upon it are rare and priceless gifts in their own right."[5] The 12 Steps can be a way to facilitate this total realization.

In the beginning, I explained Buddhist interpretations of a Higher Power from a conceptual standpoint. In Step Seven, we have to deal with it differently. This is where non-Christians, atheists, and even Buddhists have difficulty with the 12 Steps. When we talk about forming a relationship with God, they often ask, "What if I don't believe in God or a supreme being?" A lot of these people drop out of the program, and even if they stay, they feel like they're not really "in it." The criticism is that, while the 12 Steps tout a Higher Power of our own understanding, it is really a backdoor method of Christian conversion. These critics may have a point.

In the beginning of the steps, talk about a god of our understanding may seem liberal, but when you see the big picture of the steps as a whole, they presuppose belief in a god. That is, a god that we will eventually pray to, humble ourselves before, and ask for help with the most serious of our human issues. The vast majority of the more spiritual-minded recovering people talk of a Creator God, which is not conceptually different from a typical Christian viewpoint. The concept of a single Creator God that made the universe and looks over us all is presupposed, regardless of if we call it Jesus, Universal Mind, Spirit, the Divine, or something else. They all suggest the same basic principle, just with different names.

In all honesty, I'd rather have a nice, warm fuzzy feeling in my tummy about a god that loves me and will take care of me no matter what. This is what much of the 12-Step literature is aiming at: the notion that somebody's going to save you. But the Buddha said he could only show us the path; it's up to us to find our way. We can ask for some help along the way, and surely the blessings of omniscient beings are coming when we ask for them. But ultimately, we are on our own. That's a big difference right there. As the Dalai Lama says, if you're really into Christianity, that is beneficial for you. However, Buddhism challenged those beliefs for me.

Before I took any serious teachings from Tibetan lamas on any complex philosophical systems and practices of Tibetan Buddhism, I simply sat zazen. From that, I somehow got that emptiness underlies everything. But this confused me in relation to the prayers and affirmations I'd used in the past. They are still beautiful and beneficial, and I loved them then and still do now. But the fact is, the long-term results of asking God to save me and using positive thinking just didn't manifest what I needed in my life.

The question not so easily answered is: what is the Buddhist interpretation of having a relationship with a power greater than yourself that will solve your problem? I think this is the fundamental difference between the 12 Steps and Buddhism. The answer will become clearer as we progress toward the twelfth step. For now, let's focus on the principle of removing obstacles to what Buddhists call enlightenment.

Although the steps don't claim that a spiritual awakening equals total enlightenment, I think the steps have that potential when practiced with Buddhism. But we have to be very careful how we talk about the differences. I don't want to alarm anyone by saying that Buddhism will take God out of their lives. If you have God in your life and it's working for you, then that's just fine. It's not either/or; everything else as a 12-Step Buddhist can deepen your practice. But, if this is the sticking point for you in the 12 Steps and the concept of a god doesn't work for you, Buddhism has another approach. In the beginning, after we've removed the substances of our addiction, the literature talks about needing a sufficient substitute and vastly more than that. As a practicing 12-Step Buddhist, that's exactly what I've found. The mysterious "vastly more than that" is what the path delivers for me.

To be clear, Buddhism uses many different approaches, some of which do correspond, at least initially, to a more dualistic idea of subject-object, me and you, us and them. This makes it clear that

Buddhism does include the concept of asking a Higher Being for help; in fact, there are many systems that utilize such techniques. The main difference in this regard between Buddhism and the 12 Steps' Christian God orientation is that in the latter, the end goal is a good relationship with a personal God. The steps, on the surface, seem to stop there. But Buddhism goes beyond even this plateau, although it really takes a qualified Buddhist master to fully lead us into total realization of our ultimate, non-dual Buddha nature. I just want to clarify the similarities and differences, and to make sure you understand where to look for the teachings. One of the greatest Tibetan Buddhist masters of all time is Longchenpa. I don't think you'll find a more concise, pithy summary of the progression of Buddhist teachings (from dual to non-dual) than the following:

> If we analyze the Buddha's words with respect to their progression over time, we find that there are three successive cycles of teachings. As for the first cycle, when one is a beginner, one's afflictive states are reinforced by the perception of a dualism that seems to exist in its own right. Thus, there are a variety of spiritual teachings on the four truths, which demonstrate primarily the process of ethical discernment—deciding what to eliminate and what to use as an antidote—in order to protect the mind from these afflictive states. The intermediate cycle comprises the teachings that characterize phenomena as nonexistent in order to put an end to a preoccupation with antidotes. The final cycle comprises a variety of teachings that definitely ascertain ultimate truth, revealing how the fundamentally unconditioned nature of being abides. These are the three cycles.[6]

It's rather hard to ask the present moment to remove your shortcomings. I don't think we can say a prayer to karma to remove our anger. But there are principal methods in Buddhism where we deal with each and every possible type of affliction, defect, shortcoming, and obstacle. We'll address prayer and purification in Steps Ten and Eleven, but I'd like to show how to make a Buddhist prayer in the context of Step Seven that will help you integrate into self-acceptance after becoming acutely aware of the afflictions and defects in Steps Four through Six.

Buddhist Seventh Step Prayer

My intention is not to suffer from the negative effects of my shortcomings. Beyond myself, I would wish for my loved ones, friends, strangers, and enemies not to suffer from these afflictions and their effects. Beyond all these, I would wish to be of maximum benefit to all suffering beings. In order to make this aspiration real, I vow to do the best I can to act with pure compassion. I ask for help from the entire assembly of my teachers, all of the teachings, and sangha to make absolute compassion my state of body, speech, and mind as quickly as possible, for the benefit of all.

Aspects of Self: Humility

I'd like to speak to the Controller. Controller, I'd like permission to speak to Humility. Is that OK?

Please shift your body and get into the state of Humility.

What do you stand for?
What does the Self look like from your view?
Do you see beyond the character defects of the Addict?
Is your job difficult?
Do you feel that the Self hears you?
Do you ever talk to the Addict?

Sit for a little while like this.

Step 8

Made a list of all persons we had harmed,
and became willing to make amends to them all.

This step is about two things: admitting what we've done to harm others and forgiving the harm they've done to us. It's generally not talked about much in meetings as part of the eighth step, but both the NA and the AA 12-Step books emphasize forgiveness as the key principle of this step. AA says we need to live in "the greatest peace, partnership, and brotherhood." It also says, "These obstacles, however, are very real. The first and one of the most difficult is forgiveness."[1] The NA literature says, if we're still angry at people from our past, we need to practice the spiritual principle of forgiveness.[2] The logic should be clear by this point in the steps. If we want to get along in the world, if we want to learn to feel connected, rather than feel like an alien waiting for our mother ship to come back and pick us up from a planet where we've obviously been mistakenly dropped off . . . then we need to work on relationships.

I made my list and took it to my sponsor's house back in the eighties. There's not much to say about what it was like and what happened in regards to the action of that step. Instead, I'll focus on the underlying principle. I will say that, as the process of practicing all of the principles to the best of my ability became a way of life for me, the work of Steps Eight and Nine became wrapped up with Ten, where we continue to take inventory and admit where we are wrong. However, my perspective on how I practice the principles has changed over the years, and I now see it through the eyes of a 12-Step Buddhist as a practice of preventing harm, correcting mistakes, and forgiving.

Person we harmed	The harm	The defects	Need to forgive?
my partner	fell for a newcomer, broke her heart	lust, greed, pride, fear	no
my mother	didn't go to her funeral	fear, anger	yes
my friend	verbally abused	anger, pride	yes
the "other" political party	slandered, mocked, character assassinated	fear, intellectual pride, self-righteousness	yes
12-Step community	blamed for relapse	fear, pride	yes
Buddhist community	criticized	fear, pride	yes

There's always more to the step than meets the eye. Spiritual growth is almost never linear. That means that we grow on different levels at different rates. The changes are always in flux and rarely obvious while they're happening. The effect of doing Step Eight is like all the others in that it happens in small increments on the surface, but mostly, the real changes happen on a deeper level. One thing is for certain: doing Step Eight will change your life in the long run.

Where Steps Six and Seven focused more on seeing our specific defects in terms of a relationship with a Higher Power, Eight and Nine are focused entirely on our personal history. The two steps go together, but are separate in principle and in function. If you're wondering whether we have some Buddhist practices that will take us to a new level of spiritual growth in regards to these steps, I can honestly say we do. If you get nothing else out of this book, your life will change if you do the practices suggested in this chapter.

The focus of the eighth-step list is to reassess the exact nature of our wrongs and to examine how our actions affected others, so we can be free of the past and live fully in the present.[3] On the preceeding page is a chart that outlines the concept of an eighth-step list, using examples from my own life. I won't say if they're recent or not!

Principle: Forgiveness

Since we'll be focusing on the principle of admitting when we're wrong in Step Ten, the focus here will be on forgiveness. To make the relationship between the principle of the step and the practice clear, remember: the antidote to resentment is forgiveness. The way to move into forgiveness is to practice compassion. We practice compassion by putting ourselves in the other person's shoes. Whatever the wrong done to you by others, if you do these practices, the ice of your resentment will begin to melt away.

Meditation on Forgiveness: Part One

May they be free of suffering and the root of suffering

As with all the meditations in this book, the intent of this one is to loosen the "grip of self-obsession," as NA puts it. We did the meditation of maitri, or lovingkindness, earlier in a general way. It exists in many teachings, but the emphasis here is using it specifically in the eighth-step practice. I can attest to the power of this meditation, as I've used it on many people whom I've resented. Some are tougher than others to forgive, but even the slightest effort in this direction has radically altered my point of view about individuals and even groups. Talk to your sponsor, therapist, or spiritual teacher if you have trouble with any aspect of this or any other practice.

It may be helpful, but isn't required, if you have pictures of things: yourself, your pet, parents, loved ones, friends, strangers (perhaps from a magazine), those you resent, Earth, the stars, etc. You can use these to aid in the visualization. Remember, visualization in Buddhist exercises isn't necessarily about perfectly seeing something in your mind. It's more about how you feel when you think of the person, image, etc. That's one reason why practices that involve awareness of physical sensations are helpful. We start to notice feelings on progressively subtler levels. From there, we learn to notice the effects of practice and can really see concrete change in our lives.

Take out your eighth-step list. Pick someone on the list who is particularly troublesome for you, or if you're not ready, someone for whom you have less resentment. Begin with *shamatha*. Take a few extra minutes to become as calm as possible. Then, begin the practice of maitri toward yourself. Say this in your mind: "May I be free of suffering and the root of suffering." Go over this several times. It may take a whole session just on this part of the practice. It may take longer. As we say in the program, it takes what it takes. Then move to the next one—a person or pet that you feel very loving toward. Say, "May _____ be free of suffering and the root of suffering." Be calm and patient. Notice your body, the place within your heart where you feel love for this being. As you move on, bring up a close friend, "May my friend be free of suffering and the root of suffering." Really allow yourself to notice the feelings stirring within you. Try to bring the compassion from yourself, or your dog if that's easier, outward to the next being. Remember, this practice gets more powerful the more times you do it, and it's easy to incorporate into daily life.

Then, add "May all the strangers who I don't know, have never seen, and will probably never see, all the people in airports, on buses, and crowded streets, be free of suffering and the root of suffering." After allowing the feelings of compassion for yourself and loved ones to expand to strangers, take out the picture or recall from memory a person for whom you still harbor resentment. See him sitting in front of you. See what he's wearing, his hair color, a look on his face that maybe you particularly despise. Notice the feeling of compassion in your heart, but don't try to send it to him yet. Now, recall exactly what your resentment concerns. Remain still, calm, and focused. Just take notice of the resentment, don't call or email them! Just notice. Next, say the words: "May this person with whom I am resentful be free of suffering and the root of suffering." Repeat a few times. Remember, you're trying to expand the feeling of compassion from your heart out to your loved ones, friends, strangers, and to whomever you are resentful toward and need to *forgive*.

Next, say the words of lovingkindness for everyone. Take a look at a picture of the planet for example. Say, "May all beings be free of suffering and the root of suffering."

Meditation on Forgiveness: Part Two

May they enjoy happiness and the root of happiness

You can modify the next part of the maitri meditation to suit your needs. I go all the way through the "may they be free of suffering" piece for all phases of the meditation, from self on to loved ones, etc. Then, if I have time, I will go through each person once again with the following wish/prayer/intention: May _____ enjoy happiness and the root of happiness.

Because I'm an addict and have the personality defects of being overly resentful and self-centered, it's easier to wish that they not suffer than it is to actually want them to be happy. You may have a different way of thinking about it. This is what works for me, so feel free to modify. You could, for example, run through it with: May _____ be free of suffering and the root of suffering; may _____ enjoy happiness and the root of happiness.

If you do this practice every day for a month, going all the way through from self to all beings, you'll notice a shift, perhaps of attitude or of your physical experience. I found that I began to recall this feeling during the course of the day when resentments would pop into my head and before they popped out of my mouth! It's very useful. Anyone who has been in recovery for a while has heard the suggestion to pray for those with whom you are resentful. This is a way to do just that, which is very deep and practical. You can learn to do it anytime. And it works.

Buddhist Integration of Step 8

As we continue to work toward establishing a solid foundation in our relationship to other human beings, the long-term goal of Buddhism remains: to reveal and understand our true nature. The process of practicing integrity is a process of removing obstacles to total realization. One very powerful approach to this is the practice of *tonglen*, exchanging self for others. From NA, "To gain a better understanding of how we may have harmed people, we may want to 'put ourselves in their shoes.'" This is exactly the tonglen practice. *Tong* means "sending out," *len* means "receiving."[4]

This is a radical practice for anyone, let alone the self-centered addict. Trust me, it will change your feelings about yourself, the people in your life, and your place in the world. But it takes time to settle into. Don't expect to do it well immediately. If you can, that's fantastic. Buddhists would say that you must have practiced for many lifetimes to develop such ability! There are no accidents. Either way, in the context of Step Eight, you'll find that there aren't many practices that are so specifically applicable and useful to the addict in recovery.

I first learned this practice from Venerable Robina on retreat, but there are many fine teachers who can help you with this practice. This is a core practice in Tibetan Buddhism in the development of bodhicitta—compassion. It's pretty straightforward. We take in what we don't want on the in-breath, and we give away what we want for ourselves on the out-breath. As the slogans of Atisha say, "These two should ride the breath."

Setting Intention

This practice should be done in a quiet, safe setting. Work on it slowly and don't push yourself too hard. Practice willingness to do tonglen, even just a little. Before you start, think about your intention in doing this practice. You can give yourself a little lovingkindness by saying, "May I do this practice to free myself of suffering and the root of suffering." If you feel able, you can extend the intention of the practice to another person. "May this practice be of benefit to that guy I can't stand in the next cube at work," or whomever. Personalize, don't generalize.

There was an old-timer named Duffy who used to say at meetings, if you want to prove the existence of God to yourself, pray that a specific person has a better day tomorrow. Don't tell anyone you did it, especially that person. Then, watch to see if they do. If you sincerely pray, that person will have a better day. Duffy believed the prayer was that powerful. Buddhists would agree that the prayer of intention is vital to our spiritual progress, and it is extremely beneficial to the recipient. The only way to find out if it's true is to try it!

It's important to set your intention in this way before engaging in tonglen, just as it was important to understand powerlessness in Step One before moving on to the rest of the steps. I say something like, "I'm doing this because I need to work my spiritual program of action." This is a powerful action to alleviate the separating anxiety of resentment and other afflictions.

Meditation: Tonglen—Beginning Stage—Taking In

Begin with *shamatha*. Focus on your breathing, but don't change it. The in- and out-breath of tonglen doesn't have to be exactly in sync with your actual breathing. From a calm space, imagine something in front of you toward which you have an aversion. For example, visualize a dish that you normally wouldn't eat. Notice just the smell of it. Be aware of your aversion to this food. To practice tonglen, consider the willingness to just smell this food that you don't like for the benefit of others. Try to notice the smell. Feeling repulsed by this smell, you can actually practice tonglen just by acknowledging that other people feel this way too. "Other people don't like blackened Cajun catfish. It's not just me. I'm not alone." To know you are not alone in this aversion, the suffering caused by smelling Cajun catfish, is a beginning of tonglen. Remember to develop this practice at your own pace. Don't move on to the next level until you are ready.

The next stage of tonglen involves being willing to experience negativity for the benefit of all others who suffer with it. I visualize the interconnectivity of all beings. It's as if we're all in a big pool, sharing the same water. Maybe it's too cold for some of us, just right for others. My compassion—my willingness to get into the water even though it's too cold for me—will help warm it up for the others who can't tolerate its temperature. So I stick my big toe in, then my foot, eventually my whole body. As I do, my intention, willingness, and compassion begin to warm the water directly around me. As I practice tonglen, the warmth of my bodhicitta begins to affect all others in the same pool of samsara with me.

If I'm doing tonglen—on the *tong* or taking-in part—with stinky Cajun catfish, as I breathe in, I am willing to smell for the benefit of others. Be careful not to let your Dharma Pride kick in. If you hear a voice saying, "Wow, I really am an excellent practitioner. I'm totally spiritual for doing this," then you better check it before you wreck it. The practice is *not* about pumping up the ego but quite the opposite. It's about dealing with aversion and attachment, developing compassion, and the willingness to bear suffering. So take in a breath, remember not to hyperventilate. Just visualize and imagine the smell coming into your nose in the form of black, smelly, Cajun catfish smoke. Maybe it's kind of burnt and rotten. Be willing to breathe it in for the sake of all who hate it. We all hate it. Nobody likes this crappy catfish. Say, "I'm going to take it in to help everybody get over it." This is the taking-in part of tonglen. If you're able to take the practice this far, you're doing great. Don't make yourself sick; just have a little willingness.

Meditation: Tonglen—Beginning Stage—Giving Out

If willing, we practice the next level of taking-in by having the willingness to take a bite of the Cajun catfish. Take a mental bite. Chew it up, *bleh*! And swallow it for the benefit of suffering restaurant-goers everywhere. This is tonglen, taking it in. Working like this will have an impact on your sense of aversion. Perhaps the next time you're walking by something that smells foul and your stomach begins to wrench, you'll know your tonglen practice is working if you hear in the back of your mind, "I can take in this smell for the sake of others." Isn't that fascinating?

The mental effort required to do this practice is achievable by most. Just keep trying, little by little, until you can visualize the nastiest, foulest meal you never want to eat. Gobble it down for the sake of those who suffer. Then we take things a little further, by giving out what we want for ourselves. I practice by sometimes taking it in all day and sometimes giving it out. Sometimes I do an in-breath, taking in what I don't want, and an out-breath giving out what I do want. I'm flexible. If there are too many rules, I have a tendency to move on to something else.

For giving it away, the process is the same. Maybe it'd be easier in your mind to give away what you want to those you love. But, if you consider giving away your car keys, as Robina taught us, to a wino on the street, then it might be a little more of a challenge. So to practice the giving away, imagine your favorite dinner that your mom used to make you or your favorite smell or most-loved jewelry. Just make a beginning. For our purposes, we'll use the delicious macaroni and cheese I loved as a little boy.

I'm seeing the bubbling, creamy macaroni with the luscious cheesy goodness boiling over the edge of the olive green Crockware pot as my mom takes it out of the oven. It's got a nice brown, oven-baked crust on the top, and my mouth fills up with saliva as the smell wafts into my nose. I'm going to have two bowls. But wait, there's that jerk from the cubicle next to me who rocks in his squeaky desk chair all damn day. I prefer to serve him crappy Cajun catfish! But I'm now willing to try a little tonglen, so I imagine breathing out, and as I breathe out all the lovely Velveeta orangey yumminess of my mom's homemade mac 'n' cheese, it goes over the divider to his desk, where he engulfs the entire bowl, leaving nothing for me. My mom next comes around the corner with a nice big pile of disgusting Cajun catfish for me. I breathe it in, accepting what I don't want. Breathing out, I send the yummy goodness that I do want to everybody else out there who needs it.

This is in principle the practice of tonglen. You can eventually get to the point where you sit for an hour imagining all of the amazingly wonderful treats and beautiful things that you want for yourself going out in an offering to the nastiest, most hateful people in the world. Then you get to take in all of the foulest, most horrible things that anyone would have aversion to for yourself. Breathe in the pain for yourself, breathe out the pleasure for others.

There's a reason I started with a simple but more abstract version of this practice. You might not be willing to try the full version. Remember, do this at your own pace. But, in Step Nine, we'll use another level of tonglen to deepen our commitment to being of maximum benefit, developing compassion, and correcting the wrongs we've done to others.

Dedication

In Tibetan Buddhism, we dedicate the merits of our practice to the full and total enlightenment of every single suffering being. Remember, we set our intention before the practice, and now we tie up the end of the practice with the dedication. Lama Zopa Rinpoche says that the benefits of dedicating Dharma practice to the saving of all beings are immeasurable. We accumulate good karma and merits that will help us on our own path of developmental Buddhahood. To dedicate, we can say something like, "May the fruits of this practice end suffering for everyone," or "I dedicate the merits of this practice to the enlightenment of all beings." You can make one up. In our 12-Step Sangha meetings, we say, "May this practice help all suffering addicts." If all of that is too abstract, make it concrete and say, "May it help somebody."

Aspects of Self: The Victim

I'd like to speak to the Controller. Controller, I'd like permission to speak to the Victim. Is that OK?

Please shift your body and get into the state of the Victim.

Whom am I speaking to?
What's it like to be the Victim?
What have they done to make you this way?
Is there anything you can do about it?
Does it take a lot of energy to keep going?
Do you feel that the Addict listens to you?

Sit for a while like this.

Aspects of Self: The Forgiver

I'd like to speak to the Controller. Controller, I'd like permission to speak to the Forgiver. Is that OK?

Please shift your body to get into the state of the Forgiver.

Whom am I speaking to?
Do you feel soft inside? Compassionate?
How do you feel about the Victim?
What do you feel for the Resenter?
How much forgiveness do you have?
Are there any limits to what you can forgive?
Is there anyone that you wouldn't forgive?
Can you forgive the Addict?

Sit for a little while like this.

Step 9

*Made direct amends to such people whenever possible,
except when to do so would injure them or others.*

Most addicts, regardless of the type of addiction, have some history of using and abusing those in their path. The thought of directly confronting the damage we've done to others is the farthest thing from our minds when we walk through the doors into recovery. But, as we say in meetings, the steps are in order for a reason. By the time we get to these later steps, we'll be in a different headspace than when we started. NA says, "We would never be able to approach the people to whom we owe amends in the spirit of humility if we hadn't been practicing these principles before now."[1] I had a friend in recovery that used to say, "We're willing to go to any lengths to take certain steps. That means, if we're not ready to take certain steps, we're not willing to go to any lengths."

I was twenty-three when I started making amends. The way we hear about making amends in meetings is often related to finances: child support, credit cards, student loans, tapping the till. Some with gambling issues have run their tabs up and their luck out, often well into six digits. Sex addicts may have destroyed relationships and even lives with predatory behavior. Binger/purgers often cause irreparable damage to their bodies, while meth-tweakers have ripped off everything from parking meters to doorknobs. My amends the first time around were pretty run-of-the-mill.

Most of the harm I had done by the time I got into recovery was easily repairable. I fixed my credit, followed my sponsor's advice, and stayed out of my old girlfriend's life—and her family's. I got a job, paid people back, and for a time, felt like I was pretty even with the world. What I didn't see for a long time is how my attitude, and the little things I said and did, greatly affected people—even during sobriety, long into relapse, and for a considerable time into sobriety v.2.0.

What's important here is to add something new to the step work. With the God steps, we needed to draw parallels and illustrate the differences between the 12 Steps and Buddhism. This step requires actions that are intensely spiritual and totally necessary if we're to get better.

Motives

I mentioned earlier that, as Buddhists, we set our intention before doing Dharma practice. In recovery, we call it checking our motives. But the Buddhist slant is a little different, in that the teachings tell us to go beyond merely checking to actually creating new motives. There are different ways of approaching this in Buddhism. Some schools say that if you sit and be mindful long enough, eventually you'll have more compassion. Others say if we dedicate our lives to accumulating merits, we'll be able to realize the actual enlightened compassion of a Buddha. Still others say if we delve into the direct and real knowledge of our true condition, we won't have to spend time fabricating compassion—it will occur naturally. There are many methods. But the requirement to have good intentions is common to all the Buddhist teachings that I've come across. Even the lower schools, which teach enlightenment for the sake of individual salvation, say that we need to stop creating negative karma to become enlightened. The higher schools say that if we set our intention to help everybody, then we can realize the truth much faster. So we all learn to set intention as Buddhists, from wherever we start. In the ninth step, setting intention is a key part of the process.

The way we set intention in recovery is to ask ourselves what our motives are. We're making amends to the person we've harmed, so we go through the inventory process from the beginning with a sponsor. We carefully reflect on what we've done and in the process learn to become honest enough to make things right. We don't make amends just so we feel better.

The benefit of Step Nine is that we get to look the world straight in the eye again. John C. said that he wanted to die with a clean slate, and he did by working the program. "Get free or die," he used to tell me. Buddhism takes this principle to a new level with the practice of taking vows.

I found that taking Buddhist lay vows helped me with my commitment to lead a better life. These vows are for those who want to seriously enter the Buddhist path but aren't interested or able to become full-time monks or nuns. According to Venerable Robina, the nun with whom I took my vows, this practice actually acts as a deterrent to situations that would challenge our ability to keep them. In other words, the vows act as a sort of protection. They are simply: not taking what isn't given, not lying or using harsh speech, not killing anything (even bugs), not engaging in sexual misconduct (whatever might cause harm to others), and not taking intoxicants. These vows coincide nicely with the steps in that they give us a code of ethics that helps us conduct our lives with integrity.

During relapse, all the integrity I'd developed in recovery was shot. I'd just as soon lie as tell you my name. I shoplifted daily without even thinking about it. This is a typical story heard every day in meetings. That said, we do the obvious: we pay back the money, all the money. We pay child support and old bills, and tell the boss we stole from the company. But then there's the less obvious work: living amends.

The living amends is how we choose to live our life in light of all harm we've ever caused anyone, anywhere. It's about more than making apologies. It's about literally becoming a new person in how we think and act. NA says that we "mend our fences and we mend our ways,"[2] and that "amends is a two-stage process. First we make the amends and then we need to change the behavior."[3] The following illustrates methods that are non-typical but still from a 12-Step and a Buddhist perspective.

Principle: Restitution

"As a result of working the step, we are fee to live in the present moment."[4] There was no way I could tolerate my present moment without cleaning up the "wreckage" of my past, as AA calls it. Paramahansa Yogananda said that we're like radio tuners, but we have a lot of static built up. We need to tune in the station (with our meditation practice), so we can hear the spiritual truth that is always being broadcast. The steps help us tune in to the right spiritual frequency.

We can use the practices we've learned so far to prepare ourselves mentally and spiritually for making amends. We can also use this practice later as a way of altering our attitude any time we need it. NA says "the impact of realizing how deeply our actions have affected other people shocks us out of our self-obsession."[5] That's really the goal of all of the 12 Steps and Buddhism as well, as I hope you're beginning to see. There's nothing more powerful than Step Nine work to break us out of self-obsession.

Meditation on Making Amends

Begin with *shamatha*. From a place of nonjudgmental calmness, work on the maitri meditation, the one that begins with "May I be free of suffering . . ." Be flexible and simply focus on the feelings in your body as you consider the suffering you have caused others both in and out of recovery. Reflect on the damage done. Use whatever comes up from your amends list. Next, visualize one of the people that you owe amends. Think about your mother, spouse, or another close person. Acknowledge quietly to yourself that you have caused her suffering. Look at her face. Notice that she is crying from the pain you have caused her. Notice the suffering you have caused. See the tears coming down her face. Let yourself feel the emotions in your gut. Notice the tears.

Now, lining up behind this person, you can see others whom you have harmed, and they are also crying. Feel their chests heaving with the suffering they feel. Be willing to sit quietly and tolerate this moment. It's difficult, but you're just using your mind now, just imagining. See behind all the people who have suffered as the result of the action that you're considering here, and see that behind them are all the people who have ever been harmed by this type of action. They are all crying, all suffering from the pain this has caused. Stretch your imagination as far as it will go. All of these people have harmed and have been harmed in an endless, infinite cycle of suffering. The tears fall like a torrential downpour, filling up the streets with sorrow and pain just from this one type of action. Imagine for a moment that you are willing, if only you had the power, to make right all of this suffering due to this single type of action. Notice that your willingness, not just for the person on your amends list, but for everyone. This takes honesty and courage, which you've been developing. It is hard. But you can do this, at least mentally. Consider what you owe these people. You owe them more than an apology. You owe them change. Imagine that from this moment onward, you vow to abstain from that type of action. You can say to yourself and to all these crying faces before you, "I will not hurt you or anyone else in this way again. I am sorry. I want to make it right."

Next, you can tell them about the character defects that caused you to do this harm. You can ask for forgiveness. In your mind, in the quietness and privacy of your meditation, you can beg them for forgiveness. You can get down on your knees and cry. Just feel what it's like to know the suffering of others and the willingness to set it straight. Now, go back to the first person that you meditated on. Ask them, by name, "How can I make it right?" Close your meditation with openness to this question. How *can* you make it right?

There are many ways to make amends. Some of the damage can't be fixed directly. For those cases, the NA literature states that, "Many found answers in dedicating our lives to helping other addicts and other forms of service to humanity."[6] I believe that Buddhism offers a viable way to live this principle of dedicating our lives to helping addicts and everyone else. Your amends may be complete, and you might feel like you don't owe anybody anything, but if you're still suffering and you don't know why, these explorations will help you approach it from a new angle.

For example, the Buddhist explanation for why we may still be suffering after many years of sobriety, having completed the steps and done all the required work, is that we have created incalculable negative karma based on our self-centeredness—not only in this life, but in an infinite number of past lives. Because of this negative karma, we can't see our true selves, our Buddha nature. To clear away the obscurations to this truth, we need to practice the Dharma. We can practice 12-Step Dharma to good effect in and beyond our recovering community. And we can get better as we do so. I wouldn't be here to tell you if this weren't true. But spiritual work takes guts. Awareness of the pain and its causes is great motivation to change.

The NA literature on this step says that it "takes great discipline, personal sacrifice and commitment,"[7] and "We may owe amends to our community or society as a whole. We look for ways to give, not take." That is to me what the 12-Step Buddhist path represents.

Buddhist Integration of Step 9

Even though Buddhism is about awareness and compassion, you won't find the same attitude about making amends in the Buddhist community. The way addicts are used to sharing and working our recovery program seems really odd to most people who don't live the steps as a way of life. In the sanghas I've been involved with, it's rare for people to even admit they're wrong. I'm used to being around 12-Step people who more or less understand that they have to get honest and stay honest to stay clean and sober. Someone in the program may slight you or worse, but you can usually count on the fact that they'll eventually make amends. We don't sit around waiting or demanding that people owe us amends, but we do know that addicts who work a program won't let an offense go unresolved forever. They work *their* program, and that's one of the reasons why the 12-Step movement has been so enduring and successful. But many Buddhists I've met don't see it this way. I think if they did, it would be helpful.

The cultivation of an enlightened attitude
Is accompanied at the various levels

By interest, altruistic thought,
Full maturation, and likewise abandonment of the veils.[8]

Bodhicitta in Sanskrit is "awakened mind." The mind of enlightenment. Bodhicitta is divided into two aspects: relative and absolute. Relative is comprised of the intention or wish followed by the actual meditation of developing bodhicitta. Absolute bodhicitta is the realization of shunyata, or the emptiness of all phenomena.[9]

The Jewel Ornament of Liberation states, "The essence of the cultivation of bodhicitta is the desire to achieve perfect, complete enlightenment for others' benefit."[10] In the Mahayana path, which is the Great Vehicle that carries us to enlightenment faster since we're doing the work not just for our sake but for the benefit of others, bodhicitta is a widely diffused topic. I'll cover it in general here, but you'll want to explore this further with your teachers. My purpose is to connect the ideas of bodhicitta with the practices of the steps. I've found the recovery community to be an excellent and fertile ground for practicing the development of bodhicitta.

Meditation: Tonglen—Advanced Stage

The following exercise is extremely helpful for reducing my sense of victim-hood and increasing my connectedness to the world around me. This really puts us into the practice of integrating the ninth step with Buddhism. The point, as always, is to use Buddhist practices to deepen our experience of the steps in a way that isn't normally addressed in meetings.

The Tibetan lamas would say that this practice is not just for our imagination. A bodhisattva is really willing to take on the suffering of others to become a fully completed Buddha. An essential part of being on the bodhisattva path is being willing to take on the suffering of others and give up the pleasure we would want for ourselves. Talk about "What an order! I can't go through with it!" as we hear in almost every meeting. The spiritual way of life is not easy. But neither is addiction.

Do *shamatha*. Find your calm space. Next, consider a person on your eighth-step list with whom you have some serious difficulty. Pick somebody that you've harmed whom you owe amends. You may have done something to this person because you felt threatened by him on some level and wanted to retaliate. The practice will help you get over resentment and offer your forgiveness—eliminating any sense of victimhood—and facilitate willingness to make amends to them. If you don't have his picture, write his name on a piece of paper and put it in front of you.

Imagine that this person suffers, just like you do. Consider that they have their own history or baggage—whether it was a poor upbringing, bad breaks, physical or mental illness, etc. Say, "This person feels pain, just like I do. They don't want to suffer, just as I don't want to suffer." Imagine them at the worst time in their life, the most painful part of their past that you know about or can imagine. See this person getting beaten after school by a drunken father perhaps. Put yourself in their shoes, emotionally, at the time of their extreme suffering.

Next, see yourself as the happiest you've ever been, in the best time of your life. If that's hard for you, as it is for many of us with troubled pasts, try to imagine yourself with everything you could ever want. You are totally happy. You have all the money, friends, good reputation, great looks, perfect body weight, best partner, and anything else you could wish for. Now, imagine walking up to this person in his or her time of suffering, at their lowest. See yourself literally trading places with them. Give this person everything: your clothes, house keys, family, and friends. Just notice what it feels like. Next, be totally willing to take on this person's problems and fears, their past, present, and future sufferings as your own. What does it feel like to be that person? See his or her suffering in the form of black, nasty smoke that stinks from the stench of a lifetime of suffering. See the smoke oozing out of their mouth, orifices, and every pore of their body. Feel the black, acridness of their disease. Be willing to smell it. Taste it. Breathe it in. Take it on. *Be* their suffering for them. Bear it like a Buddha. Take it in, and take it on. Just let yourself consider this possibility.

As you exhale, breathe out the light within you. Imagine all of the happiness and wonderful things that you have or wished you had. Visualize a warm, rainbow light swirling up from within your heart, your breast, coming out of your mouth, through your eyes, out your ears, radiating light and hope, compassion and serenity. See this sad, suffering person, breathing out their putrid, bloody puss, vomiting it up like somebody in the cancer ward. Send them your light. Feel their pain. Give them your white, rainbow luminescence. Let it wash out of you and into him. See them breathing it in, being transformed into a beautiful array of color and beauty. As you do this, keep taking their darkness into your body. Now relax. This is hard work.

The Paramitas

Generosity, moral ethics, patience,
Perseverance, meditative concentration, and
   discriminating wisdom—
These six comprise the training in action bodhicitta.[11]

We all know that practice makes perfect. "If you want to learn it right, practice it right. Otherwise you practice your mistakes," says Dan Balmer, my guitar guru. Similar to this jazz wisdom, on the Mahayana path we practice the perfections of a bodhisattva. We "act as if" in all things as part of our spiritual development.

While the practice of all the Paramitas—perfections—is interrelated and relevant to us as recovering addicts, the practice of the Perfection of Perseverance is directly applicable to Step Nine because this step calls for intense action. To practice the ninth step requires an understanding of all the preceding principles and adds diligence and sustained effort to the list. It's easy for us as addicts to become emotionally overwhelmed at the prospect of making a direct amends. We can shut down emotionally, become physically sick, depressed. If we're paralyzed with laziness, fear, and regret, this step won't work in our life. To apply Buddhist practice in this area, it's useful to practice perseverance.

Practicing the Perfection of Perseverance

Reflection on the faults and virtues,
Definition, classification,
Characteristics of each classification,
Increase, perfection, and
Result—
These seven comprise the perfection of perseverance.[12]

Reflection on the Faults and Virtues

We start the process of reflecting on our faults and virtues in Step One and carry it through all the way to Step Twelve. It's important to realize that most people don't consider their faults and virtues in the context of spiritual growth. The non-practitioner might feel down about certain things or vain about others. An addict, however, is usually on one end of the extreme or another.

As a Buddhist, I practice the perfections as the bodhisattva path, but I already do much of this in my recovery program. As a 12-Step Buddhist, it is good to know that my efforts in recovery have wider implications as well. The Ornament of Mahayana Sutra says: "Perseverance will liberate one from the view of the transitory aggregates. If one has perseverance, one will achieve unsurpassable enlightenment quickly."[13]

Definition and Classification

The definition of perseverance is a feeling of joy in virtue.[14]

The literature says, "The joy of living is the theme of AA's Twelfth Step, and action is its key word."[15] I'll add that the joy of living is impossible to achieve without perseverance. The action of persevering taken with the intention to progress on the spiritual path, not only for our own recovery, but for the benefit of other addicts and beyond, is critical and requires commitment.

The teachings discuss perseverance as the antidote to laziness. A Zen teaching says, "Practice as if your hair was on fire." The Letter to a Friend says: "If your hair or clothes accidentally catch fire, / Postpone even this extinguishing. / Make effort to stop rebirth in samsara / Because there is no other more important work than that."[16]

In the 12 Steps, we need to understand the "hopelessness and futility" of our situation to lay a foundation for progress on the path of recovery. Similarly, Buddhism asks us to understand the futility of life in samsara as the underpinning of our evolution on the path to complete enlightenment.

Characteristics of Each Classification

Within each of these aspects, the Buddhist teachings outline examples of perseverance. One such example is called the Perseverance of Armor. The bodhisattva bhumis say: "I will be happy even if I have to stay in hell for thousands of kalpas in order to liberate the suffering of one sentient being. To say nothing of a short period of time and a small amount of suffering. This is called the perseverance of the armor of a bodhisattva."[17]

Another example is called the Perseverance of Application. This one involves dealing with afflictive emotions that are the cause of suffering. The steps are an excellent way to apply this principle. Often, in meetings, you'll hear that they don't know why it works, they just know *that* it works. When we become aware of the connections and implications of the 12-Step principles as they relate to advanced concepts in Buddhism, we can apply these principles on the path to total realization—beyond mere sobriety. I'm not saying that you need to do this in terms of your recovery. However, I do want people to know that the power of the 12 Steps when combined with Buddhism is astronomical. The further we go into this, the deeper we get into the Buddhist teachings. You're not obligated to do anything or believe anything. Just simply being aware of these connections will alter your course forever. Just like a laser beam pointed into space.

Insatiable Perseverance

If I feel that I never have enough sensual objects,
Which are like honey smeared on a razor's edge,
Then why should I ever feel that I have had enough
Merit which ripens in happiness and peace?

Gampopa[18]

My sponsor says that in order to stay sober, we need to have a spiritual thirst. I don't run across a lot of people, even in recovery, who share the same kind of thirst that I have. It's relentless, inextinguishable. Like John C. said, "I've got an itch I can't scratch." I know that it's because I'm sicker than most that I'm more desperate for spiritual answers than many others. I'm lucky, because I have to practice.

When you're suffering, it doesn't feel lucky. However, when I get goose bumps during a Buddhist teaching because I see the connections between the 12 Steps and the path of full Buddhahood, it's like getting to that spiritual sweet spot I've been looking for all of my life. It's scratching that itch, temporarily quenching the thirst—even if just for an instant. And that feeling is a taste of spiritual realization that keeps me going on the path. It's about the coolest thing ever— even better than being at Led Zeppelin on four hits of Mr. Natural, and with better results.

The Result of Perseverance

The bodhisattva bhumis say: "By fully perfecting the paramita of perseverance, bodhisattvas attained the unsurpassable, perfect, complete enlightenment, are attaining complete enlightenment, and will attain complete enlightenment."[19]

Aspects of Self: The Amender

I'd like to speak to the Controller. Controller, I'd like permission to speak to the Amender. Is that OK?

Please shift your body and get into the state of the Amender.

Whom am I speaking to?

Do you know how to make things right?

Do you have a tough job?

Do you feel that the other aspects of Self listen to you?

Do you want some help to make things right?

Would you like to ask the Addict, the Controller, the Resenter, and the others for their help to make things right?

Please ask them all now. Say, "I need your help to make things right."

Sit for a little while like this.

Step 10

We continued to take personal inventory, and when we were wrong, promptly admitted it.

I use regular psychotherapy as part of an ongoing tenth step. I see therapy as part of my recovery, not the other way around. I keep a dream journal and have practiced other forms of writing, such as Julia Cameron's "Morning Pages" from *The Artist's Way*, as part of ongoing inventory. My experience as a 12-Stepper all of these years has catalyzed the practice of introspection, and I've learned many ways to keep it alive.

One good way to stay in the awareness of self-examination is by surrounding yourself with winners in recovery. In the early years, I would befriend addicts exclusively. Few of us back then had any idea how to relate to the normies, so we stuck to each other out of habit. We honed our skills by looking inward and pointed out each other's faults with razor-quick tongues. Addicts know how addicts think, and it's hard to fool anybody when everyone's working a program.

It's hard to believe that after years of sobriety, with all the people I saw suffering in addiction, I would return to using. When we look to the literature for an explanation, NA says "some members relapse, even after long periods of clean time, because they have become complacent in recovery, allowing their resentments to build and refusing to acknowledge their wrongs."[1] The tenth, eleventh, and twelfth steps are what we call the maintenance or continuous growth steps.[2] These steps are how we maintain our sobriety and continue to grow.

The disease of addiction continues to expand and deepen its roots in us, even while we work a program. I don't know why this is so, but I can attest to it from my experience and the experience of others over the years, and knowing this wasn't even enough to keep me sober through my journey into the Funnel. This time through, I do it differently. I'm a 12-Step Buddhist. So far, so good.

The tenth step is a compilation of many recovery principles that we've worked with so far. One of the most difficult to apply for me is the principle of admitting that I'm wrong, promptly or otherwise. The step gives me the opportunity to let go of my ego and drop the normal defenses. It's opposite to what we learn in our competitive society that fosters an attitude of winning at any cost. As the *AA Big Book* says, "Common sense would thus become uncommon sense."[3] That means that the spiritual walk requires some different rules than those we learned in childhood as survival skills.

Principle: Admission

We started practicing the principle of admission in Step One. We've actually practiced admission along the way, in some form or another, in all of the steps. It is, however, useful to isolate the principle so we can examine it more closely. This is one way to amplify our awareness of the principle, so we can use it consciously as part of the ongoing recovery and spiritual program.

Admitting we're wrong is a critical skill in recovery. Our ego hates doing it. As Chuck C. said, "I'm totally convinced that the only roadblock between me and you, and me and my God is the human ego. It's the only roadblock there is. I further believe that the best definition you'll ever find for the human ego is, 'The feeling of conscious separation from God.'"[4] I can't think of a better example of ego than feeling right—more righteous than another and trying to prove them *wrong*. Step Ten is the perfect antidote.

The point of the next meditation is to create a mental atmosphere that's a little on the extreme side, so we can really feel the energy we're dealing with when we get righteous. Take out a pencil before you begin. Try to come up with the one thing in the world that you find totally unacceptable. For an addict, this shouldn't take too long.

Let's use lying as the example. I had a friend who lied to me to help another friend. He was caught in the middle and chose to protect the other person's feelings by not telling me the truth. In the past, I'd say something like, "You lied to me, you broke my trust, and therefore, you don't deserve my friendship." So this is the kind of example of righteousness I'd like you to call to mind. Pick a juicy one.

In recovery, nobody says we won't ever get angry or that we need to be perfect people or Buddhists. We need realistic expectations. So when somebody does something to us that we can't accept, and we do overreact, we've got the tenth step to fall back on, to keep our egos in check. The goal of this practice is to really feel the fires of self-righteous indignation. By this point in recovery, we're beyond saying that such a defect is not a problem for us.

Meditation on Being Wrong

Begin with *shamatha*. Find a place of relaxed calmness. When you feel calm, go ahead and call up a situation that really lights your fuse. Visualize the person in your mind who causes you this distress. As an addict you'll have no problem starting the argument in your head. See and hear yourself telling the person or group how she wronged you, how morally corrupt she is, that the situation is totally unfair, and so on. Get into it silently in your meditation space. Notice your breathing. Notice your feet on the floor. Keep them there. Don't reach for your phone to text! Just notice your respiration, heart rate, skin temperature, muscles around your face and neck as you tell them off. Are your eyes more squinted? Where do you put your tongue when you get like this? Do you clench your teeth?

Now take a mental step back. Focus on the breath. Return to a place of nonjudgmental calm. Give it a few minutes to find the calm place. How did it feel in your body and mind to be *so right*? Meditation is about getting familiar, and this one is about getting familiar with the experience of being right. Next, think about your condition as an addict on the spiritual path. Can you afford to be angry? Would you really rather be right than happy? How about the other party—their feelings? Are you willing to go to any lengths to stay in recovery? If your actions caused the other person harm, then you're wrong, and it's time to admit it.

Bring the subject of your meditation back into your awareness. From this calm place, taking into consideration all of what you've learned about yourself in the 12-Step process, look at this person with compassion. Tell her that you know you were wrong to speak harshly to her. Say it in your mind, "I am wrong." Say it over and over. The mantra is, "I am wrong, I am wrong, I am wrong." Say it with compassion for yourself, and for the person you have harmed. Notice your body as you do this meditation. Stay in the calmness. Stay with the compassion.

Take this practice with you out into your day. The next time you're wrong, it won't be so hard to admit it to others if you can admit it to yourself first.

Buddhist Integration of Step 10

In Tibetan Buddhism, we practice different methods of purification, one of which is often done as a review of the day. To study the Heart Sutra and practice Zen is a way to purify. To refresh your memory, Vajrayana practice is Tibetan. It always involves deities. The works that describe these practices are called Tantras and they always require an empowerment to be effective. It's all a part of the Dharma, or sacred truth. But the methods and timelines to enlightenment vary, according to the capacities of the individual practitioners.

A Tibetan Tenth Step

When I first learned this method, I said, "This is a tenth step!" The basic idea is that we have all the imprints of past actions in our mind stream. These karmic seeds are ready to shoot up with the right set of circumstances—dormant until the ripening conditions present themselves. Just like a walnut won't grow into a tree without the conditions of rich soil, moisture, and sunlight, our karma doesn't ripen until we act with intention. We have accumulated infinite negative karma from beginningless past lives and have been reborn in cyclic existence over and over as all manner of suffering beings. In all these forms, we've caused much harm, propelled powerlessly from lifetime to lifetime, driven blindly by our karmic imprints. For example, when we were in the state of consciousness known as the animal realm, we mindlessly killed millions of times, just to survive. The teachings say, when we become fortunate enough to be born into the human realm, we are able to find a teacher, hear the Dharma, learn the methods, practice consciously, and realize our true natural state. But there are blocks, obscurations, because of our past karma, which impede our progress despite the most valiant efforts.

There are many methods of purification, from simple mindfulness to the highest stages of Mahamudra. The concept is mentioned in the sutras, but the results are faster in the Tantras. The Tantras, you'll recall, utilize teachings that have come to realized practitioners through dreams and visions. They involve deities that represent different aspects of the enlightened Buddhas.

Vajrasattva is the main tantric deity of the methods of purification in the Tibetan Buddhist traditions and one that I have experienced. Many lamas recommend that serious practitioners do a three-month retreat to achieve a total of one hundred thousand Vajrasattva mantra recitations. That seems to be the number at which practitioners begin to get some clarity in their realizations.

By calling on the power of enlightened beings, such as Vajrasattva, we connect with their healing energy to purify negative, unripe seeds that would otherwise bring bad results. This explanation occurred to me as the result of doing this practice over time. Much like the magic mystery of why the 12 Steps work, we leave the question of Vajrasattva purification to faith—or confidence if you prefer. The only way to see if it works is to try it. What have you got to lose besides suffering?

It's important to clarify that the practice I'm about to share with you is one that I've created to give the reader a beginning. It is a compilation of ideas, derived from oral teachings I've received from different teachers. This practice is geared toward the recovering addict, so it incorporates ideas from 12-Step recovery and Tibetan Buddhism. With any of the Vajrayana practices, it's very important that the practitioner obtain a proper initiation from a qualified lineage holder in order to achieve the maximum result of the practice. I make no claim to be such a teacher. What I pass on to you is what has worked for me. I hope that you will find as much benefit as I've gained from these and similar practices. If you find that you would like to go further, please find a lama to take you to the next level.

Remember to be flexible in how you do this practice. Rewrite it for yourself if you have some ideas of how it might affect you more deeply. Sit down with a sponsor, fellow practitioner, or other friend and do it together. Make sure to give your chosen friend a copy of this book so you both have the background.

Meditation on Four Opponent Powers (Refuge, Regret, Recitation, Renunciation) and Vajrasattva Practice

This is put in the first person so you can read it aloud if you like. Take what you want and leave the rest, but this is a Buddhist practice. Rather than a watered-down version, it's amped up for those of us in recovery.

Intention

Begin with *shamatha*. Then set your intention: I do this practice because I want to be free of suffering and its causes. I would like the effect to be beneficial to as many suffering beings as possible, even those I don't know. In particular, I would like to do this practice for everyone I've ever harmed through my addictive nature.

Taking Refuge

I realize that karma is the action which has the result. Negative actions will bring negative results, while positive actions bring positive results.

Because of the afflictions—anger, attachment, ignorance, and the rest—I've caused suffering to myself and others. On my own, I'm powerless to change the past, I have little ability to live in the present, and I fear more suffering in the future. I need some spiritual help.

I feel on an intuitive level that the Buddha is trustworthy and helpful. When I meditate, hear teachings, or see a statue of the Buddha, I feel a sense of calm. For this reason, I take refuge in the Buddha. When I meditate, listen to teachings, or read the words of the Buddha, I get a sense of what he was teaching. For this reason, I take refuge in the Dharma. Because I know I can't do it (recovery/enlightenment) alone, I take refuge in my community of fellow practitioners—the sangha—in realms seen and unseen.

Regret

Through my step work, inventory process, sharing with my sponsor, prayer, and meditation, I am aware of how selfish I can be. I have good qualities too, which have often been hidden behind my shortcomings. I need to practice Dharma so I can be the best person possible and bring happiness instead of pain to others. My intention is not to wallow in regret but to stay in touch with the nature of my addiction. I need to remember the suffering I have caused in the distant and recent past. I acknowledge those past harms every day so I can be free from causing them again. Today, I will take a few minutes to recall if I've caused agitation, hurt feelings, disrespect, or other negative feelings. I don't ever want anyone to suffer because of my actions. I feel the pain that I cause others. They feel pain, just like I do. I don't want to suffer, and they don't want to suffer. I have the courage to stay in this awareness. In this way, I am connected to other beings.

Recitation and Visualization

Vajrasattva, the deity of white light and purifying, compassionate wisdom, sits before me. He is the size of a mountain. Still. Unmoving, like the profound emptiness of infinite space. His form is youthful. He is covered in amazing jewels, glistening, alive with radiant color. His body is not solid but rainbow luminescent, swirling in a glow of a billion colored lights. As I look closer, I can't find him because his body is like a diamond shimmering in the brilliant sunlight, reflecting oceans of blue, penetrating wisdom in every possible direction. He is seated on a thousand-petal, multicolored lotus flower, which represents the blossoming enlightenment of practitioners like me, the fully bloomed realizations of infinite Buddhas in a multitude of dimensions, and the imminent awakening of all future Buddhas.

Vajrasattva's face is of amazing, ethereal beauty. His eyes are blue and empty, like the sky. His mouth is red and full. All of his features are clear and pronounced. The feelings I get from looking at his face are compassion and love. Just being in his presence is a cause of peace and stillness in my mind.

From his heart a small white ball of light begins to emanate. Breathing in, I notice the light beginning to grow. As I breathe out, the ball of white light begins to emanate warmth. After a few moments, the light begins to reach out of the heart of Vajrasattva, the heart of compassion, the heart of enlightenment. The ball of white light grows larger and warmer with every breath, and I become more relaxed. I am calm. As I become more and more relaxed, the light from Vajrasattva is purifying me with its very nature. As I breathe, the light expands until it reaches my heart. Breathing in, I feel the warm, white luminescent light begin to fill my body. My own body becomes transparent, like a thin vase of the finest crystal. The light from Vajrasattva's heart fills me with warmth and clarity. I am totally relaxed. From this place of absolute relaxation, I will recite the mantra of purification as many times as possible. As I recite the mantra, I feel its energy filling my body, emanating through my speech, purifying my mind of all obstacles to enlightenment.

Note: You can do the short mantra or, when you're ready, the hundred-syllable mantra. Remember, it's more about intention than pronunciation. For an mp3 of the one correct pronunciation of the mantra, visit the12stepbuddhist.com.

The short version:

OM VAJRASATTVA HUM

The One Hundred–Syllable Mantra:

> OM VAJRASATTVA SAMAYA MANUPALAYA,
> VAJRASATTVA DENOPA TITHA, DIDO ME BHAVA, SUTO
> KAYO ME BHAVA, SUPO KAYO ME BHAVA, ANURAKTO
> ME BHAVA, SARVA SIDDHI ME PRAYATSA, SARVA KARMA
> SU TSAME, TSITTAM SHRIYAM KURU HUM, HA HA HA
> HA HO, BHAGAVAN SARVA TATHAGATA, VAJRA MAME
> MUNTSA, VAJRA BHAVA MAHA SAMAYA SATVA AH
> HUM PHAT

As you recite the mantra, imagine that you can hear more people reciting it with you. Think of all the people you have ever known, those closest to you, those distant, everyone you've harmed, and so on. Imagine they are being purified also with the light from Vajrasattva. Imagine there are many Vajrasattvas now. As you and the others recite the mantra, the air in the room and all of space becomes filled with emanations of Vajrasattva. They are all radiating light. A hundred trillion Vajrasattvas fill the universe. All the people you have karma with are saying the mantra with you. The sound is overwhelming. The hum of it is like the sound of ten trillion swords cutting through delusion. It goes on like this for a while. Then silence.

Sit in this silence for a while. Know the experience of emptiness. Feel the power of compassion. Know that you can recall this feeling anytime and bring it with you wherever you go.

Renunciation

To protect yourself from creating more negative karma, commit to walking the spiritual path, practicing your recovery program at all times. We are all interconnected. We all feel pain. We all want to be happy. For this reason, say, "I will refrain from causing suffering to any living being." If you have lay vows or bodhisattva vows, recite them with a new sense of conviction and confidence.

Dedication

I know suffering. As an addict, I have felt it and I have caused it. To all those who suffer, I send the same love that a mother has for her only child. From this sense of compassion, bodhicitta, I dedicate the merits of my spiritual practice to all suffering addicts. May they be free of suffering and the cause of suffering. May the merits of this practice extend to all beings who suffer. May we all know happiness and the cause of happiness.

Aspects of Self: The Addict

I'd like to speak to the Controller. Controller, I'd like permission to speak to the Addict. Is that OK?

Please shift your body and get into the state of the Addict.

Whom am I speaking to?

How's everything going?

We haven't talked in a while. You're still here.

What are you feeling right now?

How do you feel about this process of recovery?

What do you want to say?

What does your world look like while the Self is engaged in all this spirituality?

Don't worry. You haven't been fired. You'll always be there.

Are you willing to be more mellow, as long as you know you're not going anywhere?

Sit for a few minutes like this.

Step 11

We sought through prayer and meditation to improve our conscious contact
with our Higher Power, as we understood it, praying only for knowledge of
our HP's will for us and the power to carry it out.

Conscious contact isn't what you think it is. So what is it? There are
four aspects of this step I'd like to explore. The order of application
to achieve the maximum results of the step is: definition of the Higher
Power, prayer—of which mantras are a form of dealing with conscious
contact—and the goal: knowledge of the HP's will for us.

Definition of the HP

I've delved into the HP at great length in previous steps; however, we
are going to review the subject because Step Eleven is so central to a
long-term recovery maintenance program. Again, I'm not trying to
rewrite the steps. I've rephrased the ones that mention God because I
believe that our Higher Power should truly be "as we understand it," just
like the 12-Step literature says. The use of words like *God* and *His* limit
our ability to define *our own* concept. We've been redefining a Higher
Power in Buddhist terms all along. This step really emphasizes it, so I
want to clarify some problem areas.

Personally, I take the following statement from Narcotics Anonymous as truth: "One of the basic principles of recovery [is our] absolute
and unconditional freedom to believe in any Higher Power we choose
and, of course, our right to communicate with our Higher Power in

whatever way conforms to our individual beliefs."[1] This means that everyone, regardless of spiritual orientation, should be able not only to work the steps but also to share about their program based on their concept, or something nonconceptual, of an HP. I don't mean that we should push our ideas in meetings. We have to speak in general terms to keep the recovery message open to all, but we can establish ourselves in a tradition that works for us so that we *can* integrate it into our program. With this comes the ability to share a different, non-program HP in a way that doesn't leave us feeling like we sold out our beliefs to conform and doesn't leave others feeling like they've been proselytized. Such was the case with one young man I met in the program.

"A" is well-educated, well-traveled, multilingual, and dually diag-nosed. At a service conference for professionals in addiction, he told me that he hated the 12-Step program because of the puritanical Chris-tian patriarchal approach of most members. He had two years sober at the time and has since relapsed. He represents a recovering subculture of young, hip, politically aware addicts. As is common in all 12-Step groups, younger members like my friend find identification with each other based on social characteristics and war stories, but when it comes to spirituality, many feel a big divide between themselves and the accepted norm of the 12-Step community.

For these reasons I mention definition again, just to reiterate that there are people who don't make it due to the lack of openness and flexibility in such practices, especially compared to the original intent of 12-Step programs. By the time we've gotten to Step Eleven, we should be able to practice with our own definition, instead of feeling like we don't fit the standard.

Prayer

In meetings, we say that prayer is about talking to our HP and medi-tation is about listening. In the beginning, I did most of the talking. I often prayed to God, begging for help, making promises and negoti-ating in much the same way I did in pre-recovery. I learned more about meditation and the meaning of prayer as I worked the program. But as I said in Step Seven, this relationship with God, as I was trying to conceive it, made me feel better only temporarily. There was no lasting effect in terms of my character defects and overall sense of happiness with self and the world.

The details of how we pray in recovery are explained in the resources I recommend in this book. Although we've only talked about Buddhist meditation so far, Buddhists do pray as well. Sometimes it even sounds a bit like the way Christians pray. The difference is that in Buddhism there is a multidimensional range of methods: outer, inner, secret, and most secret. I'll focus on the ways that prayer works in Buddhism shortly.

Conscious Contact

Of all the 12-Step passages that have affected me over the years, this one is the most powerful:

> There is a direct linkage among self-examination, medi-
> tation, and prayer. Taken separately, these practices can
> bring much relief and benefit. But when they are logically
> related and interwoven, the result is an unshakable foun-
> dation for life. Now and then we may be granted a glimpse
> of that ultimate reality which is God's kingdom.[2]

The part about an unshakable foundation for life really interested me for a long time. My life before sobriety had been nothing but chaos, especially after I became a full-time addict. In early recovery, I quickly adopted the technology of self-examination, meditation, and prayer, and have used it in different ways ever since. I incorporated therapy, Emmet Fox, and other monotheistic teachings during my first recovery period. It worked while it worked. And when it didn't, things got ugly.

Conscious contact in the minds of most people I hear in meetings is about getting a sense of calm assurance that God loves them. Sometimes the reassurance comes when they notice synchronicities, or less mysterious evidence, in their lives. My sponsor saw it as a relationship wherein we could ask a question of our HP and expect an answer. This was his way of achieving conscious contact.

What's changed for me since then is that I don't see ultimate reality as God's kingdom. That language is exactly what stops some would-be recoverers flat in their tracks. It's not that they're unwilling. But the God stuff they hear in meetings creates an aversion to the whole idea of 12-Step recovery.

Connecting with an ultimate reality is better now than it ever has been. In the Buddhist Integration section of this step, I'll go into detail. As a Buddhist, I adjusted over the years as my concept of God faded and my attention to the present moment intensified. I used to worry a lot about the topic of God's will, but if I live in the present, it's not an issue.

God's Will

We're told things in the program like, "God has a plan for us." The 12-Step literature asks a lot of questions but gives almost no answers about the deeper ramifications of such statements. For example, does a loving God who is in charge of everything let babies suffer? If He's in charge, then He must be letting it happen. I know that Christian pundits have been debating these topics for centuries, but you can't ask these questions in the program. It's not the forum for it. But in the coffee shops after the meetings, these questions have dominated many a late-night discussion.

I remember a meeting where the topic was "How Do You Know God's Will for You?" I'd been meditating on that topic for over twenty years at the time. It's really a conundrum. I refer to what my sponsor told me, at six months sober, in 1985: if I ever thought I knew God's will, I was in trouble. He said, "Hitler thought he knew God's will." Since I couldn't get a definitive answer on it, I was confused about how I was supposed to find and do God's will.

In general, the answer to this question is that we come to terms with knowing what God's will isn't—anything that causes suffering. We should practice the spiritual principles of love and service in all of our affairs. And that's exactly why I was attracted to Buddhism. It's a perfect system for doing just that, and it fits into the program nicely.

Principle: Seeking

We're addicts. We have been seeking happiness in our addictions for much of our lives. Step Eleven asks us to seek within on a spiritual level. Join me for a meditation that aims to do just that as we direct our minds toward perfect spiritual fulfillment.

Meditation on Seeking

Begin with *shamatha*. After several minutes of calm meditation, think about what you're looking for on the spiritual path. Is it perfect peace? Absolute comfort? What would it be like if you found everything you had ever dreamed of? Allow your mind to freely explore the possibility that you can find absolute spiritual fulfillment. How would the sky look? Can you imagine how fresh the air would smell, how rich the colors of your world would be? Would anyone be able to make you upset? Allow your mind to move beyond an exact definition of happiness to a place within you where this absolute peace already lives. Notice it within your heart in the form of your favorite color. As you breathe in, allow the color to take on a sensation. If it's blue, perhaps that brings a feeling of coolness. If your favorite is red, it might feel warm. Notice your color as a representation of perfect spiritual peace. Feel the body sensation associated with it. Allow it to grow as you breathe in deeply and slowly. Letting out your breath, see the color coming through your nose and mouth. Let the color of perfect peace emanate out of your body to a few feet in front of you. Imagine your favorite person there. You have the desire to share this beauty and perfection with this friend. With the next breath, send out some of this colored love light to your friend. Give him or her a piece of the peace.

Allow yourself to offer this feeling, in and out of a formal meditation setting, to anyone and everyone who comes to mind. Take your favorite colored ball of love light with you anywhere. Apply it to one person per day for thirty days. Send it to difficult people instead of reacting to them. See what happens.

Buddhist Integration of Step 11

Almost all Buddhists say that there is no self. You don't even have to be a Buddhist to see the value of this definition: a power greater than self is the realization that self is an illusion. Selfishness and self-centeredness don't hold up in the face of Buddhist practices on emptiness, karma, or dependent origination. Remember, dependent origination is the practice of seeing the chain of causes for any phenomenon—even the self. Everything is dependent on a cause and its precedent, on and on through beginningless time. Of the countless Buddhist methods to gain this realization, from simple mindfulness to Highest Yoga Tantra to Mahamudra, perhaps the easiest way to integrate Step Eleven's focus on a power greater than self is the Zen practice of no-self. If you look for the self, it can't be found. In many Buddhist traditions, the purpose of meditation is to realize—not just in our heads but experientially— that our notion of self as a concrete, fixed entity is unreal. Once this is attained, we can see in every moment that the self we cherish doesn't inherently exist. That is a spiritual awakening unprecedented in the typical 12-Step view, although I see it as the whole purpose of the 12 Steps.

Prayer

The mention of prayer sounds religious to many people. The program tells us that once we're into recovery we can go back to the religion of our choice with a fresh attitude and newfound inspiration. But in meetings, we often hear, "Religion is for people who are afraid of hell. Spirituality is for people who've been there." When people refer to Buddhism as a religion, I object because I think of it as a science of the mind that leads beyond science and the mind. Buddhism is not a religion but a spiritual path—one that transcends itself.

In my Zen experience, I never heard the word *prayer*. In Tibetan Buddhism, you'll find a lot of praying, both in the conventional or "making a request" form as well as the mantra form. I could argue that, in Zen practice, sitting meditation is being in a state of prayer or offering, but your average Zen student doesn't see it that way. For example, a Zen buddy of mine was over to the house recently and noticed my stacks of books on Buddhism. He looked at one book cover and said, "I don't like that Tibetan stuff. It's too churchy." I know how he feels. But as an addict, I need to pray and to be open-minded. As it says in the AA literature, "We place prayer and meditation high on our priority list. We resolve to make [it] as much a part of our daily routine as eating and sleeping."[3]

Motivated by the suffering that is intrinsic to addiction, combined with a spiritual thirst, I've worked hard to get past some of the stumbling blocks to traditions that are foreign to me. Narcotics Anonymous says:

> We may not be aware of the many options that are open to us. Searching those options out and exploring their usefulness to us can be uncomfortable and time-consuming. It is only by being open-minded and by taking action that we are likely to find what is right for us as individuals. . . . If everything feels strange, we practice a form of prayer and meditation until it no longer seems unnatural.[4]

I had to transcend my limited view to see the richness and amazing range of methods in the Tibetan Buddhist universe. I admit that some of the rituals are long and liturgical. Some are short but beautiful and powerfully transformative. It depends on the tradition.

In the Tibetan traditions, an offering is actually considered a form of prayer. One such form is the prayer for praise. We do prayers of praise at the beginning of teachings and before practice sessions. These are recited in Tibetan or in English. For example, the Praise to Shakyamuni Buddha:

> To the founder, the endowed transcendent destroyer, the one gone beyond, the foe destroyer, the completely

perfected, fully awakened being ... I prostrate, make offerings and go for refuge.[5]

We might then recite the Heart Sutra, which is fundamental to all of Buddhism:

> Avalokiteshvara Bodhisattva, practicing deep prajna paramita, clearly saw that all five skandhas are empty, transforming all suffering and distress.
>
> Shariputra, form is no other than emptiness, emptiness no other than form.
>
> Form is exactly emptiness, emptiness exactly form.
>
> Sensation, thought, impulse, consciousness are also like this.
>
> Shariputra, all things are marked by emptiness—not born, not destroyed, not stained, not pure, without gain, without loss.
>
> Therefore in emptiness there is no form, no sensation, thought, impulse, consciousness.
>
> No eye, ear, nose, tongue, body, mind.
>
> No color, sound, smell, taste, touch, object of thought.
>
> No realm of sight to no realm of thought.
>
> No ignorance and also no ending of ignorance to no old age and death and also no ending of old age and death.
>
> No suffering, and also no source of suffering, no annihilation, no path.
>
> No wisdom, also no attainment.
>
> Having nothing to attain, Bodhisattvas live prajna paramita with no hindrance in the mind.
>
> No hindrance, thus no fear.
>
> Far beyond delusive thinking, they attain complete Nirvana.
>
> All Buddhas past, present, and future live prajna paramita and thus attain anuttara samyak sambodhi.

Therefore, know that prajna paramita is the great mantra, the wisdom mantra, the unsurpassed mantra, the supreme mantra, which completely removes all suffering. This is truth; this is not deception. Therefore set forth the prajna paramita mantra, set forth this mantra and say:

GATÉ GATÉ PARAGATÉ PARASAMGATÉ BODHI SVAHA
[Beyond, beyond, totally beyond, perfectly beyond:
Awakening. . . . Yes!][6]

Following that, we can make a mandala offering:

This ground, anointed with perfume, strewn with flowers,
Adorned with Mount Meru, four continents, the sun, and
    the moon.
I imagine this as a buddha-field and offer it.
May all living beings enjoy this pure-land!
IDAM GURU RATNA MANDALAKAM
    NIRYATAYAMI[7]

The last part is Sanskrit and, according to Yangsi Rinpoche, states our intention of offering.

Tara is a very widely disseminated deity in Vajrayana Buddhism. Her pictures and prayers are well known all over Tibet and much of the Western world. Following is an example of how to practice Buddhist prayer with Tara. OM and SOHA are Sanskrit and used to open and close a mantra. Mantras can also be considered a form of prayer. In the prayer on the previous page, we can say the mantra anytime as a meditation practice, an offering, or in the context of a request for help from Tara, an enlightened being. This is actually the opening of a practice called Praise to the Twenty-One Taras. Most Tibetans memorize this extensive prayer in early childhood.

OM TARE TUTTARE TURE SOHA
OM, I and all prostrate to the liberator,
the fully realized, transcendent subduer.
I prostrate to the glorious mother who liberates with
     TARE;
You are the mother who eliminates all fears with
     TUTTARE;
You are the mother who grants all success with TURE;
To SOHA and the other syllables we offer the greatest
     homage.[8]

The setting of intention, refuge, and bodhicitta are also considered forms of prayer and can be done formally in a session or any other time. All teachings and practice sessions are concluded with prayers of dedication. In the Mahayana path, such dedications are vital to communicating our intention of saving all beings from suffering. Additionally, we often say long-life prayers, such as the following, for some or all of our teachers. This is the Long Life Prayer for His Holiness the Dalai Lama:

In the land encircled by snow mountains
You are the source of all happiness and good;
All-powerful Chenrezig, Tenzin Gyatso,
Please remain until samsara ends.[9]

A Range of Tibetan Methods

For those who need to know more details or who feel overwhelmed by doing Tantra, the lamrim—gradual path teachings—are available in traditions such as the Gelugpa, which is the order of ordained monks and nuns that the Dalai Lama heads. These systems take their time and build to enlightenment slowly.

Across the different schools of Tibetan Buddhism, some are more focused on details and some are more direct. Not all of the schools spend vast amounts of time preparing offerings, chanting mantras, and conducting extensive rituals. The Nyingmas, for example, practice all levels but organize the teachings in a nine-yana (vehicle) system. The highest two levels of Anu Yoga and Ati Yoga contain cycles of concise teachings and practices that yield outstanding and fast results. These are more direct than the methods leading up to them and are a bit risky. But in essence, these practices contain the principles of all preceding levels.

In these levels, less time is spent on formal preparations, so there's something for everyone. Each person needs to figure out where to start. Unlike the 12 Steps, you don't have to begin at square one. It depends on your ability to understand and apply the essence of the teaching. Once you get the message, these prayers and rituals all take on a poetic spiritual magnificence that really reaches deep. To appreciate this process, we have to look beyond cultural differences to spiritual similarities. That's the step before learning about Tibetan Buddhism. We want to be sure not to practice contempt prior to investigation,[10] as AA says.

Conscious Contact through Mindfulness

We can be mindful of our breath as conscious contact with our Buddha nature. We can take this further if we practice, carefully observing ourselves in daily life. Being mindful of all our actions, wherever we are—whether it's following the ethical rules of the Eightfold Path or practicing vows—we apply mindfulness to all we do. In this sense, we are practicing Dharma. If we practice Dharma, we are practicing being in our Buddha nature. *Shamatha*, refuge, bodhicitta, tonglen, self-examination—all are methods of being mindful. And we can relate all of these practices to our recovery as 12-Step Buddhists.

Ways to go deeper into conscious contact include being present in meetings when listening to people share, living in the now instead of in resentment and fear, working on our character defects, and being of service to people in recovery—practicing all the principles of the path. If we are interested, we can take it even further in the Vajrayana practices of tantrism, which are part of the Mahayana path.

Conscious Contact through Pure Vision

NA says, "[We] believed nothing existed beyond what our limited view allowed us to see."[11] In the Tantras, we are taught to hold a pure vision at all times. What this means is that we're limited in our view when we retain the sense of a separate self, subject and object, likes and dislikes, us and them. In tantrism, we learn to view everybody as an enlightened being, thus surpassing our own dualistic conditioning. When I first started practicing Tibetan Buddhism, the monks and nuns taught that if I see the teacher as a normal person, I'll get the teachings of a normal person. But if I can see the teacher as a Buddha, I'll get teachings from a Buddha. Does that sound crazy? Wait until you start to work with it.

There is a similar principle in the 12-Step program. We try to look at everybody as a child of God or, if we're upset with someone, as a person who is spiritually sick. This transforms our vision of the person, which affects our attitude, feelings, and actions toward them. In tantrism, pure vision works the same way. We see ourselves as Buddhist deities, places as *mandalas*—the sphere of enlightened activity of a particular Buddha or deity—and other people as perfectly completed Buddhas. It's hard to put into practice, but with some effort and patience, results are inevitable. When it comes to Step Eleven, Guru Yoga is one aspect of how I practice as a 12-Step Buddhist.

Conscious Contact through Guru Yoga

In the AA literature, it states under Step Three that "we are the agents, He is the principle." The principle in this regard is God as we understand God. What is the Buddhist's equivalent? Buddhism doesn't purport the existence of a Creator God. In the 12-Step model, we externalize the responsibility for our behavior when we say phrases like, "let go and let God"; however, we're really just asking for help from a power greater than ourselves. In Tibetan Buddhism, we do this by practicing Guru Devotion, often called Guru Yoga. In the Vajrayana path, this means we become a direct representative of the guru or teacher. This is why, on one level, we need to keep the ethics of body, speech, and mind in the context of tantric samaya.

Lama Zopa Rinpoche says, "Doing this practice eliminates so much heavy negative karma and purifies all ten non-virtuous actions, broken pratimoksha vows, bodhisattva vows, and tantric vows. . . . This practice gives incredible protection." And, "If you do Six-Session Guru Yoga with lam-rim and especially lojong, the practices of thought transformation [of which tonglen is a part], the whole path is integrated into guru yoga practice. That is something that makes the Lama Tsong Khapa tradition very special, integrating the graduated path to enlightenment into guru yoga. . . . Therefore, when you integrate that into guru yoga, it makes the practice so special and so rare."[12]

The practice, as Lama Zopa outlines above, is done by reciting prayers, doing mantras and visualizations, and keeping a pure vision through all of one's activities. It's part of the commitment to the bodhisattva path and is a requirement for taking initiations in all schools of the Vajrayana. When I first took my bodhisattva vows with Lama Zopa Rinpoche, he said they amplify the benefits of all our positive actions millions of times. The reverse side is that if I "practice" my character defects, ego attachment, and other forms of negativity, the karmic backlash can be intense and immediate. Therefore, these tantric initiations are for those who are very serious about enlightenment.

For me, my condition as an addict helps me to understand my condition in samsara, and is the reason I take vows and do practices. As it says in Step One from AA, "When one alcoholic had planted in the mind of another the true nature of his malady, that person could never be the same again." And, "Under the lash of alcoholism, we are driven to A.A., and there we discover the fatal nature of our situation. Then, and only then, do we become as open-minded to conviction and as willing to listen as the dying can be. We stand ready to do anything which will lift the merciless obsession from us."[13]

An old-timer named Paz used to say, "Alcohol beat me into a state of reasonableness." In the same way that knowledge of my condition as an addict inspires me to practice the principles of recovery, the knowledge of samsara, karma, dependent arising, and impermanence instills in me a reasonableness to practice the path to enlightenment.

In the Nyingma tradition of Tibetan Buddhism, the practice of Guru Yoga is "the supreme method of generating the ultimate cognition. It is a means of entering the state of blessed empowerment. To prepare the mind for this practice, imagine your own highly endowed lama before you in space and develop a strong wish to achieve whatever he teaches. Unless you have faith in him and a sense of his pure appearance, the ultimate cannot be cognized."[14]

For us to practice Guru Yoga, we need to find our teacher—someone in whom we have complete trust. The teacher really is a doorway to the enlightened world. In the Zen tradition, my teacher used to say: "Life, just as it is, the only teacher." In the deepest sense, the point of practicing Guru Yoga, or any other Buddhist practice for that matter, is ultimately to realize this innate Buddha nature. The methods are what vary. The lamas speak very intensely of the values of Guru Yoga:

> Better than meditating on a hundred thousand deities
> For ten million kalpas
> Is to think of one's teacher for a single instant.[15]
> To practice Guru Yoga
> Exhausts all defects and perfects all attainments.[16]

Even within the various traditions, the actual practice methods of Guru Yoga vary. There have been many Guru Yoga teachings for a variety of highly accomplished teachers throughout the history of Buddhism. In the Nyingma tradition, Guru Yoga of Padmasambhava is one of the most widely practiced. It involves an initiation, samaya, offerings, visualizations, recitations, and dedications. It's up to a lama to give detailed instruction on this, but here is the prayer:

The Prayer in Seven Lines
Hum! Born in the north west land of Oddiyana

On the pollen bed of a lotus stem,
Wondrously, you attained supreme accomplishment.
You are renowned as the Lotus Born,
Surrounded by retinues of many dakinis.
Emulating you, I will perfect myself—
Come then, I pray, bestow your blessings.
GURU PADME SIDDHI HUM

This is the most revered prayer to Padmasambhava. It has many levels of meaning and constitutes a complete path itself.[17]

In the Ati (highest) Yoga path of Dzogchen, Guru Yoga is the fundamental practice. Its priority exceeds all others. John Reynolds explains:

The guru represents the manifest embodiment of all of the Three Jewels, so that by taking refuge in the Guru, all refuges are simultaneously realized. The way in which the practitioner maintains and develops a direct connection with the Guru . . . who is the source of transmission by way of empowerment and teaching, is the practice of Guru Yoga. . . . This term means the unification of Body, Speech, and Mind . . . with the state of the body, speech, and mind . . . of the master. From the viewpoint of Dzogchen, no matter what practice one does, one must link that practice with Guru Yoga. In this way, the transmissions that we have received, including the introduction to our own Primordial State, are maintained and enhanced. In this way, the Root Guru and the Lineage Gurus remain inseparably connected with our own mind, infusing our stream of consciousness with their blessings of inspiration and knowledge. Among all practices found in Tantra and Dzogchen, that of Guru Yoga is the most important and essential. And when we practice Guru Yoga properly, according to our author [Patrul Rinpoche], we thereby unify our view, meditation, and conduct.[18]

So what's an aspiring, sober Buddhist to think? Well, I've come to think of Guru Yoga as working with my own innate Buddha nature. The teacher expresses this and is, in effect, a doorway to enlightenment. It applies to the third step, the eleventh step, and all of the steps that talk about God. If you are interested in Guru Yoga, then you will have to go find your teacher. If you're at a loss about finding one, you can start praying about it. That's what I did. I went on a retreat and walked around the stupa—the statue of prayers and relics of Lama Yeshe, founder of FPMT—asking Lama Yeshe to help me find my root teacher. Then, I found many teachers, including Lama Zopa Rinpoche and Namkhai Norbu Rinpoche.

HP's Will

I think it should be obvious by now: the opposite of self-will is other-will. This thinking and action is the point of the 12 Steps. The quintessential path to helping others in Buddhism is the bodhisattva path. It's a match made in heaven, or the Pure Lands.

Try this meditation of offering aloud. You can change it in any way you like to fit your needs. I share this personal meditation with you as a taste of using offering as part of daily practice.

Meditation on Conscious Contact through Offerings

When I get up in the morning, before I take my first sip of excellent and delicious coffee, I try to remember to do a cleansing breath, letting out all the bad air. Breathing in fully, breathing out all the way, letting the breath exhale completely, and waiting a few seconds before breathing in. I go over to my altar, where I have pictures of my teachers, flowers in summer, offerings of beautiful colored stones, sacred texts, brightly colored cloth, scented and/or colored water bowls, candles, and malas—Tibetan prayer beads. Turning on my rotating, multicolored crystal Buddha light, I bow to the sacredness of all teachings and light a candle, saying OM AH HUM as I offer light. With my body, speech, and mind, I remember that I'm lucky to be alive today. I should practice! I go downstairs and grind some fresh coffee beans. Returning to my altar, I light some natural Tibetan incense, saying OM AH HUM as I imagine the lovely scent extending out to all enlightened beings in unlimited quantity. Sitting before my Dharma Desk,[19] I open a text reciting a prayer, such as the Seven Line Supplication to Guru Rinpoche (Padmasambhava). Holding my mala, I offer the practice of reciting several mantras and doing the corresponding visualizations as my teachers have taught me. Finishing whichever of these I've chosen, and looking at the pictures of deities and smelling the incense, I sit for a moment with the intention to dedicate this practice to all suffering beings, or at least one person.

After dedications, I pour myself a cup of aromatic, steaming coffee. Holding it up to my lips, I breathe deeply of the rich smell. I imagine that there are trillions of enlightened beings in the space before me. I see the faces of my teachers. I might notice Green Tara or Chenrezig or another being over my head, at my right shoulder, or in my heart. I offer in my mind all of the delicious cups of pleasure that I can imagine to all of the enlightened beings that I can possibly fathom in an instant. Noting that feeling, I acknowledge them. Then I imagine that many, many beings have been killed in the process of bringing me this simple cup of coffee. The beans were grown in ground that was tilled, killing beings. All the way through the production process, from the bugs on the windshield of the trucks to the larger animals involved in the production of all the materials and devices used to bring me this cup of coffee, many beings were killed. To them I owe a debt. May they join the path. As I take this first, best drink of early morning coffee, enjoying it thoroughly, I say, "May all beings drink deeply of the Dharma."

Aspects of Self: The Guru

I'd like to speak to the Controller. Controller, I'd like permission to speak to the Guru. Is that OK?

Please shift your body and get into the state of the Guru.

Whom am I speaking to?
What do you do?

What is your natural state?

Where are you?

What do you see?

How deep is your compassion?

Is there anyone that you don't extend lovingkindness to?

Will you send the Addict your blessings now?

Sit for a little while in the state of the Guru, the mind of enlightenment.

Step 12

*Having had a spiritual awakening as the result of these steps,
we tried to carry this message to the addict who still suffers and to
practice these principles in all of our affairs.*

Like I said in the beginning, when I saw the words *spiritual awakening* on the 12-Step list at the treatment center in 1984 and thought, "That's *cool*," I was down and strung out. Totally broken. That moment did not look like a spiritual awakening— more like some kind of death. But it was the beginning of acceptance, humility, and surrender; the onset of a strange and interesting path that I could never have imagined in my wildest high. They say in meetings, "Hold on to your ass, you're in for a helluva ride." It is not an exaggeration, but it is probably an understatement.

It's an Inside Job

By the time we reach Step Twelve, we're well into a dynamic combination of all of the preceding principles and ideas. That means we're applying them all to be of maximum service to everyone around us, not just other addicts. Growth in the steps and my understanding of them hasn't looked linear in a really long time. The comprehension and application of one principle or step can pop up, deepen, or even regress any time—seemingly out of context. There is a higher order of things, and the steps have profound implications within that structure. My best guess at how I'm doing at any given point is to look closely at my state of mind and the way people act when I'm around them. Buddhism says, if we want to know about our past life, we look at our present circumstances. If we want to know what our future will be like, we should look at our present actions.

In the same sense, I use the principles of Buddhism and the steps to examine my conditions, to receive guidance on how to act. The saying goes, "As within, so without." If people around me are agitated and not giving, I need to examine where I am spiritually. How am I causing or contributing to the experience I'm having? What is at the root of the problem? What can I do to accept or correct it? How am I at fault, and how can I contribute to the life of another? These are not questions that are natural to my state as an addict. From what I can see, they're not even questions normies ask.

I was at a meeting recently where one member said that he wished everybody in the world would work the 12 Steps. Maybe that would work, since we're all addicted or at least attached to something. But, addict egos are pretty strong, and while it can be said that the program works because we're not all crazy on the same day, in my experience, we're not all sane on the same day either. While they have power, we need to remember that the reason the 12 Steps are in our lives is because of the disease of addiction, not due to our virtue as the chosen ones, as some in recovery believe.

Buddhism emerged in response to our condition of samsara. We live in an infinite cycle of birth, suffering, death, and rebirth. On and on it goes. Where does it stop? Well, like we say to newcomers in the program, "You get to the bottom when you stop digging." I think we can learn a lot about Buddhism from the steps and a lot about the steps from Buddhism, but as to what you should do and how you should proceed, I defer to the Buddha. Let the principles, methods, steps, and teachings show the way. Walk your own walk. In the program we say, "Keep your own side of the street clean." Dilgo Khyentse Rinpoche says, "Do not have opinions on other people's actions. . . . When we look into a mirror, we see a dirty face because our own face is dirty. In the same way, the defects of others are nothing but our impure way of seeing them. By thinking in this way, we should try to rid ourselves of this perception of the faults of others, and cultivate the attitude whereby the whole of existence, all appearances, are experienced as pure."[1]

The program offers a lot of ways to be of service, from setting up chairs and making coffee to being on the national delegate committee for world conferences. Some are circuit speakers; some never talk at meetings. Some sponsor everybody; some have never been asked to sponsor anybody. Within the normal context of a 12-Step program, we have all of these options. The point is to treat the "disease of self"; the solution is always to work for others. Always. But the application of that, namely giving up our self-centered focus, is, as Joko used to say, "the last thing we want to do." So why do we even try to do it?

For addicts, we have a limited set of options: death, insanity, or spirituality. No matter how we dress it up, intellectualize it, or externalize it, the spiritual solution is always about doing for others. It is, in essence, the practice of selfless, unconditional love that the program offers. It's no coincidence that that's what the Mahayana path of Buddhism prescribes as well.

Principle: Unconditional Love

If we're able to practice the principle of unconditional love when it's most needed, we can truly say we've had a spiritual awakening. But for most of us, it's useful to run through the steps mentally as often as we need. The following type of meditation is similar to reviewing all the steps in the AA and NA step books. Using these principles as a meditation, with our intention to practice them in all of our affairs, we can review them individually. This will deepen our experience of the steps.

Meditation on the 12-Step Principles

Depending on how much time is available, you can make this meditation as short or as long as you like. It can take thirty minutes to do thoroughly, or just a few minutes to hit the major points at any given time. You can interrupt this meditation to go to therapy, call your sponsor, or wash the dishes as the need arises. Be present. Be willing. Do the footwork. That's all we can ask of ourselves.

Begin with *shamatha*. From a place of calm abiding, consider the spiritual principles of the 12 Steps, one by one.

Step One: Acceptance

Thinking back to my last experience of using, I open my heart to the first step of recovery. I remember what it was like the last time. My body was sick. My mind and behavior were out of control. The people around me had turned away in disgust or despair. They had given up on me or were about to, and so had I. There was no way to know that this was the first step in recovery. But it was.

I think about that time. What I was wearing, what the room smelled like, the feeling in my stomach, maybe the smell of my own vomit, excrement, or the taste of blood. I was finished. Truly powerless. I see that I was and am truly unable to control and enjoy my addiction. Being in that awareness, I notice that, untreated, my addiction makes my life totally unmanageable. Knowing that I can never go back to my addiction in ignorance, I notice the Addict as present within me. I reaffirm and accept the truth about it, even if it makes me a little afraid. There is a solution to be followed on the spiritual path, so it's OK. This is acceptance.

Spend a few moments being present with your body, speech, and mind to the total awareness of addiction as a condition of your life. When you're ready, move on to the next step.

Step Two: Confidence/Faith

Reflecting that alone I am powerless to manage my addiction without spiritual help, I turn resolutely to the Higher Power of my own understanding. No matter what my childhood religion, regardless of the opinion of others in my life or in 12-Step meetings, the definition of my Higher Power is for me to choose. I'm not free of addiction until I use this freedom of choice to discover my own Higher Power. In its simplest forms, my Higher Power can be the group of 12-Step practitioners, the sacred presence of the only moment of truth, the now, my management team, or the laws of cause and effect. However I choose to view a Higher Power, I have confidence that no matter what I am feeling, there is always a power greater than my disease and the current situation. My problems have never been permanent, no matter how concrete they may seem in my mental drama. Knowing this is the second step.

My Higher Power is fluid. I give myself permission to allow it to change and grow with me as long as I cultivate its presence in my life. One day it may be compassion, love, willingness, or just the necessity to go to a meeting. Other days, the confidence in my Higher Power may come from the smile of a small child or even the giggle of a crazy street person. By my willingness to know that there is always a Higher Power, I practice Step Two. This gives me faith and confidence to continue practicing the path of recovery.

Spend a few moments being present with your body, speech, and mind to the total awareness of faith in a Higher Power as a solution in your life. When you're ready, carefully move on to the next step.

Step Three: Surrender

I return to the breath for a few moments. This is my path. I do what I need to do. Nobody's going to do it for me. Knowing this, I draw my attention inward. Looking inside my self and reviewing my history— I see that my Addict has dominated every aspect of my life. It has been the guiding influence of so much suffering and destruction. Yet, through the process of the steps, I can see that it is the Addict who suffers too. Because of the pain of my addiction, I have been brought to my knees many times. This time, I choose to get up with the help of a Higher Power.

In whatever form I imagine my Higher Power, I allow it to make me feel comfortable, trusting, and happy. Maybe it's the idea of a kindly person or a ball of colored light. It could be a big, beautiful redwood tree, the ocean, or the vast night sky. I'm open to however my Higher Power chooses to reveal itself. Breathing in, I am present in the presence of my Higher Power. Breathing out, I surrender to the love that is present before me. Breathing in, I surrender to the love that is present within me. Breathing out, I connect with spiritual power.

I am confident in my decision to allow this power to guide me through principles, written or spoken words, synchronicity, or whatever means are necessary. The choices I make will be guided by my Higher Power. I feel safe in turning over all aspects of my life to this pure spiritual essence. In this way, I practice surrender. I live in Step Three.

Spend a few moments being present with your body, speech, and mind to the gentle presence of your Higher Power in whatever form it takes. When you're ready, move on to the next step.

Step Four: Self-Examination

Knowing the condition of my addiction and the presence of a power greater than my self and my addiction, I turn my eyes inward. I rest for a few moments in gentle, calm, abiding meditation. My awareness turns to the physical sensations in my body. I can quickly recall a resentment or a fear. Sitting silent, being still, I can call up the face of a person I resent. I see this person in full detail: the folds in their clothes, the color of their eyes, and the shape of their mouth. I sense the tension in my body with this person in mind.

Remembering the skills learned in my inventory process, I mentally see paper and pen. I watch myself jot down the resentment. *I don't like what they did that day, and they should have treated me better.* Now I notice that in the stillness, I can discover my own participation in this dilemma. I feel resentful. I expected this person to be different. I raised my voice or my hand. I acted out in defense of myself and made the situation worse. What did I do to get myself into that situation in the first place? Sitting silently, I allow the memory to surface. *Yes. I did play a role. My part was . . .*

Keep saying it, "My part was . . ." until it becomes clearer. Spend a few moments being present with your body, speech, and mind turned inward. When you're ready, slowly move on to the next step.

Step Five: Self-Honesty

Breathing in, I notice the energy in my body. Where are my feet? Without looking, I can feel my hands, my legs. With my eyes still, my mind is still. Noticing the breath entering the nose, letting it out, slowly relaxing, being still. In this presence I abide.

In my heart, with my spiritual eyes turned in on myself, I see my sponsor, trusted friend, or spiritual adviser sitting before me. They are comfortable, at peace, ready to listen. I ask mentally if they suffered as I have suffered. They seem to hear my question, seeing the look in my eyes, and as I look back, I know in my heart that they too have suffered just as I have. I know that I can trust this person. I realize they have been down a similar road. I have total faith and confidence that my secrets are safe with them.

Sitting before me on a table, I see my written inventory. It is hundreds of pages thick. As I pick it up and thumb through it, I see that the pages go on forever back through time to a beginning that I cannot find. All the negative, painful things I've wanted to do, have thought about doing, tried to do, or have done are written in this secret document. It is *all* there. I open the book and begin to read from page one. From the corner of my eye, I catch my sponsor looking at me with compassion. A tear is rolling down his face. He feels my pain. Knowing this, I proceed. As I read, I hold nothing back. Every action, every fear, every secret, all resentments, everything I have ever done or feel guilty about is revealed in this sacred space between us. When it is done, I look up. My sponsor is still looking at me, still caring, still listening. They ask if I am done. I say yes. Together, we sit for a while in Noble Silence, contemplating the trust and sacredness of what has been shared.

Spend a few moments being present with your body, speech, and mind in awareness of the relationship of trust between you and your fifth-step listener. There is no judgment. Only peace. Rest in that peace for a little while. Let the tears fall if they need to. You are safe. When you're ready, continue to the next step.

Step Six: Willingness

Being in the state of presence, knowing that I have just shared my entire history back as far as I could possibly remember and even some harms I had forgotten, my fifth step is done. I bid my sponsor farewell, embracing him. These next steps need to be done in solitude. My sponsor reminds me that I am on the right path and encourages me to go on. The pain of reading my inventory has diminished somewhat; the pervading sense of embarrassment is all but gone. But the sense of anxiety about my actions toward myself and others is still tugging at me. I can feel this tension nagging at my guts. There is more work to be done. Sitting in the resolute awareness of all of these defects of character, I go through them as they come to mind.

I notice one by one, all of my defects of character. As they come up, I am willing to acknowledge them. Maybe they take the form of little pieces of sludge that I am willing to release. Where I was ignorant, I am willing to see the truth. Where I was angry, I am ready to become tolerant. Where I have been selfish, I am honestly going to try to think of others. I feel these defects of character as deep in my bones as anything I've ever felt in my life. Maybe for the first time in my life, I am willing to let myself feel the effects. I am willing to try something different. With this awareness, I am entirely willing and completely ready to ask for help to get rid of these problems that cause so much pain.

Spend a few moments being present with your body, speech, and mind in the absolute awareness of the character defects. They can take a visual form, like a chunk of gray dirt lodged in your throat. Whatever visual or sensory experience comes to mind, let it. There is no judgment, only a desire to do better, be better. Rest in that willingness for a little while. When you're ready, go to the next step.

Step Seven: Humility

Breathing in, I know that I am an addict. Breathing out, I know that there is a path. The path is clearer to me now than ever. Sitting in a calm, silent space, knowing the root of my delusions as never before, I see in front of me a long road. I imagine my favorite setting, perhaps a natural place, a pond or a mountain trail. Maybe it's a park or a lake that I love or the walk to a corner store that I used to take with my dad. However the path manifests before me, I know from Step Six that I am willing to take the next steps. This is a path that is illuminated with honesty and the light of an awareness that I've always had deep within but was never allowed to Shine.

I am grateful for the steps, appreciative of my sponsor, and have the honest desire to do better. Humility is knowing the truth about myself. Through the love and tolerance of my 12-Step community, I know that people sicker than me have become much better through the practice of humility. I know that humility is not self-deprecation but the subtle acknowledgment of my strengths and my weaknesses. Through the 12-Step process so far, I have made such acknowledgment. Sitting still and silent in this view of the path before me, I turn to the Higher Power that I have been working to understand. If it's a person, a tree, a color, or a feeling, I notice it before or within me. Knowing these truths about myself, I utter my prayer in the most humble manner possible, asking for help from whomever or wherever it may come. In this space, I remain open.

Spend a few moments being in your body, in the presence of your Higher Power. In this awareness, ask for help to move past your shortcomings. Rest in humility for as long as you like. When you're ready, slowly proceed to the next step.

Step Eight: Forgiveness

Drawing from the humility I've gathered from looking inward in the previous steps, I turn my focus outward again to consider those I have harmed. I sit for a few moments in the rich, pure awareness of the present moment. I notice all the sounds around me. I see clearly the objects in front of my eyes. My body is rooted in its position, and my mind is firm in its resolve. I will continue through this process. I now imagine before me one person I have harmed. I speak their name. How have I hurt them? What have I done? I look into their eyes, searching for the effects of wounds I have inflicted. Breathing in, I feel the hurt I have caused them. At first, it's a little twinge in my throat. The feeling begins to grow and sinks deep down into my bones. I know the pain I have inflicted. I feel it and I accept it back for myself.

This isn't self-abuse; I'm not trying to punish myself. On the contrary, this is the path to freedom. For, as it says in the St. Francis prayer, *only by self-forgetting can I find*. I must be willing to take on the suffering of the other in order to find my own freedom. I know and feel the pain I've caused, and in my heart, I know that I am truly sorry. I want to make it right. I will make it right. I will not give up until this person is healed from my actions against them. I feel the presence of my Higher Power in my body, speech, and mind, and know that I am protected. I can feel what I need to feel, and it will be OK. I will survive, and I will make it right.

I bring up another person whom I have harmed through resentment. I have not forgiven them but must in order to make amends. In my heart, I feel darkness where there should be light. I am willing to visualize this person before me. They are close. Close enough for me to see the pores of their skin. They too are human. They too feel pain. Just like me, they want to be happy, joyous, and free. But they can't because they are bound by their own issues, limitations, and problems. How can I learn to forgive this person? I must reach within and find the strength to forgive. What will I lose if I give up my resentment toward this person? Only strain.

Where is the tightness that I feel in regard to this individual? Searching within my body, I feel a ball of tension surrounding my thoughts of this person. I imagine it as a dark gray ball about the size of a baseball. It seems hard on the surface, but if I poke my finger in it, it makes a little hole in the center. In front of me is a pitcher of a white, glowing liquid representing the spiritual power of unconditional love. I can reach this elixir and pour some into the hole of this ball that is my crusty resentment. Pouring, I fill the hole of anger up with healing love and light. This is my true nature—the same as the person I resent. I feel the resentment softening, and the ability to forgive grows stronger in my heart. I can return to this feeling anytime I need to practice forgiveness.

Being aware of your thoughts, feelings, and sensations in your body, notice gratitude in the presence of your Higher Power. From this place of calm awareness, know you can forgive any wrong done to you, as you're about to ask to be forgiven for your own in Step Nine. When you're ready, slowly move on to the next step.

Step Nine: Restitution

Before I worked these steps, I thought everything I did was justified. I was rarely willing to admit my part. It's always been about what others have done to me. That's common sense. But the steps ask me to look at relationships another way. They give me a way to see how I can be free and how I can free others from the problems I have caused them. With the courage I've developed in Steps One through Eight, I have a new strength with which to face those I've harmed. I breathe in to become aware of this precious moment of human existence. So rare. I've wasted so much time. Through addiction, I have caused enough harm. It's time to get right with the world. As I breathe out, I release the fear of facing all the people I've damaged.

I take a few moments to settle into a relaxed state. From this position of total calmness, I imagine the person I owe the biggest amends to. What do I owe them? If it's money, I imagine that I am holding part of it in my hand. I'd rather spend it on myself, but I want to stay in recovery more than I want whatever that money would buy. I can say to them, "This is a small part of what I owe you, but is a big piece of what I have available." I visualize or feel them becoming angry with me, but I remain calm and patient. I've done the work. I know that the restitution process isn't about me.

I continue by saying to myself, breathing in, "I accept the anger and disappointment that is coming at me right now. I have no need to defend myself. I'm here to make amends, to make it good." I look at the person and say, "What else can I do to make it right?" Whatever they say, I agree to it and move on to the next amends on my list. Moving down the list, I bring up the next person into my mind's awareness. What is the exact nature of the wrong I have committed to this person? I remember what my sponsor told me about this one. I look at them and ask, "How can I make it right?" This is how I practice meditation of restitution.

Attentive to your physical body, emotions, and thoughts, draw up strength from your Higher Power with imagery and feeling. From this place of calm awareness, know that by making an honest effort to walk the spiritual path in Step Nine, no matter what the response of those to whom you make amends, you can forgive yourself for any wrong you have done just as you have forgiven others in Step Eight. Now you're ready for the maintenance steps.

Step Ten: Admission

As I breathe in, I acknowledge that I am often wrong. Holding my breath for just a moment, I see how I hold on to my rightness. I hold and hold and hold, but to live, I eventually have to let go. Exhaling, I practice letting go. Through the process of the steps, I have been shown that my perceptions have often been wrong. As I cling to my sense of righteousness in arguments over small things, I've made myself out to be more important, more of a victim, and less responsible than is reasonable. In relationships, I've had a pattern of taking more than I have given. Even when my actions have been helpful to others, deep down my expectation was what I could gain. Outwardly, I've let my disappointments be known. I've lied, manipulated, stolen, and hurt people I love and who have loved me. I have been wrong when willing to fight to prove that I was right.

Breathing in, I acknowledge that my perceptions about myself have been inaccurate. Holding my breath for just a moment, I emphasize how I've held on to mistaken views time and again. I relax. I let go. I give it all back.

In order to practice the principle of admission for Step Ten, I practice now in my own private, relaxed meditation space. My words will be spoken with true conviction. When the person whom I've wronged hears me, they will know I'm speaking from the heart because I am truly working a program. As I inhale, I think the words, I am wrong. Holding my breath for just a second, I feel the words resonate: I am wrong. Letting out the air, I let out the need to be right and I say out loud, "I am wrong." I can do this many times, over and over, getting it ingrained, needing to practice this with conviction and sincerity. *I am wrong. I am wrong. I am wrong.*

Spend a few moments being present with your body, speech, and mind to the total awareness of addiction as a condition of your life. You will be an addict for life. If your addict voice says otherwise, practice saying, "I am wrong." Your DNA will not change. Therefore, the spiritual path is something you vow to take seriously. Being humble, honest, accepting, and admitting when you're wrong is being on the path. In this sense, we practice the path of Step Ten by admitting when we're wrong. When you're ready, take the next step.

Step Eleven: Seeking

In the silent solitude of any present moment, I notice where my feet are planted. In the grounding presence of reality, I know what day it is and where I have to be next. Being in this magical present moment, I celebrate my life today. My life is very different than when I entered into recovery. But the condition of addiction is only dormant so long as I maintain my willingness to practice spiritual principles. I've experienced many problems as a practicing addict and some in recovery. Troubles and challenges will keep coming, like the rising of the tides, until I take my very last breath. I know that moment will come, and it will be my last. But I don't know when that's going to happen. With this mindfulness, I intend to practice seeking in Step Eleven as much as possible. My sobriety is contingent on my spiritual condition. My spiritual condition is maintained by spiritual practice. Meditation is spiritual practice. I can meditate anywhere, anytime, using the methods I have learned in this process.

When I wake up in the morning, I am mindful of the miracle that I am still alive and still in recovery. When I brush my teeth and my mind wanders, I bring my attention to the task at hand. I give myself fully to making my breakfast, dressing, and planning my day. Even as I plan, I am aware of my feet, aware of my breath, aware of the preciousness of my life. As I walk to my car to go to work, I am mindful of my steps. Throughout the day, my practice is to be aware, awake, alert, and attentive to my precious sober life. With every action I practice mindfulness. When I get upset, I am mindful. I follow my program, doing the spiritual actions that have brought me this far. Everything passes. One day, I will pass. In a hundred years, most of the people who are alive today will be gone. Nothing stays the same. Breathing in, I am aware of the changing nature of existence. Breathing out, I practice acceptance.

In this way I practice conscious contact. To make contact, I need to be conscious. To be conscious, I practice mindfulness all the time. Then when the big questions come, I can rely on the intuitive understanding that is the fundamental underlying current of the spiritual life for everyone on the path. For me as an addict, it is as important as the air I breathe.

Spend a few moments being present with your body, speech, and mind. Kindle the awareness that prayer and meditation is a constant and regular part of your recovery program. Rejoice in the opportunity. Say a prayer of gratitude. An addict just died while you were doing this meditation. Dedicate the benefits of this practice to him. When you're ready, advance to the next step.

Step 12: Selfless Service/Unconditional Love

Sitting in silent awareness, I practice my spiritual awakening. In this moment, my presence of body, speech, and mind is sharp. I am mindful that I am an addict and cannot change that fact. I bring my awareness to this condition every day. There is a power greater than my disease, and I can call it into my awareness every moment as long as I remember to do so. The best way for me to remember my addiction and my recovery is to stay in contact with and in service to my community of recovering addicts. The steps have given me a chance to live a life that I always thought was just for others. I owe myself the self-esteem that comes only from carrying the message of recovery to those who still suffer.

Sometimes the person I need to connect with is new, sometimes not. We are all in the same boat. We all need a hug, a smile, and a warm greeting no matter how long we're in recovery. I practice the integration of all of the spiritual principles of the 12 Steps. I therefore nurture my constant spiritual awakening by staying present in recovery, keeping commitments to the group, working with others, and being an example of the amazing power of the 12 Steps. Anything less would be a waste of this precious life. May I work always to make my sobriety a spiritual action and a benefit to everyone I come in contact with.

The disease of addiction is not temporary no matter how long I'm in recovery. Breathing in, I accept that fact. The main character defect of addiction is self-centeredness. Holding, I notice how it feels when I hold on to old ideas. Breathing out, I realize that I must let go of self absolutely, all day, every day, by making the focus of my life about others and not about myself. In this way, I practice unconditional love. Whenever there is an opportunity to forget my self and be of service to others, I take it without complaint. In this way, I am mindful of selfless service.

Spend a few moments being in your body. Know your addict. Know your Higher Power. Breathe in acceptance; breathe out gratitude. Live mindfully in love and light and peace and healing.

At the end of the above meditation, 12-Step Buddhists can go right into the Bodhisattva Vow.

Buddhist Integration of Step 12

The Bodhisattva Vow: Prayer to Generate Bodhicitta
With the wish to free all beings
I shall always go for refuge
to Buddha, Dharma, and Sangha,
Until I reach full enlightenment.
Inspired by wisdom and compassion,
Today, in the Buddha's presence,
I generate the mind of full awakening

For the benefit of all sentient beings.
As long as space remains
As long as sentient beings remain
Until then may I too remain
And dispel the miseries of the world.
—by His Holiness the Dalai Lama[2]

In my opinion, the ultimate solution of the 12 Steps is to find the bodhisattva path to complete enlightenment. I didn't know this for a really long time. It took over twenty years, some hard falls, and a lot of suffering. As a fellow addict said in a meeting recently, it takes what it takes, until it takes. The main practice of the bodhisattva path is to dedicate your life to others. This notion is echoed in typical 12-Step focus: "Our very lives, as ex-problem drinkers, depend on our constant thought of others and how we may help meet their needs,"[3] and "learning how to live in the greatest peace, partnership, and brotherhood with all men and women."[4] That's what a bodhisattva does. The path is the means by which a bodhisattva practices all the Paramitas. If you take the above statements literally, the argument can be made that the 12 Steps are, in fact, the bodhisattva path. This is how it looks to me, but it's not necessary that you see it that way. I think if you've followed along this far, however, it's hard to miss some very interesting parallels.

In the steps, we learn to practice selfless, unconditional love to stay in recovery. We've examined this concept through this treatment of the steps and through meditative examination of their principles. In Buddhism, we learn that our condition—samsara—is hopeless and our only salvation is to forget about our selves and dedicate our existence— no matter how long it takes—to saving literally every single conscious sentient being. Every one without exception. Sentient beings are numberless. I vow to save them all. That's the bodhisattva way, be it Zen, Tibetan, or another form of Buddhism.

If you're at all like I am, you probably think that this kind of commitment is only for more spiritual people. Those with more patience, less anger, and so forth. For me, I was much too angry for much too long to really consider myself spiritual.

Bokar Rinpoche says, "If we consider that ill will, anger, and hatred are defects, we are ready. We must take the vow. The vow helps us to improve. It will be useless for a person who has no ill will, who is good by nature, or who is not stained by conflicting emotions to take the vow. We take the vow precisely because we recognize the presence of ill will and conflicting emotions that we want to eliminate within ourselves. The more anger and aversion we see within ourselves, the more we must be determined to take the Bodhisattva vow."[5]

I could never understand, as I've said, how I could apply such sincere 12-Step work along with therapy and meditation for so long and still have so much trouble with thoughts and emotions. Then, in my second decade of sobriety, I met the lamas. I continued therapy and my program of recovery while taking teachings, doing meditation, and deep studying. I knew then that there was a way to integrate all of these solutions and to apply them to my amalgam of problems. The culmination of this search is to practice the bodhisattva path as a recovering addict.

From my perspective as an addict, for a normie, this path would seem impossible, but as an addict, I have all the motivation I need to really commit to serious Buddhist practice. I realize there are millions of Buddhists around the world, but I can't imagine—for myself—having the motivation to surrender at the level that Buddhism demands without the condition of addiction as the impetus. I can only guess what it's like for non-addicts, because I am an addict. As an addict through and through I can share that the discovery of the deeper aspects of Buddhism, by way of these amazing teachers, has made all the difference in my recovery. That difference is life rather than an excruciating, slow death—in or out of recovery.

The Ten Bhumis[6]

If we are to practice the bodhisattva path, we should be aware of the stages that we can expect to experience along the way. The Bhumis are the grounds or stages of the bodhisattva path. They are linked to the practice of the Paramitas, which can easily be linked with the 12 Steps via some meditation. That is, if you're willing to do a little work, as they're not always direct correlations. It's my understanding that the sequential stages outlined in Buddhism, be they from the lamrim or otherwise, aren't literally steps in the sense that one must achieve perfection at one level to progress to the next. In my own experience, spiritual progress has always been on different levels and at different speeds. Since everything is interrelated anyway, it seems that progress on one level facilitates understanding on another, but we must begin somewhere, and as the Buddha said, the journey of a thousand miles begins with the first step. These stages are outlined in brief below. I invite you to study them with a qualified teacher as you work a diligent program of recovery.

First Bhumi: "Joyful. A Bodhisattva embarks upon his career with the production of the thought of enlightenment—bodhicitta." We can relate this to any aspect of our steps by keeping in mind that the purpose of recovery is to become happy, joyous, and free. Anything we do in our program can be viewed as a positive step in that direction. We can supercharge that notion and our efforts if we view such actions as part of the bodhisattva path to complete enlightenment.

Second Bhumi: "Pure/Stainless. All immoral conduct and dispositions are eradicated." This might sound like a conflict with what is said in recovery about progress rather than perfection. Be sure not to overthink it. The full attainment of this stage comes after a long span of highly developed bodhisattva practice and is not necessarily something you can achieve in one lifetime. But maybe you can. Talk to your teacher about it and make sure to be realistic in your expectations.

Third Bhumi: "Luminous/Radiant. Through meditation, the Bodhisattva strengthens and deepens their insight." The 12-Step Buddhist can begin practicing this luminosity from day one. The light only gets brighter with time and effort. Make sure you Shine it everywhere you go. A smile is a great way to practice luminous radiance!

Fourth Bhumi: "Brilliant. All good qualities are vigorously pursued." I'd say that if we practice any of the principles of the 12 Steps with as much vigor as we pursued our addiction, we're progressing on this aspect of the bodhisattva path.

Fifth Bhumi: "Hard to Conquer. The Bodhisattva devotes their self to their own development and to the welfare of others." Here we don't get attached to or conditioned by the experiences and behaviors of others. A bodhisattva who has perfected this stage is able to truly walk anywhere on earth as a free being.

Sixth Bhumi: "Facing Forward/Obviously Transcendent. Great Wisdom into the true nature of phenomena is attained." If we take just one moment to really reflect on any crisis in our lives with "this too shall pass," we are practicing along this path. When a bodhisattva really knows this in his bones, he's said to have transcended samsara and nirvana.

Seventh Bhumi: "Going Far. The power of skillful means is attained." This is where the bodhisattva is said to be on the one-way path. The analogy of a snake stuck in a bamboo tube is applicable here. In this story, there are only two ways to go: up or down. As a 12-Step Buddhist, every move I make is either a step toward recovery or a step toward relapse.

Eighth Bhumi: "Immovable. The possibility of falling back [into samsara] is gone forever." A bodhisattva at this level is always able to abide in her Buddha nature and is thus immovable. She's not totally enlightened yet but is never going to relapse into samsara. In recovery, I don't think it's safe to think of ourselves as immovable in the sense of never being able to relapse. No matter how spiritual we may be or think we are, the only way to prove the point of transcending addiction is to engage in it as a test. I'm not willing to take that chance. Ever. In this I am immovable. We practice being immovable in our recovery when we don't let the preponderance of addictive tendencies sway us. But be careful; the Addict within may convince you otherwise.

Ninth Bhumi: "The Good/Discriminating Wisdom. The Bodhisattva teaches the doctrine to beings." At this stage, the bodhisattva is a dedicated teacher of the Dharma. We might liken this to making recovery our sole vocation, which the program warns us not to do, so don't make that mistake. When a bodhisattva gets to this level on the path, he is said to understand and speak all languages in all dimensions so that he may teach the Dharma to all beings. So I guess if you're an addict and you can make the claim to know all languages, you might be well on your way. Even if you feel like you can teach the Dharma to addicts in the street, before you decide that you're at this bodhisattva level, you'd better talk to your sponsor!

Tenth Bhumi: "Cloud of the Dharma. The Bodhisattva reaches full perfection and becomes a fully enlightened Buddha." You are said to "shower the rain of Dharma like a cloud and pacify the dust of afflicting emotions of sentient beings." There's no 12-Step equivalent to this, since Buddhism is a path that transcends itself. But we never graduate from recovery in the normal way of thinking. If you learn to rocket into the fourth dimension by practicing as a 12-Step Buddhist, you may become a Buddha faster than the average yogi. If you get to this level and become a Buddha, look me up. I'll gladly let you buy me a Starbucks.

We find ourselves on the path as 12-Step Buddhists by simply being mindful in meetings and in our daily lives, setting up chairs or being a greeter at our home group meeting or working in the trenches with suffering addicts in a detox unit. Selfless activity is the hallmark. If we take just a little of the Buddhist teachings into our recovery, we can cause a shift in the direction of our laser beam—our lives—that will surely put us in a different place from where we would be had we not been exposed to the Dharma. As Venerable Robina said, "The Buddha made statements that are outrageous! But we have to check ourselves to see if he was right. If we can apply even one percent of it in our lives, fantastic!"

Meditation: Pausing When Agitated

Begin with *shamatha*. Read this Christian prayer excerpt slowly, aloud, several times:

> Yea, though I walk through the valley of the shadow of death, I shall fear no evil, for thou art with me.[7]

Take a moment to let the meaning sink in. In Buddhist terms, the valley is samsara. The shadow of death is ever present, that is impermanence. Fear is evil, an incorrect assumption about the nature of reality, seemingly concrete, ever illusory. "Thou" are the Buddhas and bodhisattvas of the universe, the totally enlightened beings who have transcended ignorance and, in so doing, have developed the capacity to have, live, and be universal compassion/unconditional love—like a mother has for her only child—for every single pathetic, suffering being in all places and at all times. The victorious ones have the ability to bestow blessings, that is, to Shine the light on the path before me. But it is up to me to walk the path, to take the steps. Nobody can do it for me. The omniscient ones can send love and light, but it is entirely up to me to deal with the rotting vestiges of resentment that lurk in my heart like a black soul sentenced to a billion years of separation from all that is good and pure. This is all an illusion, a dreamlike apparition. I'm like a blind crazy man running into the streets, looking frantically for himself, not seeing that what he's looking *for*, he's looking *with*.

I can look back and see that my parents could have, should have, done a better job. I can continue to blame my conditions on everyone and everything except my own ignorance. But the steps and the teachings have made that deception impossible. Just as they say that AA will ruin your drinking, Buddhism will ruin your thinking. I am no longer able to construct the walls that keep me imprisoned in my own version of hell. What can I do?

I start where I am; feet on the ground; breathing in; breathing out; Buddha eyes open, looking deeply for the truth; Buddha ears, listening to the cries of sufferers in every realm with great compassion.

This breath may be my last. What should I do? What teaching can I remember that will help me now? I can think of the Buddha, the calmness, the smile, the sense of ease. I see a blue luminous figure over my head, sitting on a thousand-petal lotus of enlightenment. I see the white nectar of infinite compassion and wisdom pouring down over my body, filling it with light. Controlling my speech, I recite the mantra of the pure, the stainless, the Bhagavan, Tatagatha, Arhat, Perfectly Complete Buddha, Glorious Conqueror Shakyamuni Buddha.

TAYATA OM MUNI MUNI MAHA MUNIYE SOHA

Chanting this mantra over and over, I use my mind to visualize sending this light out to the hell realms—the realms where beings suffer uncontrollably with no hope for salvation. I know this hell; I know this suffering. My addiction has taken me there, and I never want to return.

The light radiates out now to the hungry ghost realms, where starving crackhead beings wander, infinitely searching for a little hit of whatever they think will cure them, searching in eternity for little white crack crumbs on the indoor-outdoor carpet of the universe, finding only lint. I've lived as a hungry ghost in my addiction. Even in recovery, I sense this aspect of my addict alive within me. May it never take me over again.

I send the compassionate and infinite Buddha light of universal, endless love to the animal realms, where beings chase each other and shred each other in an endless struggle for survival, parents eating their newborn young, tearing and ripping at each other's flesh, never realizing that there exists a path out of this suffering. I have lived as an animal in my addiction, fighting and clawing my way through life to get to the next fix, pill, drink, porno website, piece of cake, bet, person, or project. May I never have to live that way again, and may I do everything I can with this knowledge to free others from similar suffering.

My compassioned light of Buddha nature extends then to the human realm, where all reasoning human beings wander around the planet sucking up resources, taking what's not theirs, killing and causing misery on each other even though they alone have the capacity to learn and practice Dharma—the means to end this suffering. Through the process of inventory, I can see that there is nothing that any human has wanted to do, thought about doing, tried to do, or done that I have not at least considered myself. We are all in the same boat. My Buddha light goes out to them. May they hear the teachings.

The light extends to the jealous gods, who exist with great power and duration, but like everyone else in samsara, cannot be happy with what they have. I've lived in jealousy and envy and know how it feels to want what others have, only to get it and find out that this too cannot end my suffering. I send my light to these beings.

Continuing, out to the god realm, where formless beings sit in a sleepy state of pseudo-enlightenment for countless aeons—until their karmic tanks are empty and the merit of the past is entirely exhausted, sending them spiraling back into the lower realms. I've been spaced out, strung out, and flat-out crazy in my addiction. When I've been at my highest, I've felt like a formless god, out there in the cosmos dwelling on a temporary buzz that will only end in misery. To you gods, I send Buddha Light. May you be free.

The Buddha knows all this—all this suffering and the causes of suffering and the path that leads to the cessation of suffering. To the Buddha, I turn and take refuge. To the Dharma teachings, I turn and take refuge. To the noble Arya Sangha, I turn and take refuge, not only for myself but for all suffering sentient beings in all realms. No matter what it takes, I vow to save them all.

Aspects of Self: The Addict

I'd like to speak to the Controller. Controller, I'd like permission to speak to the Addict. Is that OK?

Please shift your body and get into the state of the Addict.

Whom am I speaking to?

How are you doing?

Well, we've had a nice long conversation with a lot of aspects, haven't we?

How do you feel about all of that?

Know that you are acknowledged. You are part of the whole.

Aspects of Self: The Bodhisattva of Compassion

I'd like to speak to the Controller. Controller, I'd like permission to speak to the Bodhisattva of Compassion. Is that OK?

Please shift your body and get into the state of the Bodhisattva of Compassion.

Whom am I speaking to?
Are there any limits to your compassion?
Is there anyone you do not love?
Please send the Addict some love.

Sit for a little while like this, in the state of absolute compassion.

Afterword:
Mindfulness—The Key to Compassion
Compassion—The Tool for Healing

With its release in 2009, the principles and practices of *The 12-Step Buddhist* laid the foundation for a way to integrate Buddhism with 12-Step recovery without necessarily having to leave traditional meetings behind. Since then, many thousands of people interested in Buddhism have come into recovery with the door wide open. Further books about Buddhism and recovery and subsequent workbooks have been written that have helped people work a Buddhism-oriented recovery program. Still, Buddhism is not for everyone. There are millions who suffer who will never set foot in an AA meeting or a Refuge Recovery or anything that seems remotely religious in orientation. A lot of them will die for lack of a solution that they can embrace. We need to do something about that. Any good Buddhist would.

What Is Spirituality?

The main problem I've heard in over thirty-four years in the recovery field is that people shut themselves off from healing because of bad experiences with religious figures, parents, and authority figures. As I mentioned earlier, the number of teachers gone bad in Buddhism, yoga, and other communities is staggering. Even some who have done much good and reached many people have effectively poisoned the well for new teachers and new students alike.

You can define your own spirituality. Just be sure to separate religion from spirituality. Religions are often about control and dogma. Spirituality is about being alive, whole, and free.

An artist taps deep into their soul to create poetry, music, or paintings but may be a devout atheist. Are they not spiritual? The spirit is the mystery, the unseen forces. No one knows where we came from, how we got here, or where we're going. These are the real questions of science, art, philosophy, and religion. In my view, they're also spiritual questions.

We can actually practice spirituality within the confines of a strict religious system. Or we can practice it outside of any system. We have total freedom in our choices as to how we approach our healing.

Though the principles of Buddhism are in their essence universal, psychological, and practical, difficulty remains for the general public in making the leap from a "religious" idea to a simply human way of being, such as compassion. I've personally never thought of Buddhism as a religion or of myself as belonging to a religion. There have been many who have made Buddhism pretty religious looking. I am, however, convinced of the power of a spiritual way of life in recovery. I wouldn't be here without one. But the question remains, can we cull the essential meaning out of practices that have been delivered in the "cup" of tradition and culture?

When I first got sober in 1984, I studied with fiery curiosity the tenets of metaphysical Christianity via writers like Emmet Fox and Ernest Holmes. I studied the Bible, the Psalms, and the Sermon on the Mount from a view quite different than that of Middle America in the 1970s when I grew up. I'm not Christian. But I'm not not-Christian. I still feel the spiritual power of Christ's message and that of the enlightened poets of the Psalms. The common threads of those teachings and those of the Buddha, and other masters, still fascinate and delight me after all these years of trying to work with and understand them.

In the background of this Buddhist emergence into recovery, clinicians have begun to study the science of things like mindfulness, compassion, self-compassion, and lovingkindness. Advances in brain imaging have given researchers the tools they need to observe changes in the brain that occur during meditation practices. Clinicians like Bessel van der Kolk, Peter Levine, and many others have a clear understanding of the benefits and limitations of traditional Western methods. You can't just take a pill and be all better. But a pill can possibly help you get to the root of the problem. Psychology can help you understand the problem. But a spiritual experience will make meaning that nothing else comes close to.

Rather than an either-or solution—either Western medicine or Eastern philosophy—those of us who want to help heal ourselves and each other have been calling for an integrated solution. Because people, situations, karma, and DNA are possible in an infinite variety of combinations. There is no one size fits all.

Sometimes it's like this. Sometimes it's like that.

We need to have a dynamic, adaptive, open system for healing that utilizes every possible tool to do what all good bodhisattvas are committed to doing: save all beings from suffering. The Buddha taught a certain thing at a certain time to a certain people. But as an enlightened being, was he limited? How could the Buddha be enlightened and limited? That means we can let go of things like fundamentalist notions and exclusive membership regulations. We in the helping professions need to find ways to be less limited when we define the audience we want to help and how we want to help them. We need a universal, dynamic, and adaptive approach that still has enough focus to be empirically tested.

To get there, we can look at what we have in common for clues to a common healing paradigm. We are all alive. We all suffer. If we don't get that, we have never heard a word that the Buddha said. When we do understand the Truth of Suffering, then we have an opportunity to practice being present to our own suffering with compassion. Then the door to wisdom can creak open just a bit. We begin to see things as they are, not as we wish them to be.

The Buddha taught that attachment is the root of suffering. If we understand that, then we know the basis of our common humanity. As AA says, look for the similarities, not the differences. Attachment is the root of addiction. Again, addiction is attachment gone wild. If we understand attachment—truly understand it—then we understand the nature of addiction. To heal addiction, we must understand the nature of attachment. It's a spectrum of what we share in common as sentient beings. From this point of view, there is no such thing as the "real addict" vs. the "normy." We're all addicts, sucking on the crack pipe of samsara with the same desperation of any good junkie.

Just as we have a common problem, suffering, we have a common solution, compassion. In essence, it really is that simple. But we need a program that helps us help each other without the limitations we've been using so far. AA hasn't changed its literature or thinking in over seventy-five years. They use the "singlemindedness of purpose" tradition as a way to keep focus, but it also serves as a roadblock to countless people who could otherwise be helped. I'm not suggesting that we get rid of AA meetings or that we try to make them change. That thought will get nowhere. What I am proposing is that we can use what we have learned that is good and effective from the 12-Step movement, along with what we know about Buddhism—and other spiritual, psychological, and scientific domains—to open up a path of healing that is truly universal, unlimited, and open to new things as we learn them.

The Spectrum of Attachment Addiction

There's healing from the attachments that keep us locked into a cycle of suffering that happen on different levels. At one level, the long-term meditator can eventually, maybe after decades or lifetimes, learn to let go of the sense of "I" that keeps her bound, until she becomes absorbed in the universal oneness of the great totality, or something like that. The man who can't stop taking painkillers long after his surgery is complete and long after he's lost his home, wife, and children can't worry about something as esoteric as the attachment to an "I." He needs to let go of the addiction to the drug that is killing him and work on getting his life back together.

There are stages of attachment and stages of addiction. But it's all one big continuum. Attachment simply means that we hold on to something. It can be physical, emotional, or mental. You can hold on to a rope in a tug of war, or a feeling of fear, or the belief that things will never get better. As we know from trauma research, we can be holding on to our trauma without even knowing that we have it. But our bodies know. And we suffer.

Is all attachment bad? From the Buddhist point of view, we must ultimately learn to let go of all attachments from the most obvious things, like material possessions, to the more subtle, like our ideas of who and what we are.

In psychology the theory of healthy attachment that I spoke about earlier deals with the human need to bond with our caregivers. This attachment theory says that if we bond with parents and mates in a way that helps us feel secure in the world, then we're doing good. As mammals, we cannot exist independently. We need love, bonding, and nurturing. When we don't learn how to form healthy attachments, we alternatively form anxieties, fears, and phobias. If we experience traumas, that can later lead us to form a sort of replacement attachment to something like a drug or toxic people, as we discussed in some detail.

But the aims of psychology and spirituality have traditionally been different. Although things are changing—in that the field of psychology has become more informed about the benefits of spiritual practices, such as compassion—the main point of psychotherapy has typically been focused on crisis intervention, learning to cope and manage and get back to your job. The psychotherapist is not your guru, isn't trying to lead you—let alone all beings—out of the infinite ocean of cyclic existence to a place of liberation. Therapists are beginning to realize, and some have always known, how hard it is to really help people long term. The science is starting to show how spiritual practices, reworked into a secular context, are powerful factors in healing.

Making Science of Spiritual Practice

I feel that it would be very useful to develop instruments to measure the spectrum of attachment addiction. In order to test the efficacy of practices such as mindfulness and compassion, psychologists have secularized the practices. This way they're open to anyone from any religion or background. The practices can be measured, along with states of being before, during, and after the research studies. I've participated in one of these that has helped me along in my understanding of many things such as compassion, self-compassion, and the value of bringing the benefits of tools that started in Buddhist and other systems to more people who can and do benefit. I was helped in meaningful and measurable ways. We are all in the same boat, and we need to help each other.

Thupten Jinpa, PhD, is the CEO of Compassion Institute. The author of *A Fearless Heart: How the Courage to Be Compassionate Can Transform Our Lives* and the Dalai Lama's translator since 1985, Jinpa worked with Stanford's Center for Compassion and Altruism Research and Education to help carry out the Dalai Lama's wish from years earlier. The Dalai Lama had met with Western psychologists and told them they were spending so much time studying the pathology of the human condition, why not study things like the benefits of mindfulness and compassion? The science has been going on for many years now and has been part of a massive shift in the consciousness of clinicians, researchers, healthcare workers, law enforcement officials, economists, and policy makers. In an effort to bring the science of compassion to more people, the Compassion Institute was formed as a separate organization, but still closely connected with Stanford.

The institute devised a course called Compassion Cultivation Training, which has reached more than ten thousand people in nineteen countries and nine languages. From their site:

What is Compassion Cultivation Training?

Compassion Cultivation Training (CCT) is an eight-week program designed to develop the qualities of compassion, empathy, and kindness for oneself and for others. CCT integrates traditional contemplative practices with contemporary psychology and scientific research on compassion. The CCT protocol was developed at Stanford

University by a team of contemplative scholars, clinical psychologists, and researchers.

Compassion

Compassion is a process that unfolds in response to suffering. It begins with the recognition of suffering, which gives rise to thoughts and feelings of empathy and concern. This, in turn, motivates action to relieve that suffering.

Cultivation

Humans have a natural capacity for compassion. However, everyday stress, social pressures, and life experiences can make it difficult to fully express this capacity. Each of us can choose to nurture and grow the compassionate instinct, like a plant that is carefully cultivated from a seed. This process requires patience, steady care, proper tools, and a supportive environment.

Training

The process of cultivating compassion involves training our own minds, developing specific skills in how we relate to others and ourselves, and intentionally choosing compassionate thoughts and actions. In CCT, the training process includes:

- Daily meditation practices to develop lovingkindness, empathy, and compassion.
- A two-hour weekly class that includes lecture, discussion, and in-class exercises.
- Real-world "homework" assignments to practice compassionate thoughts and actions.[1]

I took this course for eight weeks with a group of healthcare workers, mostly nurses, hospice workers, and social workers. We met on Wednesday evenings in the blustery cold and wet San Diego February and did simple meditations that I've been practicing, and teaching, for many years. I was amazed from the very beginning at how easy it was for non-addicts, non-Buddhists, and non-meditators to grasp and develop, as AA says, simple tools for healing. We met and did simple settling practices such as grounding in our bodies and with our breath. We talked a little bit about the science but not too much. We mostly did practices about lovingkindness and shared gently with each other about our experiences, limitations, and breakthroughs. We broke off into dyads and triads, looked into each other's eyes, and said things like, "May you be free of suffering. May you be happy." Sometimes we cried a little. People wrote and read poems. Nobody went on with personal dramas or dominated the group. The facilitators compassionately and skillfully guided us to go a little deeper and practice a little softer with ourselves and each other.

It was a game changer for me. I learned that if you distill the essence of spiritual practices, they can still be powerful and effective tools for healing. If you do things in a set way, test them out, measure the effectiveness of the tools, and try different models, you can create a sequence and a system that really works. Many of the nurses have done the course several times. They're all beautiful caregivers who really want to help others yet have run into the same old walls that each of us faces within ourselves.

I also learned something else that one would think a long-term Buddhist in recovery who writes books on the subject would well have mastered by now. I learned that to be compassionate is different than being an empath. I am an empath. I feel what other people feel. I read energy and have impressions—visual, emotional, visceral— from my environment constantly. Being an empath, as monk Matthieu Ricard says, is like having an electric motor that just burns itself up. We need to infuse our empathy with love and compassion. Because to be compassionate is to suffer with, to want to change or help the suffering of another. But the real wisdom here is that ultimately, we may not be able to "fix" anything. So our mindfulness, our ability to simply be present to suffering in ourselves and each other, is the key that opens the door to compassion. We can suffer with, bear witness to, and care deeply about others without getting overwhelmed by what is happening inside ourselves. Let me tell you, this was quite an eye-opener for me, and I can see the potential for a lifetime of healing as the result of the awareness that I've gained from this experience.

Compassionate Recovery Is the Next Step

The next step in recovery, beyond the concepts and practices of *The 12-Step Buddhist* and other works in the field, is to create a collaborative worldwide community of healers, scientists, and practitioners who work together to support compassion and its healing powers.

This isn't a one-person problem, so it's not a one-person solution. Attachment to one degree or another is everyone's problem. Compassion is a solution that everyone can learn, practice, and embrace. It helps so many things. Compassion is universal. The Dalai Lama has spent his lifetime traveling and teaching us this simple truth. We don't need to be religious or even call ourselves spiritual to be kind to ourselves and each other.

Compassionate Recovery isn't meant to be a replacement for any other program that people use to get better, so let's talk just a little about what it is. After that, I'll see you in the next book to go into more detail.

What Is Compassionate Recovery?

Compassionate Recovery (CR) is a set of principles that anyone can practice to loosen the grip of attachment and addiction. Attachment is defined as an unhealthy bond, fixation, obsession, or preoccupation that causes a life disruption. In CR, addiction is defined more loosely as any attachment to a process, event, substance, or person that the individual wants to be free of. Recovery is defined as any reduction, elimination, or progress on the path of healing. One can opt to claim one or more "clean dates" for different afflictions or opt out of the traditional timelines altogether. CR seeks to reduce the sense of shame, one of the main components of trauma and addiction.

What's Different? 12-Step vs. Compassionate Recovery

12-Step	Compassionate Recovery
Has love and tolerance as a principle	Is based on compassion from the beginning with the understanding of trauma as a strong correlate to addiction
Is service oriented; helps a lot of people	Takes service and community-level involvement as a basic foundation
Is theoretically non-dogmatic; integrates spiritual principles into everyday life	Openly welcomes any and all tools in a way that's safe for everyone
Integrates spiritual principles into everyday life	Integrates principles based on science, psychology, *and* anything else that works
Has meditation as a tool	Begins with meditation as a foundation
Exclusive; one must identify as an alcoholic or addict to be a member, share at meetings, and feel a part of the program	Inclusive; no identification is required or encouraged; a person can participate if they feel they have an attachment that is problematic in any place on the spectrum of attachment–addiction
Monotheistic, patriarchal, male-dominated	Poly- or nontheistic, no hierarchy, sensitive to language that is neutral and welcoming to women, people of color, LGBTQ, and others who may be considered marginalized

12-Step	Compassionate Recovery
Steps must be worked in order	No steps, only principles that can be dipped into, learned, experienced, and practiced in any amount of time by anyone
Ignorant of science	Utilizes scientific understanding of trauma, addiction, and compassion as it develops
Fixed	Open to change
There are no leaders; the blind leading the blind	Use of trained facilitators as well as community-led groups and meetings
Unaware of underlying trauma that contributes to addiction	Cognizant, embraces the role of trauma from the beginning of the recovery process
Sees sobriety from a limited perspective; "As long as I don't take a drink, that's all that matters"	Sobriety from one thing, such as a substance, is one aspect of many that can be addressed and healed; the wholeness of the individual is considered
Literature is limited	Open to any literature or training that can provide support
Closed to "outside issues"	Open to all issues that address the total human and the ultimate evolution of people on the planet
Recovery is seen as abstinence only	Other models, such as harm reduction, can be used

Continued on next page

12-Step	Compassionate Recovery
Recovery is measured in time off from a particular substance; simple program for complicated people	Recovery is seen as a complex path for complex people and can be measured in terms of happiness and an overall sense of wellness and wholeness setting the stage for long-term recovery; the tools are simple but the individual is never minimized and problems are not oversimplified
Very little cooperation with research	Where possible, evidence-based research is used to create skill trainings and practices for Compassionate Recovery; encourages members to be open to helping out with research so that the best possible programs can be developed to help the most people over time; this is always optional but is recommended; the best data gives us the most information in order to be of maximum benefit to all beings; now that we have smartphones, tablets, and watches, we can submit anonymous data to researchers to fine-tune the trainings and groups as we go; this is a pretty exciting time to be in recovery!

What's Different? Refuge Recovery vs. Compassionate Recovery

Refuge Recovery	Compassionate Recovery
Specifically Buddhist; too "hipster Buddhist" for some	Open to any tool from any tradition; secular to light spirituality
Author and teacher discredited; teaching rights revoked	Non guru-centric; principles based, rather than dogma based
Schisms and wounding in the community	Committee oversight
Issues with rewriting the book; copyright lawsuits	Fresh slate, no legal issues
Is meditation based and, to an extent, compassion oriented	Is meditation based but also science based
More open than AA to alternative thinking	Even more open to integrate into communities and existing modalities
Is popular and growing	Not about a brand or an alternative as much as an integration to reach more people and relieve suffering

Compassionate Recovery Meetings

CR has at least two kinds of community meetings available. One is without a facilitator, and one uses someone who has different levels of training, depending on the skills being used. For example a non-facilitated meeting will have a meeting leader, much like a traditional 12-Step meeting. They read the format, introduce a topic, and facilitate meditation and sharing, not as a teacher, but as a peer with some training.

The *Compassionate Recovery* book can be used to read from. Other books and materials are also welcome if approved by the group. Various meeting formats as well as guided meditations can be downloaded from the website. Simple practices can be followed with easy-to-read written guidelines. Since Compassionate Recovery uses skills that you don't find in 12-Step style groups, we offer skills trainings. These are available online and in person and will be for peers to help run meetings. For deeper understanding with more science and technical skill focus, skills trainings for clinicians and treatment centers are also available. See compassionaterecovery.net for more. This is where the collaboration with the larger community is of benefit. A CR committee will vet and guide the process of creating new trainings and cooperating with researchers to get measurable results.

The meetings are dynamic in that they can focus on specific topics, addictions, or principles such as life skills, meditation, breathing, mindful eating, yoga, or nonviolent communication. Topics can be based on the needs of the community. Therapists and treatment centers can be certified in Compassionate Recovery and can offer specific groups led by trained facilitators. This collaboration serves the community, rather than being at odds with it as has been the case between 12-Step groups and 12-Step-based treatment programs.

The book and support groups walk readers through discussions and exercises, meditations, and goal setting on topics such as smoking, weight loss, relationships, meditation, financial health, emotional well-being, nutrition, and brain health as well as the more common issues of substance abuse. The big picture of a spectrum of recovery is visible from the beginning. There's more to be developed, and I'm very happy to be able to offer this work to the recovery community and everyone else who can benefit.

As Chuck C. said, "We have as far to go as we have come."

Stay tuned at compassionaterecovery.net.

I'll leave you with a practice that you can try right now and which ties together a lot of what I've learned as a 12-Step Buddhist and what I'll be sharing more about in *Compassionate Recovery*.

Stance of Self-Compassion

Stand with your feet separated. Bend your knees a little. Push down into your feet so you feel rooted. Lift up your torso from the waist up. If you're unable to stand, modify in whatever way you can so you feel strong.

This is your power stance. You are not a victim. You have power, the power of compassion. Say the following words.

I am self-empowered.
I live in the heart of compassion.
My choices are mine to make.
I allow myself the freedom and self-compassion to choose not to
    practice my attachments, just for today.

Breathe in deeply. Feel a warm, rosy-colored light at your heart center. Exhale. Let go of wounds. Let go of suffering. Repeat a few times, slowly.

Put your hands on your chest, face, or belly. Think of how you would treat a friend who was suffering. Now, how do you feel about yourself when you are suffering?

Ask yourself what you need.

What do I need?

Give it to yourself. Bring online any sense of generosity, patience, or kindness that you would offer a friend or loved one. Say the following words out loud or silently to yourself:

May I live in compassion.
May I be happy.
I am at peace.
May I be free of suffering.
I am strong.
May I feel strong.
From this center I live and move and have my being.
May all beings be free of suffering.
May we all know our own strength.
May all beings be happy.

Peace out and Namaste!

—Darren Littlejohn
San Diego, CA
March 1, 2019

Acknowledgments

Writing and publishing are collaborative efforts. The process of getting one's thoughts in a clear form for readers is not, in my opinion, possible without the help of kind and astute people who share the same vision or at least carry a great appreciation for it. To all of these people I owe a great debt.

I wish to thank Tysa for the patience and compassion of a bodhisattva since the day we met in 1997. Without her support on many levels, I would not have found myself in conditions favorable to writing or to the spiritual process in general.

Thank you Dr. Thurman for the beautiful foreword. In reading it aloud (in between tissues), it struck me that the goal of this book had been reached. If this were indeed my last breath, I would go out knowing I did something. One couldn't ask for a better understanding from a more respected teacher. As my lamas say, many *Tashi Delegs*.

John Nelson, editor extraordinaire, clarified my thinking and the language of the book's text. Ever trimming and adding, he also helped get the proposal in a shape that landed me an agent. John also coined the title, which is perfect. Thank you, John.

My literary agent, Barbara Neighbors Deal of Literary Associates, gave me excellent advice to seek out and work with an editor of her choice. After I followed it and we provided a work worthy of her consideration, she had further tips to shape both the proposal and first draft. I also thank Barbara for her belief in me and in the importance of this work, and for winnowing the selection process down to Beyond Words Publishing.

Cynthia Black at Beyond Words saw the potential in the book's proposal and in me. Literally, on her way out of town one afternoon, she squeezed me in for a short meeting. It turned out to be long enough, combined with the sample chapters, for her to make a decision to publish this book. May all beings benefit.

Thank you to my test readers: David Valdez, sax genius, and Vajra sisters Suzca Zamecnickova, Beth Norris, and Sharon Cardamone—who read the most—Kate Ryder, Sarah Meyer, and Michele Happe. Without your feedback and encouragement, this book would have been less accessible to those who need it most. Thanks to Donald Altman, author of *Loving Kindness*; Elaine Jackson at Vajrapani; Cutty and Diane Hyde and Ron Baker—thank you for helping finance the late-stage editing. The project would be dead in the water without you.

John Carney, who was there for me every time I needed him from 1985 until his passing in 2005. John Peterson, for being my friend since 1991 and picking up where John C. left off—but mostly for teaching me about the Funnel and the spiritual thirst necessary for progressive recovery. To all my sober friends throughout the years: thank you for keeping me alive.

Craig Zarling, who told me to go for it in my recovery and writing, has consistently helped me to see that life is not about black or white, all good or all bad but, in effect, is both. Thank you for your compassion, patience, flexibility, and skill.

My teachers: Joko Beck for never letting me believe my negative thoughts, Rubin Habito for helping me when I was down, Larry Christensen for being my Zen therapist/teacher/friend for all these years. To Lama Zopa Rinpoche who stimulated the idea for this book and beamed like a radiant jewel when I told him I was really doing it; Venerable Ingrid, who told me it needed to be done and I was the one to do it; Venerable Robina, of course, who challenged me enough to get my attention and make me think more deeply about so many things.

Yangsi Rinpoche for teaching me meditation in the Tibetan style, as well as for his encouragement to find my own path; Chogyal Namkhai Norbu Rinpoche, without whose direct transmission I would still be floundering, confused in the sea of Dharma teachings. Thank you,

Rinpoche, for your clarity and your wish that this book would help many people.

To all Buddhas and bodhisattvas of the past, present, and future. May your blessings continue to fall like rain until every suffering being is free.

NAMO GURU BHYE—homage to all the teachers. Please continue to turn the Dharma wheel for knuckleheads like me.

Glossary

Addict: As used here, more comprehensive than the term *alcoholic*. An addict is any person who is unable to control participation in addiction of any kind, including alcohol.

Addiction: The inability to control frequency and/or duration of use and subsequent results of any substance, event, process, or person/relationship, despite negative consequences.

Attachment: An unhealthy bond, fixation, preoccupation, or obsession that causes a life disruption.

Arhat: An enlightened yogi in the Hinayana tradition. Some traditions define Arhat as synonymous with a Buddha, but according to the Mahayana, an Arhat is not yet a completed Buddha.

Buddha: Awakened one, has omniscient (but not omnipotent) mind with total clairvoyance. Has the capacity to see the minds of sentient beings so that they may be helped along the path to awakening.

Compassion: The willingness to be present to the suffering of others, and the desire to help.

Compassionate Recovery: From the book by Darren Littlejohn, a universal, inclusive, trauma-informed approach to healing from any attachment or addiction.

Calm abiding: See Shine.

Chenrezig: A male deity in Tibetan Buddhism. See also Avalokiteshvara (Sanskrit). The female aspect of Chenrezig is Kuan Yin, mostly practiced in China.

Deity: In Tibetan Buddhism, a deity is considered a manifestation of the Buddha. We practice the deity that corresponds to the particular condition we are faced with. For example, some deities are peaceful and some are wrathful. The practice of any one deity could be seen as a complete system leading to enlightenment.

Dependent origination: Everything in the universe comes into being as the result of a previous cause. Nothing stands autonomously, on its own, from its own side. This is the basis for testing reality that eventually leads the practitioner to a realization of emptiness.

Dharma: Generally refers to the Buddha's teachings; may also mean phenomena, attributes, qualities, or mental objects.[1]

Dzogchen: "In Tibetan, literally 'great perfection'; the primary teaching of the Nyingmapa school of Tibetan Buddhism. This teaching, also known as Ati Yoga [extraordinary yoga] is considered by its adherents as the definitive and most secret teaching of Shakyamuni Buddha."[2] Namkhai Norbu Rinpoche said, "To know or discover the real sense of the Dzogchen teaching . . . you listen well and try to understand the meaning of the teaching, and then use the methods. . . . That is the only way you can discover the real meaning of Dzogchen."[3]

Empathy: The ability to feel the suffering of another as if it is happening to ourselves.

Emptiness: The not finding of an inherently existing self, or any other internal or external phenomenon. Emptiness is not nothingness, however. The realization of emptiness is seen as the pinnacle of spiritual development in many Buddhist traditions. In Dzogchen, it is seen as a necessary prerequisite for Buddhahood but not adequate by itself.

Enlightenment: The state of complete awakening or Buddhahood.

Four Schools: The four main schools of Tibetan Buddhism are Nyingmapa, Kagupa, Sakya, and Gelugpa. See Reginald Ray, *Indestructible Truth*.

Green Tara: A female deity in Tibetan Buddhism whose practice is widely used. See Step 11 for a type of Tara practice.

Guru: Pali for spiritual teacher.

Higher Power: Often abbreviated as HP in recovery literature. Refers to God, Creator, and Father.

Hinayana: Lesser Vehicle, focus on becoming an Arhat for the sake of ending one's own suffering.

Karma: Literally, action. Physical, verbal, or mental acts that imprint habitual tendencies in the mind.[4]

Kaya: Body or aspect of a Buddha. See Trikaya.

Koan: A Zen puzzle, impossible to solve through cognition. A koan is designed to confound the mind to the point of awakening.

Lama: Tibetan for teacher/guru.

Lineage: "The tracks of a teaching, a text, or a person backward in time to its point of origin is the Buddhist mechanism for authority. The heir to a direct line of transmissions, leading often back to the Buddha himself, is the legitimate holder of that lineage."[5]

Mahamudra: A system of Tibetan Buddhism that utilizes the union of compassion and emptiness through Vajrayana practices. See Dzogchen Ponlop's *Wild Awakening*, (Shambala, 2003).

Mahayana: Great Vehicle, where the practitioner works on enlightenment not just for his/her own sake but for the benefit of all suffering beings.

Meditation: The practice of (Tib: gom pa) becoming familiar with one's own condition through observing and working with mind and experiences.

Mindfulness: Placing the attention on an object, the breath, the body, or a concept like compassion and letting other thoughts quiet.

Nirvana: Absolute happiness, the realization of our true condition, complete awakening, wherein the realms of sight and sound, cause and effect, birth and death are seen as empty of inherent existence and no longer bind the individual to samsara through the misperception of dualistic vision.

Normie: A non-addict, one who is not addicted to anything.

Paramita: Literally, reaching the other shore; refers primarily to the six transcendent actions of generosity, discipline, patience, diligence, meditative concentration, and knowledge.[6]

Post-traumatic stress disorder (PTSD): A syndrome that develops following exposure to an extremely horrific event(s) in which the person has flashbacks of the trauma and perceives a heightened threat long term to the point of having a negative effect on his or her lifestyle. Can also appear as complex PTSD, in which the individual also struggles with emotional regulation and self-worth as a result of the trauma(s).

Recovery: The lifelong healing process of letting go of attachments and addictions. It may or may not include total abstinence from particular substances.

Refuge: The act of seeking help and turning to someone or something for shelter from suffering. In Buddhism there are many forms of refuge. See *The Power of Vow* by Darren Littlejohn.

Refuge Recovery: A Buddhism-based program of recovery with worldwide meetings, based on the book by Noah Levine.

Rinpoche: A title given to a Tibetan lama who is a recognized Tulku (reincarnate lama). Often given in name only as part of the monastic tradition. See Reginald Ray for an excellent treatment of this topic.

Samaya: A tantric commitment to do certain practices and maintain vows and views until complete enlightenment is achieved.

Samsara: The infinite cycle of suffering, birth, and death. The freedom from samsara is nirvana.

Shamatha: The practice and result of focusing the mind on a single object. Higher forms of Tantra teach objectless or formless *shamatha*. The result in either is Shine (calm state) and eventually integration with all experiences.

Shine (shi-nay): Tibetan for "the calm state," also called calm abiding. Achieved primarily by practicing *shamatha* but not exclusively.

Single-pointed concentration: See Shamatha.

Sponsee: One who is sponsored in a 12-Step program. See Sponsor.

Sponsor: An experienced person in a 12-Step program whose main responsibility is to act as a spiritual guide and mentor through the process of the 12 Steps.

Sutra: The scriptures of Buddhism focused mainly on individual liberation in the Hinayana—liberation for all beings in the Mahayana—through the path of renunciation.

Tantra: Literally, continuation of energy. In Sanskrit, "continuum."[7] Tantra can refer to a scriptural text or a system of practice. It is an expedited method of the Mahayana, where enlightenment can be achieved more rapidly than through lower methods.

Tantrism: The practice of Tantra in the Vajrayana tradition of Tibetan Buddhism. It emphasizes the path of transformation through practice of certain deities through visualizations, mantras, offerings, and dedications. Advanced practices include breathing techniques in combination with the above to coordinate energies within the gross, subtle, and most subtle body (levels of energy) of the practitioner. Consult a lama for more details.

The program: The 12-Step program, whichever of the hundred or so that are currently available.

The rooms: Where 12-Step program meetings are held.

The steps: The 12 Steps, created by Alcoholics Anonymous.

Tibetan Buddhism: Tibetan Buddhism is the body of religious Buddhist doctrine and institutions characteristic of Tibet and the Himalayan regions.

Tonglen: The practice of exchanging self for others. Breathe in their suffering, breathe out your happiness or goodwill. Note: This can be done for the self as well. See *Compassionate Recovery* by Darren Littlejohn.

Trauma: Unhealed emotional, psychological, and spiritual wounds.

Trikaya: The Three Kayas. In Sanskrit, literally "the Three Bodies: the three aspects of Buddhahood: dharmakaya, sambhogakaya and nirmanakaya."[8]

Tulku: Literally the emanated body of a Buddha. In Tibetan culture, a Buddhist master can reincarnate deliberately at the right place and time in order to be of compassionate service to beings. Tulku is not synonymous with Rinpoche, but they are often used interchangeably.

Vajrayana: In Sanskrit, "Diamond Vehicle."[9] The systems of Vajrayana practice utilize initiations and samaya, mantras, and visualizations to achieve the perfection of a deity.

Yana: In Sanskrit, "Vehicle,"[10] in which the practitioner travels on the way to enlightenment.

Yoga: "Any form of spiritual discipline aimed at gaining control over the mind with the ultimate aim of attaining liberation from rebirth."[11] Yoga, as treated in Buddhism, is not limited to Hatha Yoga, as popularized in the West. Really any form of practice can be thought of as a type of yoga. You can call the work in this book the Yoga of Recovery if you like.

Yogi: Male yoga practitioner.

Yogini: Female yoga practitioner.

Zen: *Chan* in Chinese. A branch of Buddhism that emerged in Japan in the Samurai days, but the practices differ from region to region, particularly from East to West. Zen is Japanese interpretation of Chan and is a tradition of meditation that emphasizes no-thought, no-mind, no-self. The intention is to move beyond thought to the realization of Emptiness through direct experience and observation. Zen practice is almost entirely non-scriptural in that recitation and study of texts is not emphasized, particularly in American Zen. Some traditions use koans to this end.

Notes

Introduction

1. *Alcoholics Anonymous: The Story of How Many Thousands of Men and Women Have Recovered from Alcoholism*, 4th ed. (New York: Alcoholics Anonymous World Services, Inc., 2002), 84. Most 12-Steppers will refer to this as "The Big Book" or "The Basic Text."

2. Nora D. Volkow, "Addiction and Co-Occurring Mental Disorders," *NIDA Notes* 21, no. 2 (February 2007), http://www .drugabuse.gov/NIDA_notes/NNvol21N2/DirRepVol21N2.html.

3. American Psychiatric Association, "Criteria for Substance Abuse," *Diagnostic and Statistical Manual of Mental Disorders*, 5th ed. (Arlington, VA: American Psychiatric Association, 2013), 483.

4. *Alcoholics Anonymous: The Story of How Many Thousands of Men and Women Have Recovered from Alcoholism*, 4th ed. (New York: Alcoholics Anonymous World Services, Inc., 2002), 25.

5. Ibid., 275.

6. Chuck C., *A New Pair of Glasses*, 9th ed. (Irvine, CA: New Look Publishing Co., 2003).

7. Alcoholics Anonymous, *Twelve Steps and Twelve Traditions*, 13th ed. (New York: The AA Grapevine, Inc. and Alcoholics Anonymous World Services, Inc., 1999), 15.

8. Bessel van der Kolk, *The Body Keeps the Score: Brain, Mind, and Body in the Healing of Trauma* (New York: Viking, 2014), 559.

9. *Denver Post*, "California Yoga Mogul's Mysterious Death: Trevor Tice's Drunken Last Hours Detailed," January 27, 2017, https:// www.mercurynews.com/2017/01/27/coroner-death-trevor-tice -colorado-native-corepower-yoga-founder-accidental/.

Chapter 1

1. *Alcoholics Anonymous: The Story of How Many Thousands of Men and Women Have Recovered from Alcoholism*, 4th ed. (New York: Alcoholics Anonymous World Services, Inc., 2002), 25.

2. Ibid., 60.

3. Ibid., 30.

4. Margalis Fjelstad, *Stop Caretaking the Borderline or Narcissist: How to End the Drama and Get On with Life* (Lanham, MD: Rowman & Littlefield, 2013), 41.

5. Amir Levine, *Attached: The New Science of Adult Attachment and How It Can Help You Find—and Keep—Love* (New York: Tarcher Perigree, 2010), 44.

6. Janna Lawrence, "Psychedelics: Entering a New Age of Addiction Therapy," *Pharmaceutical Journal* 293, no. 7834 (November 1, 2014), https://www.pharmaceutical-journal.com/news-and-analysis/feature/psychedelics-entering-a-new-age-of-addiction-therapy/20066899.article.

7. *Alcoholics Anonymous: The Story of How Many Thousands of Men and Women Have Recovered from Alcoholism*, 4th ed. (New York: Alcoholics Anonymous World Services, Inc., 2002), 164.

Chapter 3

1. Joseph Califano, interview by Charlie Rose, June 2007, *The Charlie Rose Show*, Public Broadcasting System, https://charlierose.com/videos/11605.

2. The White House Office of National Drug Control Policy (ONDCP), "What America's Users Spend on Drugs" (September 1997), http://www.whitehousedrugpolicy.gov/publications/drugfact/retail/c_conclusion.html (page discontinued).

3. Substance Abuse and Mental Health Services Administration and Office of the Surgeon General, *Facing Addiction in America: The Surgeon General's Report on Alcohol, Drugs, and Health* (Washington, DC: U.S. Department of Health and Human Services, 2016), https://www.ncbi.nlm.nih.gov/books/NBK424860/.

4. U.S. Centers for Disease Control and Prevention (CDC), "Drug Use, HIV, and the Criminal Justice System" (August 2001), http://www.thebody.com/content/art17049.html.

5. Alcoholics Anonymous, "Estimated Worldwide A.A. Individual and Group Membership"(2018), https://www.aa.org/assets/en_US/smf-132_en.pdf.

6. National Institute on Drug Abuse (NIDA), "Treatment Histories: The Long View of Addiction," *NIDA Notes* 12, no. 5 (September/October 1997), https://archives.drugabuse.gov/news-events/nida-notes/1997/10/treatment-histories-long-view-addiction.

7. Alan I. Leshner, "Addiction Is a Brain Disease," *Issues in Science and Technology* 17, no. 3 (Spring 2001), https://issues.org/leshner.

8. National Institute on Drug Abuse (NIDA), "Treatment Approaches for Drug Addiction," NIDA InfoFacts (June 2008, accessed October 16, 2008), http://www.drugabuse.gov/Infofacts/treatmeth.html.

9. U.S. Department of Health and Human Services, "Key Findings: The Neurobiology of Substance Use, Misuse, and Addiction," Surgeongeneral.gov, accessed March 20, 2019, https://addiction.surgeongeneral.gov/key-findings/neurobiology.

10. Bessel van der Kolk, *The Body Keeps the Score: Brain, Mind, and Body in the Healing of Trauma* (New York: Penguin, 2014), 55.

11. Ibid., 60.

12. Fulton T. Crews, T. Jordan Walter, Leon G. Coleman Jr., and Ryan P. Vetreno, "Toll-Like Receptor Signaling and Stages of Addiction," *Psychopharmacology* 234, no. 9–10 (May 2017), https://doi.org/10.1007/s00213-017-4560-6.

13. Substance Abuse and Mental Health Services Administration and Office of the Surgeon General, "The Neurobiology of Substance Use, Misuse, and Addiction" in *Facing Addiction in America: The Surgeon General's Report on Alcohol, Drugs, and Health* (Washington, DC: U.S. Department of Health and Human Services, 2016), https://www.ncbi.nlm.nih.gov/books/NBK424849/.

14. There are numerous studies surrounding the long-term effects of drug and alcohol addictions on the brain and body, including DNA damage. http://www.time.com/time/magazine/article /0,9171,1640436,00.html.

15. Clearview Treatment Programs, "The 5 Stages of Drug & Alcohol Addiction" (2019), https://www.clearviewtreatment.com /blog/stages-drug-alcohol-addiction/.

16. Maren A. Masino and Janina Fisher, "Addictive Disorders and the Traumatized Brain," July 6, 2018, slide 9, accessed March 28, 2019, https://www.slideshare.net/iCAADEvents/maren-masino.

17. PTSD United, "PTSD Statistics" (2013), http://www .ptsdunited.org/ptsd-statistics-2/.

18. Sidran Institute, "Traumatic Stress Disorder Fact Sheet" (November 2018), https://www.sidran.org/wp-content/uploads /2018/11/Post-Traumatic-Stress-Disorder-Fact-Sheet-.pdf.

19. Lisa M. Najavits, *Recovery from Trauma, Addiction, or Both: Strategies for Finding Your Best Self* (New York: Guilford Publications, 2017), 104–105.

20. "About the CDC-Kaiser AVE Study: ACEs Definitions," Centers for Disease Control and Prevention website, last modified June 14, 2016, https://www.cdc.gov/violenceprevention/childabuseand neglect/acestudy/about.html.

21. Maren A. Masino and Janina Fisher, "Addictive Disorders and the Traumatized Brain," July 6, 2018, slide 9, accessed March 28, 2019, https://www.slideshare.net/iCAADEvents/maren-masino.

22. World Health Organization, "Post Traumatic Stress Disorder," ICD-11: International Classification of Diseases, 11th Revision, June 18, 2018, https://icd.who.int/browse11/l-m/en#/http%3a%2f%2fid .who.int%2ficd%2fentity%2f2070699808.

23. World Health Organization, "Complex Post Traumatic Stress Disorder," ICD-11: International Classification of Diseases, 11th Revision, June 18, 2018, https://icd.who.int/browse11/l-m/en# /http%3a%2f%2fid.who.int%2ficd%2fentity% 2f585833559.

24. Maria Olga Sakellariou and Athena Stefanatou, "Neurobiology of PTSD and Implications for Treatment: An Overview," *Pulsus* (2017), https://www.pulsus.com/scholarly-articles/neurobiology-of-ptsd-and-implications-for-treatment-an-overview.html.

25. Christine A. Courtois, "It's Not You, It's What Happened to You: Treatment for Adults Interpersonally Traumatized as Children" (PowerPoint presentation, Melissa Institute for Violence Prevention and Treatment conference, University of Miami, Coral Gables, FL, May 5, 2017).

26. Michael Pollan, *How to Change Your Mind: What the New Science of Psychedelics Teaches Us about Compassion, Dying, Addiction, Depression, and Transcendence* (New York: Penguin, 2018), 360.

27. Global Ibogaine Therapy Alliance, "What Is Ibogaine?" accessed March 22, 2019, https://www.ibogainealliance.org/ibogaine/.

28. Lance Dodes, "Is Addiction Really a Disease?" *Psychology Today* (December 17, 2011), https://www.psychologytoday.com/us/blog/the-heart-addiction/201112/is-addiction-really-disease.

29. Nora D. Volkow, "The Addicted Brain: Why Such Poor Decisions?" *NIDA Notes* 18, no. 4 (November 2003), https://archives.drugabuse.gov/news-events/nida-notes/2003/11/addicted-brain-why-such-poor-decisions.

30. American Psychiatric Association, "Criteria for Substance Abuse," *Diagnostic and Statistical Manual of Mental Disorders*, 4th ed. (Arlington, VA: American Psychiatric Association, 2000), 199.

31. Nora D. Volkow, "Addiction and Co-Occurring Mental Disorders," *NIDA Notes* 21, no. 2 (February 2007), https://archives.drugabuse.gov/news-events/nida-notes/2007/02/addiction-co-occurring-mental-disorders.

32. Substance Abuse and Mental Health Services Administration and Office of the Surgeon General, *Facing Addiction in America: The Surgeon General's Report on Alcohol, Drugs, and Health* (Washington, DC: US Department of Health and Human Services, 2016), https://www.ncbi.nlm.nih.gov/books/NBK424849/.

33. *Alcoholics Anonymous: The Story of How Many Thousands of Men and Women Have Recovered from Alcoholism,* 4th ed. (New York: Alcoholics Anonymous World Services, Inc., 2002), 67.

34. National Institute on Drug Abuse (NIDA), "Addiction Is a Chronic Disease," *Drug Abuse and Addiction: One of America's Most Challenging Public Health Problems* (August 2008), https://archives .drugabuse.gov/publications/drug-abuse-addiction-one-americas -most-challenging-public-health-problems/addiction-chronic-disease.

35. Alan I. Leshner, "Treating the Brain in Drug Abuse," *NIDA Notes* 15, no. 4 (September 2000), https://archives.drugabuse.gov /news-events/nida-notes/2000/09/treating-brain-in-drug-abuse.

36. Nora D. Volkow, "The Addicted Brain: Why Such Poor Decisions?" *NIDA Notes* 18, no. 4 (November 2003), https://archives .drugabuse.gov/news-events/nida-notes/2003/11/addicted-brain -why-such-poor-decisions.

37. National Institute on Drug Abuse (NIDA), "Addiction Is a Chronic Disease," *Drug Abuse and Addiction: One of America's Most Challenging Public Health Problems* (August 2008), https://archives .drugabuse.gov/publications/drug-abuse-addiction-one-americas -most-challenging-public-health-problems/addiction-chronic-disease.

38. Alan I. Leshner, "When the Question Is Drug Abuse and Addiction, the Answer Is 'All of the Above,'" *NIDA Notes* 16, no. 2 (May 2001), https://archives.drugabuse.gov/news-events/nida -notes/2001/05/when-question-drug-abuse-addiction-answer-all -above.

39. *Alcoholics Anonymous: The Story of How Many Thousands of Men and Women Have Recovered from Alcoholism,* 4th ed. (New York: Alcoholics Anonymous World Services, Inc., 2002), 19.

40. Telephone conversation with Deepak Chopra on Saturday, June 23, 2007, during his Wellness Radio show on the Sirius Satellite network.

41. National Institute on Drug Abuse (NIDA), "Treatment Approaches for Drug Addiction," NIDA InfoFacts (June 2008),

accessed October 16, 2008, http://www.drugabuse.gov/Infofacts/treatmeth.html.

42. Ibid.

43. *Alcoholics Anonymous: The Story of How Many Thousands of Men and Women Have Recovered from Alcoholism*, 4th ed. (New York: Alcoholics Anonymous World Services, Inc., 2002), 164.

44. Ibid., 19.

Chapter 4

1. *Alcoholics Anonymous: The Story of How Many Thousands of Men and Women Have Recovered from Alcoholism*, 4th ed. (New York: Alcoholics Anonymous World Services, Inc., 2002), 17.

2. Ibid., 55.

3. Telephone conversation with Deepak Chopra on Saturday, June 23, 2007, during his Wellness Radio show on the Sirius Satellite network.

4. *Alcoholics Anonymous: The Story of How Many Thousands of Men and Women Have Recovered from Alcoholism*, 4th ed. (New York: Alcoholics Anonymous World Services, Inc., 2002), 82.

5. Ibid., 84.

6. Ibid., 60.

7. Alcoholics Anonymous, *Twelve Steps and Twelve Traditions*, 13th ed. (New York: The AA Grapevine, Inc. and Alcoholics Anonymous World Services, Inc., 1999), 98.

Chapter 5

1. *It Works: How and Why, Twelve Steps and Twelve Traditions of Narcotics Anonymous* (Van Nuys, CA: Narcotics Anonymous World Services, Inc., 1993), 51.

2. Robert A. F. Thurman, trans., *The Tibetan Book of the Dead: Liberation Through Understanding the In Between* (New York: Bantam Books, 1994), 13–14.

3. John Myrdhin Reynolds, trans., *The Golden Letters* (Ithaca, NY: Snow Lion Publications, 1996), 23.

4. Ibid., 86.

5. John Myrdhin Reynolds, trans., *Self-Liberation Through Seeing with Naked Awareness* (Ithaca, NY: Snow Lion Productions, 1996), 41.

6. Thich Nhat Hanh, *The Heart of Buddha's Teaching* (New York: Broadway Books, 1998), 169–175.

7. Bhikkhu Bodhi, *In the Buddha's Words: An Anthology of Discourses from the Pali Canon* (Somerville, MA: Wisdom Publications, 2005), 22–23, 336–337.

8. Reginald A. Ray, *Indestructible Truth: The Living Spirituality of Tibetan Buddhism* (Boston: Shambala Publications, Inc., 2000), 337–346.

9. Chogyal Namkhai Norbu, *Dzogchen Teachings* (Ithaca, NY: Snow Lion Publications, 2006), 23.

10. Ibid.

11. Reginald A. Ray, *Indestructible Truth: The Living Spirituality of Tibetan Buddhism* (Boston: Shambala Publications, Inc., 2000), 194–196.

Step 1

1. Yangsi Rinpoche, *Practicing the Path: A Commentary on the Lamrim Chenmo* (Somerville, MA: Wisdom Publications, 2003), 217.

Step 2

1. *Alcoholics Anonymous: The Story of How Many Thousands of Men and Women Have Recovered from Alcoholism*, 4th ed. (New York: Alcoholics Anonymous World Services, Inc., 2002), 23.

2. Alcoholics Anonymous, *Twelve Steps and Twelve Traditions*, 13th ed. (New York: The AA Grapevine, Inc. and Alcoholics Anonymous World Services, Inc., 1999), xxiv.

3. *Alcoholics Anonymous: The Story of How Many Thousands of Men and Women Have Recovered from Alcoholism*, 4th ed. (New York: Alcoholics Anonymous World Services, Inc., 2002), 24.

4. Glen H. Mullin, *The Dalai Lamas on Tantra* (Ithaca, NY: Snow Lion Publications, 2006), 2.

5. This was from one of Eckhart Tolle's talks at a retreat. He makes this point quite often, throughout several sources.

Step 3

1. This concept is from Namkhai Norbu Rinpoche, who often revisits this concept at his retreats.

2. *Alcoholics Anonymous: The Story of How Many Thousands of Men and Women Have Recovered from Alcoholism*, 4th ed. (New York: Alcoholics Anonymous World Services, Inc., 2002), 30.

3. Ibid., 63.

Step 4

1. *It Works: How and Why, Twelve Steps and Twelve Traditions of Narcotics Anonymous* (Van Nuys, CA: Narcotics Anonymous World Services, Inc., 1993), 36.

2. *Alcoholics Anonymous: The Story of How Many Thousands of Men and Women Have Recovered from Alcoholism*, 4th ed. (New York: Alcoholics Anonymous World Services, Inc., 2002), 70.

3. Ibid., "Doctor's Opinion."

4. *It Works: How and Why, Twelve Steps and Twelve Traditions of Narcotics Anonymous* (Van Nuys, CA: Narcotics Anonymous World Services, Inc., 1993), 38.

5. Eknath Easwaran, trans. and ed., *The Dhammapada* (Tomales: Nilgiri Press, 1985), 78.

6. Lama Yeshe, *Ego, Attachment and Liberation: Overcoming Your Mental Bureaucracy* (Weston, MA: Lama Yeshe Wisdom Archive, 2006), 93.

7. Yangsi Rinpoche, *Practicing the Path: A Commentary on the Lamrim Chenmo* (Somerville, MA: Wisdom Publications, 2003), 217.

8. Lama Surya Das, *Buddha Is as Buddha Does: The Ten Original Practices for Enlightened Living* (San Francisco: HarperOne, 2007), 18.

9. Gampopa and Khenpo Konchog Gyaltsen Rinpoche, *Jewel Ornament of Liberation: The Wish-Fulfilling Gem of the Noble Teachings* (Ithaca, NY: Snow Lion Publications, 1998), 206.

10. This was from a retreat with Lama Zopa Rinpoche, Maitripa Institute, in November of 2006.

11. Namkhai Norbu Rinpoche, "Longchenpa's Commentary of Gampopa's Four Dharmas" (public webcast, December 2007), https://webcast.dzogchen.net.

12. *Alcoholics Anonymous: The Story of How Many Thousands of Men and Women Have Recovered from Alcoholism*, 4th ed. (New York: Alcoholics Anonymous World Services, Inc., 2002), 84.

13. This was from a retreat with Venerable Robina Courtin, in July of 2005.

14. Namkhai Norbu Rinpoche, "Longchenpa's Commentary of Gampopa's Four Dharmas" (public webcast, December 2007), https://webcast.dzogchen.net.

Step 5

1. *It Works: How and Why, Twelve Steps and Twelve Traditions of Narcotics Anonymous* (Van Nuys, CA: Narcotics Anonymous World Services, Inc., 1993), 51.

2. *Alcoholics Anonymous: The Story of How Many Thousands of Men and Women Have Recovered from Alcoholism*, 4th ed. (New York: Alcoholics Anonymous World Services, Inc., 2002), 62.

3. Ibid., "The Doctor's Opinion."

4. *Alcoholics Anonymous: The Story of How Many Thousands of Men and Women Have Recovered from Alcoholism*, 4th ed. (New York: Alcoholics Anonymous World Services, Inc., 2002), 83.

5. Kevin Griffin, *One Breath at a Time: Buddhism and the Twelve Steps* (Emmaus: Rodale Books, 2004).

6. Geshe Rabten Rinpoche, "The Twelve Links of Interdependent Origination," Lama Yeshe Wisdom Archive (2005), http://www.lamayeshe.com/article/twelve-links-interdependent-origination.

7. Ibid.

Step 6

1. *Alcoholics Anonymous: The Story of How Many Thousands of Men and Women Have Recovered from Alcoholism*, 4th ed. (New York: Alcoholics Anonymous World Services, Inc., 2002), 75.

2. Friends in Recovery, *The Twelve Steps for Christians* (Centralia, WA: RPI Publishing, 1988), 103.

3. Alcoholics Anonymous, *Twelve Steps and Twelve Traditions*, 13th ed. (New York: AA Grapevine, Inc. and Alcoholics Anonymous World Services, Inc., 1999), 64.

4. A note about the notion of heaven in Buddhist thought: Some forms of Buddhism, mainly the sects of Pure Land and Nichiren in China, actually practice for the purpose of being reborn in a Pure Realm. In this realm, they will be able to receive teachings directly from the Buddha and will be guaranteed enlightenment. The Pure Land Buddhists are possibly the largest group of Buddhists in China currently.

5. Thich Nhat Hanh, *The Heart of Buddha's Teaching* (New York: Broadway Books, 1998), 73–74.

6. Patrul Rinpoche, "4.2.4: The suffering of death," *The Words of My Perfect Teacher* (Boston: Shambala Publications, 1994), 84.

Step 7

1. *It Works: How and Why, Twelve Steps and Twelve Traditions of Narcotics Anonymous* (Van Nuys, CA: Narcotics Anonymous World Services, Inc., 1993), 69–75.

2. Al-Anon, *How Al-Anon Works for Families & Friends of Alcoholics* (Virginia Beach, VA: Al-Anon Family Groups Headquarters, Inc., 1995), 56–57.

3. *The Encyclopedia of Eastern Philosophy and Religion* (Boston: Shambala Publications, 1989), 179–180.

4. Ibid., 251.

5. *It Works: How and Why, Twelve Steps and Twelve Traditions of Narcotics Anonymous* (Van Nuys, CA: Narcotics Anonymous World Services, Inc., 1993), 75.

6. Longchen Rabjam, *The Precious Treasury of Philosophical Systems* (Junction City, CA: Padma Publishing, 2007), 30.

Step 8

1. From "Step Eight," Alcoholics Anonymous, *Twelve Steps and Twelve Traditions*, 13th ed. (New York: AA Grapevine, Inc. and Alcoholics Anonymous World Services, Inc., 1999), 78.

2. *It Works: How and Why, Twelve Steps and Twelve Traditions of Narcotics Anonymous* (Van Nuys, CA: Narcotics Anonymous World Services, Inc., 1993), 78.

3. Ibid., 78–84.

4. Chögyam Trungpa, *Training the Mind and Cultivating Loving-Kindness* (Boston: Shambala Publications, Inc., 1993), 26.

Step 9

1. *It Works: How and Why, Twelve Steps and Twelve Traditions of Narcotics Anonymous* (Van Nuys, CA: Narcotics Anonymous World Services, Inc., 1993), 85.

2. Ibid., 88.

3. Ibid.

4. Ibid., 95.

5. Ibid., 94.

6. Ibid., 91.

7. Ibid., 92.

8. Gampopa and Khenpo Konchog Gyaltsen Rinpoche, *Jewel Ornament of Liberation: The Wish-Fulfilling Gem of the Noble Teachings* (Ithaca, NY: Snow Lion Publications, 1998), 149.

9. *The Shambhala Dictionary of Buddhism and Zen* (Boston: Shambala Publications, 1991), 23.

10. Gampopa and Khenpo Konchog Gyaltsen Rinpoche, *Jewel Ornament of Liberation: The Wish-Fulfilling Gem of the Noble Teachings* (Ithaca, NY: Snow Lion Publications, 1998), 147.

11. Ibid., 179.

12. Ibid., 213.

13. Ibid., 214.

14. Ibid.

15. Alcoholics Anonymous, *Twelve Steps and Twelve Traditions*, 13th ed. (New York: AA Grapevine, Inc. and Alcoholics Anonymous World Services, Inc., 1999), 106.

16. Gampopa and Khenpo Konchog Gyaltsen Rinpoche, *Jewel Ornament of Liberation: The Wish-Fulfilling Gem of the Noble Teachings* (Ithaca, NY: Snow Lion Publications, 1998), 215.

17. Ibid., 216.

18. Ibid., 218.

19. Ibid.

Step 10

1. *It Works: How and Why, Twelve Steps and Twelve Traditions of Narcotics Anonymous* (Van Nuys, CA: Narcotics Anonymous World Services, Inc., 1993), 97.

2. *Paths to Recovery: Al-Anon's Steps, Traditions, and Concepts* (Virginia Beach, VA: Al-Anon Family Group Headquarters, Inc., 1997), 102.

3. *Alcoholics Anonymous: The Story of How Many Thousands of Men and Women Have Recovered from Alcoholism*, 4th ed. (New York: Alcoholics Anonymous World Services, Inc., 2002), 13.

4. Chuck C., *A New Pair of Glasses*, 9th ed. (Irvine, CA: New Look Publishing, 2003), 7.

Step 11

1. *It Works: How and Why, Twelve Steps and Twelve Traditions of Narcotics Anonymous* (Van Nuys, CA: Narcotics Anonymous World Services, Inc., 1993), 108.

2. Alcoholics Anonymous, *Twelve Steps and Twelve Traditions*, 13th ed. (New York: AA Grapevine, Inc. and Alcoholics Anonymous World Services, Inc., 1999), 98.

3. *It Works: How and Why, Twelve Steps and Twelve Traditions of Narcotics Anonymous* (Van Nuys, CA: Narcotics Anonymous World Services, Inc., 1993), 107.

4. Ibid., 109.

5. The Foundation for the Preservation of the Mahayana Tradition, *Essential Buddhist Prayers: An FPMT Prayer Book* (Queensland, Australia: Mandala Books, 2007), 3.

6. From "Four Chants," Lama Surya Das. Translation from http://www.dzogchen.org/chant/heartsutra.htm (page discontinued).

7. The Foundation for the Preservation of the Mahayana Tradition, *Essential Buddhist Prayers: An FPMT Prayer Book* (Queensland, Australia: Mandala Books, 2007), 15.

8. Kathleen McDonald, *How To Meditate: A Practical Guide* (Somerville, MA: Wisdom Publications, 1984), 174.

9. The Foundation for the Preservation of the Mahayana Tradition, *Essential Buddhist Prayers: An FPMT Prayer Book* (Queensland, Australia: Mandala Books, 2007), 23.

10. *Alcoholics Anonymous: The Story of How Many Thousands of Men and Women Have Recovered from Alcoholism*, 4th ed. (New York: Alcoholics Anonymous World Services, Inc., 2002), Appendix II.

11. *It Works: How and Why, Twelve Steps and Twelve Traditions of Narcotics Anonymous* (Van Nuys, CA: Narcotics Anonymous World Services, Inc., 1993), 105.

12. Lama Zopa Rinpoche, *Six-Session Guru Yoga* (Ithaca, NY: Snow Lion Publications, 2006), 17–22.

13. Alcoholics Anonymous, *Twelve Steps and Twelve Traditions*, 13th ed. (New York: AA Grapevine, Inc. and Alcoholics Anonymous World Services, Inc., 1999), 23–24.

14. Khetsun Sangpo, *Tantric Practice in Nying-ma* (Ithaca, NY: Snow Lion Publications, 1996), 167.

15. Patrul Rinpoche, *The Words of My Perfect Teacher* (Boston: Shambala Publications, 1994), 309.

16. Ibid., 311.

17. Ibid., 395.

18. John Myrdhin Reynolds, trans., *The Golden Letters* (Ithaca, NY: Snow Lion Publications, 1996), 70–71.

19. See my website for free Dharma Desk plans: the12stepbud dhist.com.

Step 12

1. Dilgo Khyentse Rinpoche, *Enlightened Courage* (Ithaca, NY: Snow Lion Publications, 2006), 75.

2. The Foundation for the Preservation of the Mahayana Tradition (FPMT), *The Bodhisattva Vows* (Queensland, Australia: Mandala Books, 2004), 19.

3. *Alcoholics Anonymous: The Story of How Many Thousands of Men and Women Have Recovered from Alcoholism*, 4th ed. (New York: Alcoholics Anonymous World Services, Inc., 2002), 20.

4. Alcoholics Anonymous, *Twelve Steps and Twelve Traditions*, 13th ed. (New York: AA Grapevine, Inc. and Alcoholics Anonymous World Services, Inc., 1999), 77.

5. Bokar Rinpoche, *Taking the Bodhisattva Vow* (San Francisco: Clear Point Press, 1997), 25.

6. From Damien Keown, *Oxford Dictionary of Buddhism* (New York: Oxford University Press, 2004), 35, and Gampopa and Khenpo Konchog Gyaltsen Rinpoche, *Jewel Ornament of Liberation: The Wish-Fulfilling Gem of the Noble Teachings* (Ithaca, NY: Snow Lion Publications, 1998), 263–277.

7. Emmet Fox, *Power Through Constructive Thinking* (New York: HarperCollins, 1968), 44.

Afterword

1. Compassion Institute, "Compassion Cultivation Training" (2017), accessed February 5, 2019, https://www.compassioninstitute .com/cct.

Glossary

1. Chokyi Dragpa, *Uniting Wisdom and Compassion* (Somerville, MA: Wisdom Publications, 2004), 196.

2. *The Shambhala Dictionary of Buddhism and Zen* (Boston: Shambala Publications, 1991), 61.

3. Chogyal Namkhai Norbu, *Dzogchen Teachings* (Ithaca, NY: Snow Lion Publications, 2006), 43.

4. Chokyi Dragpa, *Uniting Wisdom and Compassion* (Somerville, MA: Wisdom Publications, 2004), 198.

5. Jacob P. Dalton, "Uses of the Dgongs pa 'dus pa'i mdo in the Development of the Rnying-ma School" (PhD diss., University of Michigan, April 2002).

6. Chokyi Dragpa, *Uniting Wisdom and Compassion* (Somerville, MA: Wisdom Publications, 2004), 199.

7. *The Shambhala Dictionary of Buddhism and Zen* (Boston: Shambala Publications, 1991), 217.

8. Patrul Rinpoche, "Translator's Introduction," *The Words of My Perfect Teacher* (Boston: Shambala Publications, 1998), 436.

9. Ibid., 242.

10. Ibid., 251.

11. Damien Keown, *Oxford Dictionary of Buddhism* (New York: Oxford University Press, 2004), 340.

Recommended Resources

Recovery

Compassionate Recovery: compassionaterecoveryproject.com

Refuge Recovery: refugerecovery.org

Alcoholics Anonymous: aa.org

Narcotics Anonymous: na.org

Teachers, Centers, and Publishers

Lama Zopa Rinpoche: fpmt.org

Yangsi Rinpoche: maitripa.org

Chagdud Gonpa Foundation: tibetantreasures.com

Tibetan Incense: tibetanincense.com

Compassion and Mindfulness Training

Compassion Institute: compassioninstitute.com

Jim Hopper: jimhopper.com

Jamie Marich: traumamadesimple.com

Books

Alcoholics Anonymous: *Basic Text, 12 Steps and 12 Traditions*

Narcotics Anonymous: *It Works: How and Why*

Joko Beck: *Everyday Zen, Nothing Special*

Claudia Black: *Unspoken Legacy: Addressing the Impact of Trauma and Addiction within the Family*

Patrick Carnes: *The Betrayal Bond: Breaking Free of Exploitive Relationships*

Thupten Jinpa: *A Fearless Heart: How the Courage to Be Compassionate Can Transform Our Lives*

Noah Levine: *Refuge Recovery: A Buddhist Path to Recovering from Addiction*

Jamie Marich: *Trauma and the Twelve Steps: A Complete Guide to Enhancing Recovery*

Lisa Najavits: *Recovery from Trauma, Addiction, or Both: Strategies for Finding Your Best Self*

Namkhai Norbu: *The Crystal and the Way of Light, Dzogchen Teachings, The Supreme Source*

John Reynolds: *The Golden Letters, Self-Liberation Through Naked Awareness*

Patrul Rinpoche: *The Words of My Perfect Teacher*

Yangsi Rinpoche: *Practicing the Path*

Reginald Ray: *Indestructible Truth, Secrets of the Vajra World*

Bessel van der Kolk: *The Body Keeps the Score: Brain, Mind, and Body in the Healing of Trauma*

Also by Darren Littlejohn

The Power of Vow
Perfect Practice
How to Gain Nothing from Buddhist Practice
The Yoga of Self Compassion
The Yoga of Letting Go
The Yoga of Being a Badass
How to Find a Spiritual Teacher
Compassionate Recovery

Podcast

The 12-Step Buddhist Podcast is on iTunes, YouTube, and Spotify as well as the12stepbuddhist.libsyn.com.

Join our mailing list for free meditations and updates on trainings, retreats, and other resources at the12stepbuddhist.com.

Index